Easy-to-Make
STUFFED ANIMALS
& All the Trimmings

Jodie Davis

Williamson Publishing • Charlotte, Vermont 05445

Copyright © 1992 by Jodie Davis

Library of Congress Cataloging-in-Publication
Data

Davis, Jodie, 1959–
    Easy–to–make stuffed animals and all the
    trimmings/ Jodie Davis
        p.   cm.
    ISBN 0-913589-56-X
    1. Soft toy making.   2. Stuffed animals
        (toys)   I. Title.
    TT174.3.D3728 1991
    745.592'4—dc20   91–21738   CIP

Cover and interior design:
Trezzo-Braren Studio
Cover illustration: Loretta Trezzo
Back cover photograph: Bruce Conklin
Interior photographs: Bruce Conklin
Project design: Jodie Davis
Printing: Capital City Press

Williamson Publishing Co.
Box 185
Charlotte, Vermont 05445
1-800-234-8791

Manufactured in the United States of America

10 9 8 7 6 5 4 3 2

CONTENTS

DEDICATION

♥

*To my wonderful publishers,
Susan and Jack, whose enthusiasm makes
work feel like play.*

♥ ♥ ♥ ♥ ♥ ♥

*W*hy stuffed animals?

Well, just look at me. Here I sit at my trusty Macintosh, with a Jack Russell Terrier enjoying an afternoon nap in my lap. (She just finished her noon siesta, which followed her morning rest.) A calico kitty sunbathes outside in the window box, and a Gouldian finch I hand fed from 10 days of age serenades me from my shoulder, hopping as he sings. From the living room/ bird room baby Zebra finches beg food from their parents and every so often the Silver-eared Mesia voices his jubilance to the sweet spring breeze.

Soon, when the clock reads four, Lil Bit will reach up with a canine slurp to remind me of her daily soccer game. Outside, five kitties are assembled in the barn in anticipation of our walk, and Caesar trims the grass by the gate, anxious for his grain.

You see, animals are essential to my life. And so, after writing books full of teddy bear and doll designs, animals seemed the natural progression.

Some of the animals in this book are life-like, others incorporate a bit of artistic license. All overflow with personality and embody the characteristics unique to their species.

On page 8, each animal is listed with a number that corresponds to a rating of the skills required for the task. If you are unsure of your sewing skills, you may wish to choose your first project from those marked level 1. Level 2 animals involve an extra step or two, have more intricate pattern pieces, require machine applique, or have small parts which require very accurate stitching.

Have fun populating your home with these friendly creatures. They make extraordinary decorating accessories never dreamed of by an interior designer. Hang the bat upside down in a dark corner, assign a cow the job of keeping watch over an old-fashioned milk can, or warm your pillow with a sleepy reclining kitty. Each will help make your house home.

♥

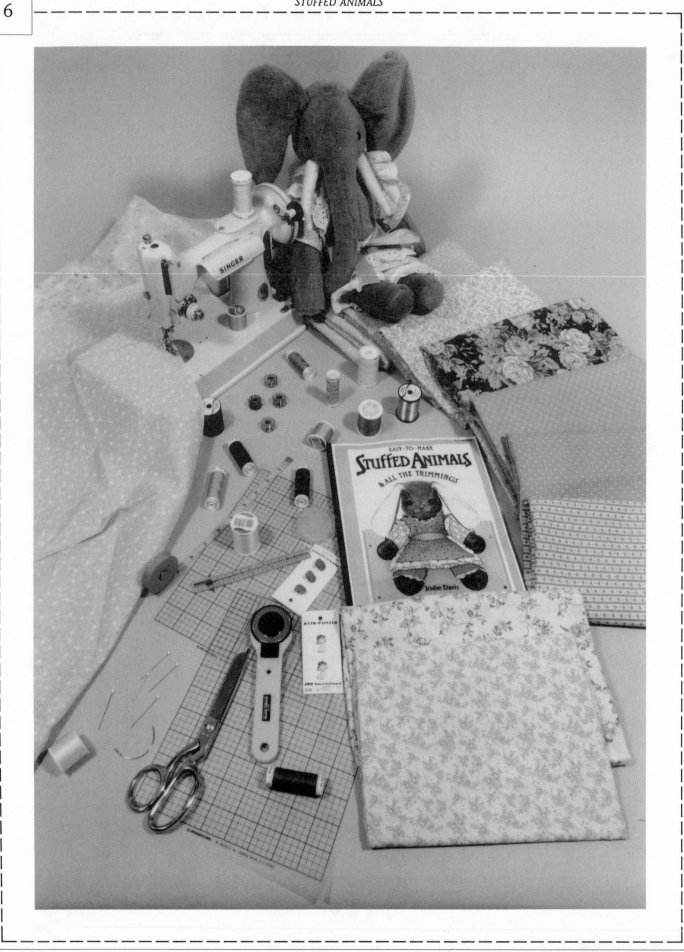

♥

The Basics

Here are the essentials for constructing the animals and clothes in this book: a review of the necessary basic sewing skills and tools needed, and a few time- and aggravation-saving methods. This book holds all you need to make this colorful kingdom of animals. Anyone who loves these whimsical creatures can feel comfortable with the projects. For additional reference, there is a bibliography of excellent general sewing books available at your local bookstore or library. Before you begin, assemble all of the tools and materials needed for your project. Then follow the instructions one step at a time.

DEGREE OF DIFFICULTY

Some of these projects take a bit more skill than others, although I feel certain anyone can make an adorable animal from these patterns, no matter what their skill level. Still, there are times when you might prefer a less fussy project, so I have labeled all of the projects - 1 for simpler, 2 for a bit more detail and more challenge. Whichever you decide to do, enjoy the process as well as the results!

Level #1	Level #2
Brontosaurus	Unicorn/Horse
Triceratops	Penguin
Lamb	Rooster
Lamb Doll	Bat
Fox Doll	Cow
Dog Doll	Jointed Bunny
Teddy Bear Doll	Kitty Doll and Reclining Animal
Bunny Doll	Fox Doll and Reclining Animal
Mouse Doll	Lion Doll and Reclining Animal
Piggy Doll	Cow Doll and Reclining Animal
Elephant Doll	Fawn/Rudolph Doll and Reclining Animal
	Horse/ Unicorn Doll and Reclining Animal

GENERAL SUPPLIES

Essential

Sewing machine: Be sure to use a needle appropriate for fur. Depending upon the brand of machine you use, choose a size 90 or a 14.

Bent-handle dressmaker's shears: A good quality shear, 7" or 8" in length is recommended for general sewing purposes. Reserve these shears for cutting fabric only, as paper will dull them quickly.

Scissors: For cutting paper, cardboard, and other materials, these inexpensive scissors will save your shears from a lot of wear and tear.

Dressmaker's tracing paper: For transferring markings from patterns to fabric.

Dressmaker's tracing wheel: A device used with the tracing paper.

Straight pins: To hold paper pattern pieces in place as you cut out the fabric.

Hand-sewing needles: For general hand sewing. Choose a fine, size 10-8, sharp for lightweight fabrics such as calico, and a medium, size 8-6, sharp for heavier fabrics such as fur, corduroy, flannel, and denim.

Embroidery needle: For embroidering the animals' noses and mouths.

Dollmaker's needle: Five inches or longer. Needed for installing glass eyes. Also helpful in embroidering mouths. Available from CR's Crafts (see Sources).

Awl: Used for making holes in the fur for eyes, plastic noses, and joints. Though a seam ripper can be used in its place, an awl makes a clean, round hole without breaking threads. You can buy an awl at a hardware store or local fabric store. A small version costs less than half the price of the large ones and will do the job nicely.

Wooden Spoon: You will find the handle end indispensible in stuffing those hard to reach noses and paws and in packing the stuffing. If you plan to make many stuffed animals or bears, you may wish to invest in special T-shaped stuffing tools offered by Edinburgh Imports and CR's Crafts (see Sources).

Fray Check®: A few drops of this nifty product secures threads that might otherwise unravel.

Glue: A general purpose white glue for fabric, felt, wood, and paper is available at any dime, crafts, or fabric store under a variety of brand names.

General purpose thread: The all-purpose size 50 will fill most of your general hand and machine sewing needs. Always choose the highest quality.

Carpet thread, quilting thread, or waxed dental floss: Has the strength required to withstand the tugging needed to install eyes, gather the necks of animal heads, and close openings in fur. The dental floss will slide through the fur easily.

Paper: For clothing and other patterns.

5" or longer dollmaker's needle: Needed for thread-jointing the doll.

Tag board (oak tag) or cardboard: For durable animal patterns. These can be laid on the backing of the fur and traced around. This is easier and produces a more accurate transfer of pattern to fabric.

Hammer and socket or nut and washer: To secure metal lockwashers to plastic joints, for long-wearing, healthy joints. Turn to jointing section of this chapter for more information.

Nice to Have

Seam ripper: A sharp, pointed tool used to tear out temporary basting stitches and goofed seams. I list this as non-essential because you can substitute the thread clipper listed below.

Pinking shears: Cuts a ravel-resistant zigzag, used for finishing seams in animal doll clothing. A good choice is the 7½-inch size.

Thread clippers: A variation on a small pair of scissors, thread clippers are handy for trimming threads at the sewing machine, for clipping into seam allowances, and for making buttonholes. If you do much sewing, I highly recommend a pair.

Thimble: This is listed as non-essential though many, including myself, will argue that this little piece of equipment is in fact essential in guiding the needle and guarding against painful pin pricks.

HOW TO TRANSFER PATTERNS
• MARK & CUT •

All of the patterns in this book are shown in their actual size. It is suggested that you make your animal patterns out of a heavy cardboard, such as oak tag (tag board) or cardboard cereal boxes, since accuracy is extremely important. By tracing around the cardboard pieces you will transfer the patterns very accurately. Paper will suffice for the clothing patterns as you will pin them to the fabric and cut out the pieces.

Note: These days reducing and enlarging patterns with perfect accuracy is simple with a photocopy machine that has these capabilities. A teddy bear maker once sent me a photograph of a family of more than a half dozen bears she made using this method. Ranging in size from 18" to ³/₄" (yes, ³/₄"!) tall, they were exact replicas of each other. Quite impressive!

MATERIALS

Tracing paper

Dressmaker's tracing paper

Cardboard or paper for patterns

INSTRUCTIONS

1. Lay a piece of tracing paper over the pattern in the book. Carefully trace the pattern onto the tracing paper, including all pattern markings.

Note: Those patterns that are too large to fit on one page are cut in two or more pieces and labeled (for example: body side part 1 of 2, body side part 2 of 2). When you come across such patterns, simply trace them from the book as in step 1 above, cut them out, and butt and tape the edges together as instructed on the pattern pieces. Then, continue on to step 2 below to make a permanent pattern that will be easy to use.

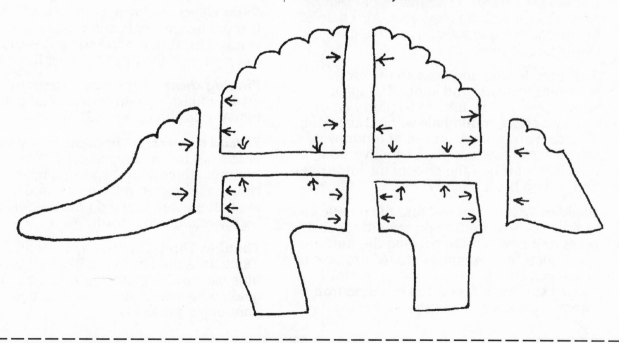

2. Lay the cardboard (for clothing patterns, paper) on your work surface. Place a sheet of carbon paper on top and your tracing over that. To avoid the possibility of slippage you may wish to tape the two top sheets to the bottom cardboard or paper, or to the work surface. With a pencil or dressmaker's wheel trace the pattern, pressing firmly. Pick up a corner of the two top layers to be sure that the pattern is being transferred clearly to the bottom surface. Transfer all markings and instructions to the pattern.

3. Cut out the cardboard pattern. Mark each pattern piece with the name of each animal or garment. Add all markings and helpful instructions. For easy transfer of dots and eye and joint markings to fur backing, bore holes through the pattern at the markings. When you position the pattern over the fur you can simply push the tip of your marking pencil or pen into the hole to mark the fur.

4. Lay the fur, backing side up, on your cutting surface. Point the nap of the fur toward you. If you stroke the fur as you would a dog, the fur should lie smoothly toward you, as if you were standing behind the dog.

5. Place the pattern pieces on the fabric, arranging them in the best way to economize on the fur. Make sure all arrows point toward you, in the direction of the nap. Remember: all seam allowances (¹/4") are included in the patterns.

6. With a white or dark fabric marking pencil, depending upon the fur color, trace the pattern pieces. Cut out the fur pieces. For accuracy, cut just inside the drawn lines. Slide the lower blade of the scissors along the backing of the fur, being careful not to cut the fur itself.

7. Transfer all eye, joint, and other placement markings to the wrong side of the fur backing. Instructions in the chapters themselves will instruct you when you need to transfer markings to the right, fur, side of the fabric. To do this, simply fill your sewing machine bobbin or thread your hand needle with colored sewing thread and, from the backing, or wrong side of the fur, baste over the markings. For eye markings, all you need is one stitch, leaving the thread tails hanging from the fur side of the fabric.

8. In some instances you will be instructed to trim the animal's fur. To do this, from the right side of the fabric, simply hold your scissors parallel to the backing of the fur and cut the nap of the fur to within ¹/4" of the backing. Picture yourself giving the fur a crew cut.

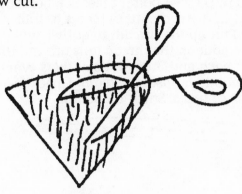

TIP: Manila envelopes (great opportunity for recycling) and ziplock sandwich bags are great places to store your patterns. Label them and store them away for lots of future use.

Note: The illustrations in this book follow the customary practice of depicting the wrong side of fabric dotted. The right side is left plain.

SEWING TECHNIQUES

Darts
Fold the fabric along the center line of the dart, right sides together. Beginning at the raw edges, or widest point of the dart, sew the dart along the broken lines to the point and backstitch to secure the stitching. For clothing, press the dart to one side.

Gathering

Using a long stitch, make a row of stitches between the marks indicated on the pattern, leaving the thread tails long enough to grasp so you can pull them. Repeat close to the first stitching, inside the seam allowance. Pin the two pattern pieces together, matching the two pattern pieces as indicated. Pull up the threads to gather the fabric and loop the thread tails around the pins at each end. Adjust the gathers evenly and smoothly. Baste the seam. Check for puckers or tucks. Stitch the seam.

Trimming and Clipping Seams

After stitching a seam, seam allowances are trimmed and clipped for a number of reasons. For clothing, trimming with pinking shears will reduce the bulk of the seam and, in some fabrics, prevent raveling of the raw edges. For clothing and animals, clipping into the seam allowances of convex (outward) curves permits the edges to spread when the item is turned right side out. Notching the seam allowances on concave (inward) curves allows the edges to draw in when the item is turned right side out. Trimming across corners insures a smooth finished seam and square, crisp corners.

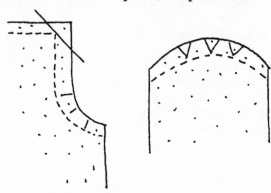

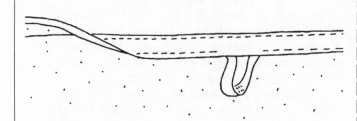

Elastic Casings

The casing is a tunnel of turned under fabric through which flat elastic is threaded.

To make an elastic casing, press the edge of the garment under $1/4$". Then turn and press the edge under an additional $3/4$" or desired amount. Machine stitch the lower edge of the casing, leaving a $1/2$"-wide opening for threading the elastic. Stitch a second row close to the top fold.

Next cut a length of elastic as indicated in the instructions for the garment. Attach a safety pin to one end of the elastic, push it into the casing and work through, taking care not to twist the elastic.

Safety pin the two ends of the elastic together, overlapping the ends $1/2$". Try the garment on the animal, adjust the elastic if necessary. Your animal's measurements may vary according to how you stuff it, so double check the fit. Machine stitch the ends of the elastic together, back and forth to secure them. Pull the elastic through the casing. Machine stitch the opening closed, being careful not to catch the elastic in the stitching.

STITCH DICTIONARY

Basting Stitch
Use this long (¼" by hand or longest possible by machine), temporary stitch to mark and stitch together two pieces of fabric to make sure they fit properly before the final stitching.

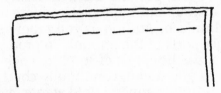

Ladder Stitch
Use this stitch to close the openings in the animals' bodies and limbs that had been left open for turning and stuffing. This easy stitch results in professional-looking seam closures. After brushing the seam you'll hardly be able to see it!

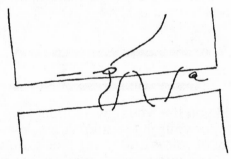

Running Stitch
This stitch is similar to the basting stitch, though it is a shorter, even stitch, for fine, permanent seaming.

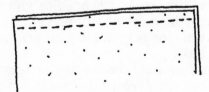

Overhand Or Whipstitch
Use to join two finished edges, as when closing the turned under edges of the ear.

PREWASH

For clothing only: Before cutting your fabric wash, dry, and iron it according to the manufacturer's instructions to avoid shrinkage and running of colors when the finished item is laundered.

SEWING THE ANIMALS

Use a regular machine stitch and a high quality thread for sewing your stuffed animals. Always choose the appropriate size needle and a brand recommended by the manufacturer. For most furs choose a size 90/14; for most clothing fabrics, an 80/12. A properly tuned and equipped machine will produce seams with the strength needed to withstand stuffing and loving.

JOINTING THE ANIMALS

The simple plastic joint pictured here will allow your animal's head, arms, legs, etc. to move. The joint consists of a stationary disk with a threaded post, topped by a large plastic washer, a plastic lockwasher to hold the joint together, and, for long term strength, a topmost metal lockwasher.

The metal lockwashers are not packaged as part of the plastic joint set. Buy extra sets of safety eyes that have the correct size metal lockwashers and discard the eyes. This is worth the effort. Without them the animals will contract the "sleepy teddy bear" syndrome, especially noticable in the legs; over time the all-plastic joints will loosen and the animal will nod forward.

Assemble the joint by inserting the stationary disk into the limb (head, arm, or leg) so the post pokes out of a hole in the fur (placement is marked on the patterns).

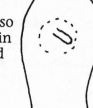

Next poke another hole through the corresponding body placement marking.

Working from inside the body, slip the large plastic washer over the stationary disk post. Then snap the plastic lockwasher onto the threaded post.

To snap it snugly, put the entire assembly, animal and all, on a hard surface, with the post pointing up. Place your thumbs on the lockwasher and, using the weight of your body to help you, push the washer down onto the post until it snaps - maybe more than once.

Next, snap the metal lockwasher onto the threaded post. Tighten the metal lockwasher by placing either a socket from a socket wrench set or a large nut over the post, on top of the metal washer. Hammer the socket or nut. Check the joint by trying to move the head, arm, or leg. It should be very difficult.

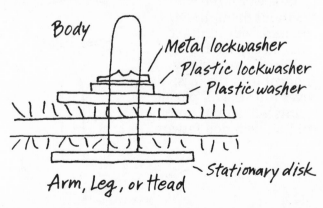

Body
Metal lockwasher
Plastic lockwasher
Plastic washer
Stationary disk
Arm, Leg, or Head

STUFFING

The art of stuffing is a learned skill. First, start with a quality stuffing — one of even, fluffy consistency. Always begin at the extremities: noses or paws, using smaller bits of stuffing for small parts, packing them in tightly with the aid of your stuffing tool. Graduate to larger chunks of stuffing as you progress to the larger parts of the animal. To produce less lumping, use handfuls of stuffing. Pack the stuffing as you add it, continually checking for lumps and evenness. Hold whatever part you're working on at arm's length to check for symmetry. You may have to unstuff your first attempts to get it right. Ladderstitch the openings closed when you are satisfied with your work.

Just take your time. With a bit of experience you will develop a feel for stuffing and will progress more quickly.

VOICES

Would you like your cow to moo, your lamb to baa, or your pig to sing? A giggle-evoking variety of voices and music boxes are sold at craft stores and through mail order catalogs. Sources are listed in the back of this book.

Voices are easy to install. Just slip them into the leg of a discarded pair of panty hose, knotting it at each side of the voice box. Center the box in the body as you stuff it. The panty hose fabric will prevent the stuffing from clogging the mechanism in the voice box.

Push button music boxes are inexpensive and easy to install. Place the music box inside the unstuffed animal with the silver button against the fur backing. The music box can be placed in the center of the tummy or over the heart. (Since Rudolph's music box is attached to his blinking red nose, his music box is located at the back of his head.) When the music box is in position, stuff the animal. This should hold the music box in place. For extra support, stitch through the holes at the corners of the music box and through the fur before stuffing the animal.

INSTALLING EYES

Install plastic safety eyes before the head is stuffed, glass eyes after stuffing but before attaching the the head to the body.

For plastic safety eyes, use an awl or seam ripper to make holes at the eye markings on the backing or wrong side of the fabric. Turn the animal right side out. From the right side of the head, push the eye post into the head. Place the head on a hard surface, eye down, with a towel or a few thicknesses of fabric under the eye to protect it from possible scratches. Push the lockwasher onto the eye post. You may need a large spool of thread or a large nut centered over the post to help you push harder. I can usually snap the washer in place by positioning my thumbs on each side of the washer and standing up to make use of my body weight in pressing the washer down.

For glass eyes (one eye on each end of a wire), cut the wire with wire cutters about 1" from each eye. Use needle-nose pliers to bend the last third of the wire back on itself and bend it down again.

With an awl or a seam ripper, make holes at the markings for the eyes. Remove the colored thread markings. Apply a drop of Fray Check® and leave to dry. Double thread a long dollmaker's needle with heavy thread or waxed dental floss. Push the needle through the fabric covering the disk at one side of the base of the neck (the fur will hide the knot) and come out the eye hole you made on the same side of the head.

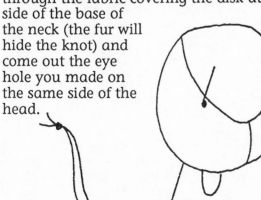

It will take a few stabs to get the needle to come out exactly in the hole. Put the needle through the loop in the eye wire (or, if the needle is too large for the hole in the loop, just work the thread onto the loop as you would if linking one paper clip to another) and push the needle back into the eyehole. Push the needle out through the base of the neck near where you started it. Pull the thread very tightly, seating the eye flatly and firmly against the head. Pull again to be sure the eye is secure. Make a stitch in the fabric covering the disk to secure the thread. Take another stitch, emerging on the edge of the disk at the other side of the head. Install the eye as above. Be sure both eyes are tight before knotting the thread at the neck.

INSTALLING PLASTIC NOSES

To install plastic noses, use an awl or seam ripper to make a hole at the nose marking. From the right side of the head, push the nose post into the head. From inside the head, push the metal lockwasher onto the post and snap it in place.

EMBROIDERING NOSES & MOUTHS

The easiest method to begin and end embroidery is to start with a long needle threaded with unknotted floss or perle cotton. Poke into the fur anywhere on the side of the head. Emerge anywhere a few inches away. Pull the thread just until the tail disappears into the fur. Go back into the fur just next to where the thread emerged. Come out somewhere near where you will start your embroidery. Repeat, emerging at the starting point of your embroidery. Pull on the thread.

Finish embroidery in the same manner, clipping the thread close to the fur after it emerges from the fur for the final time.

If you use embroidery floss, do use the full six strands; otherwise the floss becomes lost in the fur. I prefer the heaviest weight of perle cotton. Don't limit yourself to black. How about a pink or rust? When you finish the embroidery, brush and trim the fur to display your handiwork.

In most of the individual instructions for the animals you will make either of the two noses and/or mouths below. Both are very easy. Use your long dollmaking needle. You may need some pliers to pull the needle out of the fabric. Follow the step-by-step illustrations for a perfect nose and mouth. Thread a length of embroidery thread or perle cotton on a tapestry needle. Knot it. Push the needle into the fur under the nose and emerge at center top of the nose, in the fur off the felt. As illustrated, work side-to-side across the nose area using satin stitches, putting a stitch on one side of the nose and then the other, checking to be sure the nose is turning out even, until the felt is covered. After the last stitch, come out just under the center of the bottom of the nose. Continue on with the mouth instructions for your specific animal.

For the cow, horse and fawn:

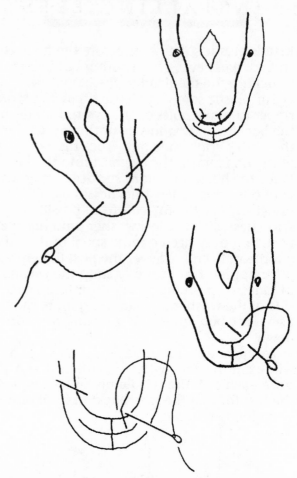

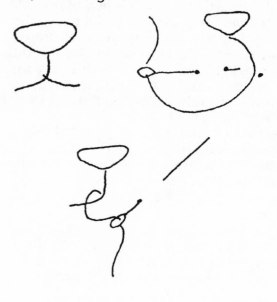

For the fox, lion, dog, bunny, mouse, fawn, panda, and kangaroo:

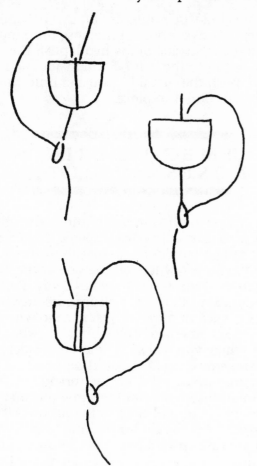

E A R S

Some animals' ears are stitched into the seams of the heads. Others' ears are added after the animal is stuffed. With the latter, first turn the bottom edges of the ears ¼" to the inside at the bottom open edges and whipstitch with heavy thread. When you finish do not cut off the thread. (See Stitch Dictionary for whipstitching.)

Next stitch the ears to the head. Place the ear on the head. With the thread coming out of the ear at one end, stitch into the head, front to back.

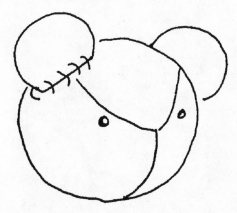

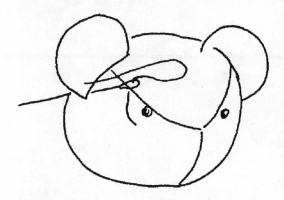

Now, stitch through the bottom of the ear, back to front.

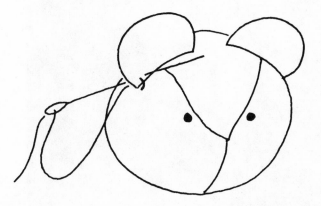

You may wish to hold the ear in a cupped shape as you sew to mimic the natural shape of an animal's ear. Continue until you reach the other end of the ear. Knot the thread in the fur and clip it.

F I N I S H I N G

The final touches for your animal may be likened to primping and preening. First, you can mold the stuffed animal with your hands. This is usually the cure for a slightly lopsided head, most often squashed in the jointing process. Much character can be added to an animal by molding the arms, for instance, to bend inward, or the elephant's tusks to point inward and upward.

Brushing the animal for a professional finish, with a special brush (see Sources) will hide seams and smooth fur in the proper direction. Scrub the fur back and forth, up and down along the handstitched seams to pull the caught fur from the seam. Pull the fur caught in the curved ends of the ears, paws and feet. Brush fur away from the eyes, clipping any that obscures the animal's vision.

Above all, take your time and have fun!

♥ ♥

Kids' Favorites

♥ ♥

B R O N T O S A U R U S

The brontosaurus stood 15 feet tall — at the hips. He measured 75 feet long, including his 30-foot tail. Weighing in at 30 to 40 tons, he was 12 times the weight of a large elephant. The brontosaurus lumbered along at two to four miles an hour, leaving behind him yard-long footprints. Our bronto measures 16 inches tall and 41 inches long. He is made of a soft fabric that simulates the look of suede.

MATERIALS

1¼ yards doe suede

Matching thread

Two 6 mm eyes

Polyester fiberfill stuffing

INSTRUCTIONS

Note: All seam allowances are ¼" unless otherwise instructed.

Prepare patterns as instructed on page 10. Pin them to the fabric. Cut out.

1. Right sides facing, pin and stitch two inner back legs together along marked edge as shown.

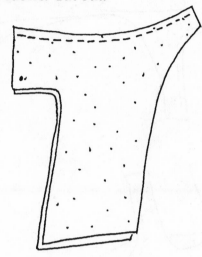

2. Right sides together, fold underbody gusset along dart foldline. Stitch dart in underbody gusset.

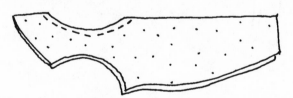

3. With right sides together, pin inside back legs to underbody gusset as shown, matching dots L. Stitch.

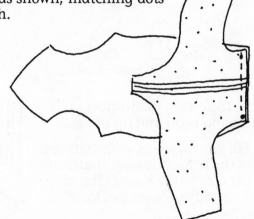

4. Matching dots A and B, pin inside front legs to underbody gusset. Stitch.

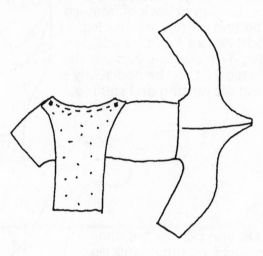

5. Right sides facing, match and pin dot D on front of underbody gusset to dot D on one body side, on the underside of the neck. Continue pinning down the front of the front leg to the bottom of the foot. Stitch. Repeat for other body side.

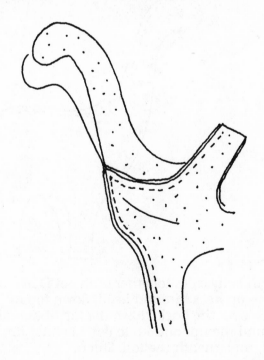

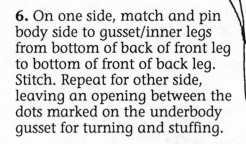

6. On one side, match and pin body side to gusset/inner legs from bottom of back of front leg to bottom of front of back leg. Stitch. Repeat for other side, leaving an opening between the dots marked on the underbody gusset for turning and stuffing.

7. On one side, match and pin dots E on inner back leg and one body side. Continue pinning to bottom back of back legs. Stitch. Repeat for other side.

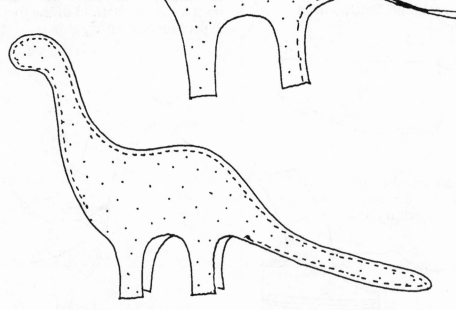

8. Pin body sides together from dot D at chest, up neck, around head, down top of neck, over the back, down the top of the tail, around the tip, and up to dot E behind hind legs, underneath the tail. Stitch.

9. Trim seam allowances to ⅛" around head and tip of tail.

10. Pin foot soles to the bottoms of the legs, as shown, matching the dots to the seams. Stitch. Trim seam allowances to ⅛".

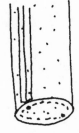

11. Make holes for eyes at markings. Turn brontosaurus right side out.

12. Install the eyes at the head markings as instructed on page 15.

13. Start stuffing at the head, using walnut-sized pieces to stuff the head evenly. Double the size of the pieces of stuffing to fill the neck. Stuff the neck, checking it for smoothness.

Stuff the legs firmly.

Stuff the tail as you did the head and neck.

Stuff the body with large handfuls of stuffing.

Check to be sure the brontosaurus stands squarely.

14. As instructed on page 13, ladderstitch the opening in the body closed.

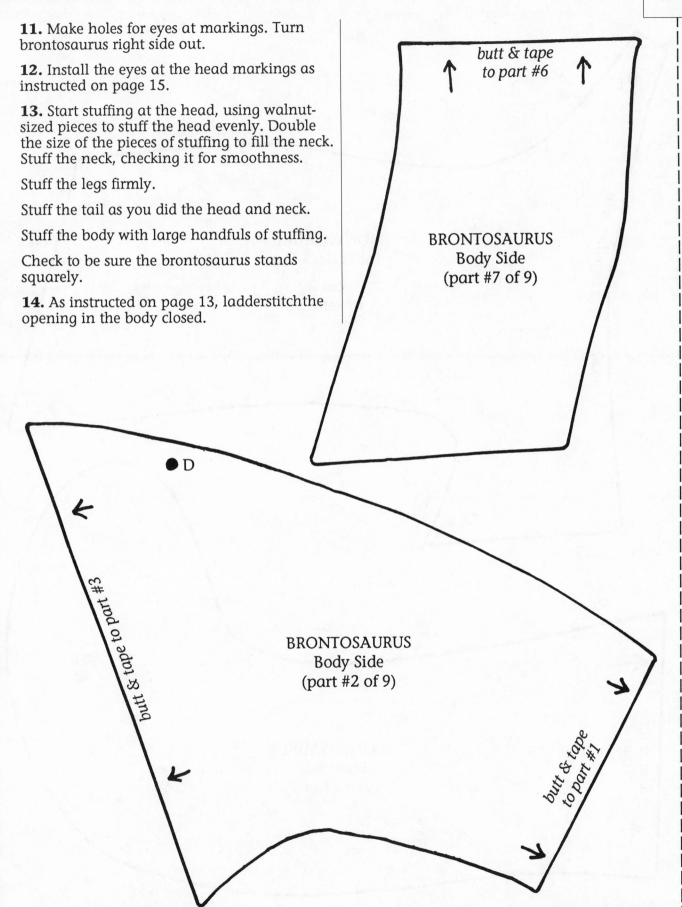

butt & tape
to part #6

BRONTOSAURUS
Body Side
(part #7 of 9)

● D

butt & tape to part #3

BRONTOSAURUS
Body Side
(part #2 of 9)

butt & tape
to part #1

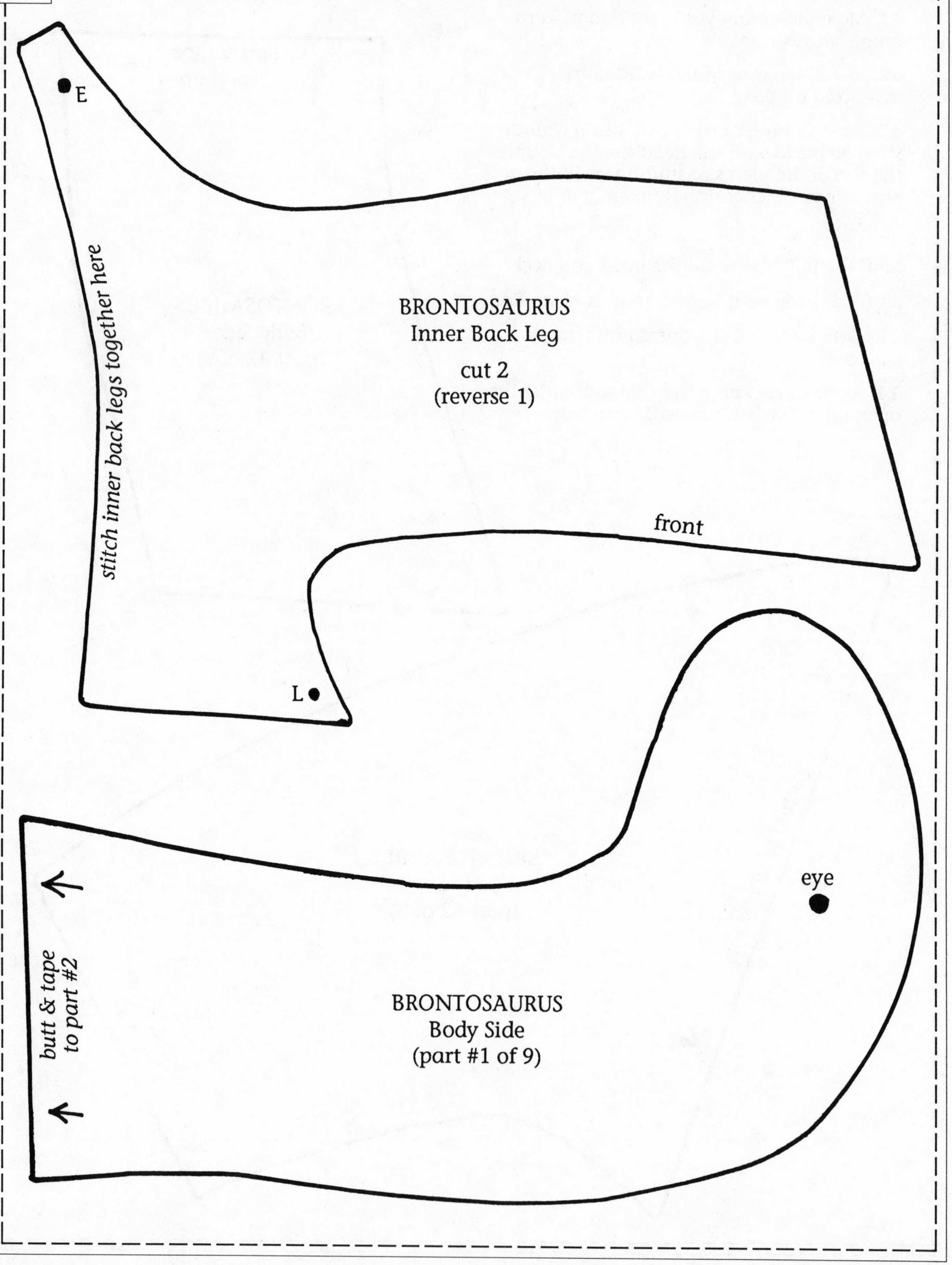

E

stitch inner back legs together here

BRONTOSAURUS
Inner Back Leg

cut 2
(reverse 1)

front

L

butt & tape
to part #2

eye

BRONTOSAURUS
Body Side
(part #1 of 9)

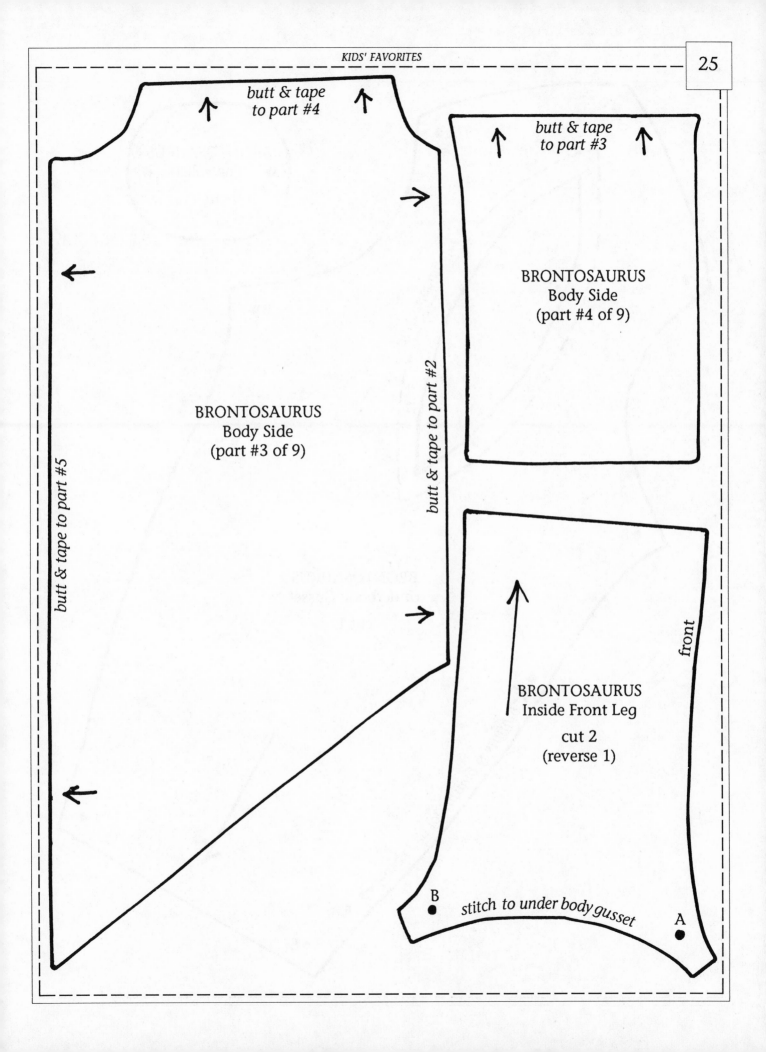

butt & tape
to part #4

butt & tape
to part #3

BRONTOSAURUS
Body Side
(part #4 of 9)

butt & tape to part #2

BRONTOSAURUS
Body Side
(part #3 of 9)

butt & tape to part #5

front

BRONTOSAURUS
Inside Front Leg

cut 2
(reverse 1)

B

stitch to under body gusset

A

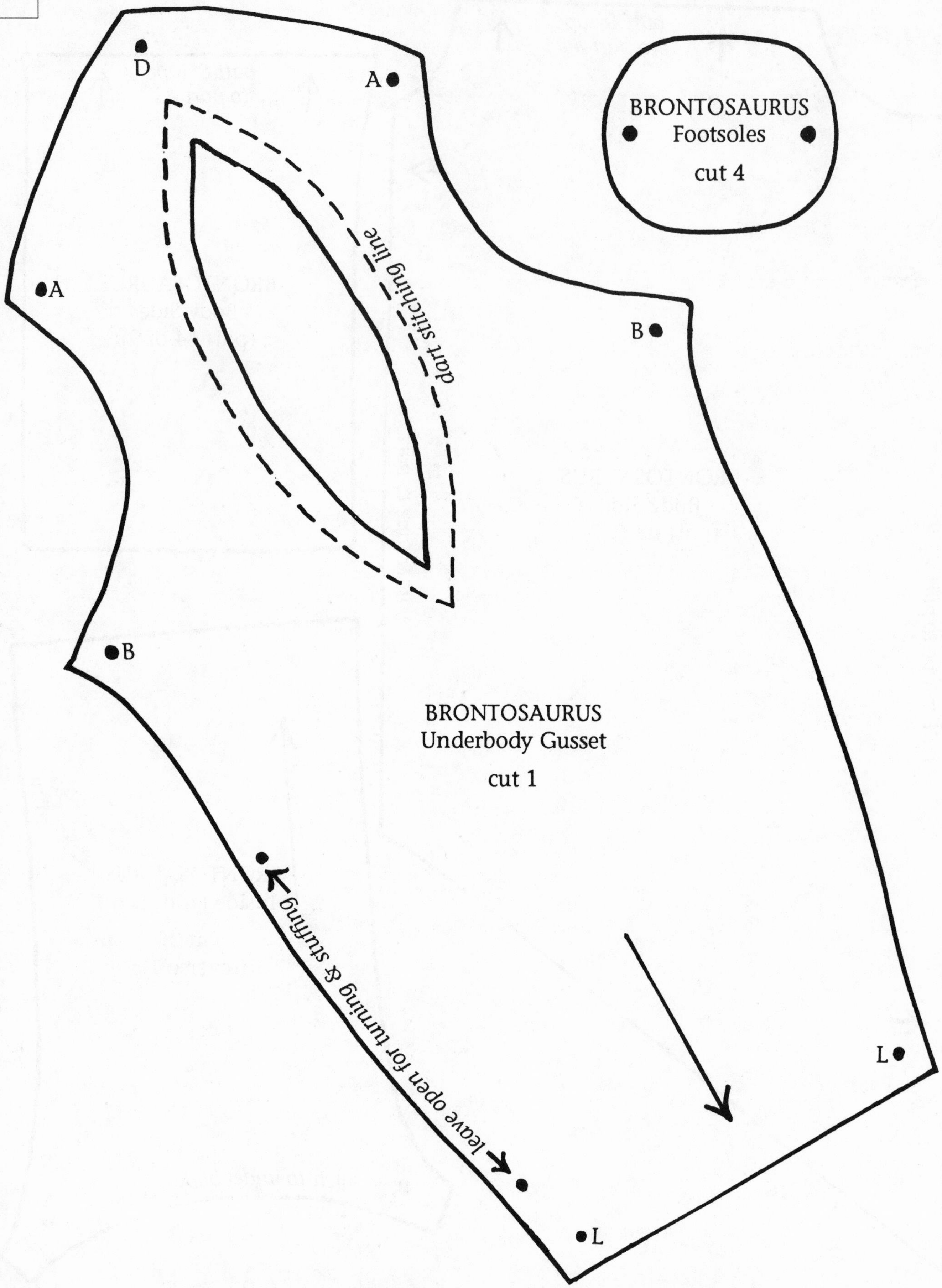

D

A

A

dart stitching line

BRONTOSAURUS
Footsoles

cut 4

B

B

BRONTOSAURUS
Underbody Gusset

cut 1

leave open for turning & stuffing

L

L

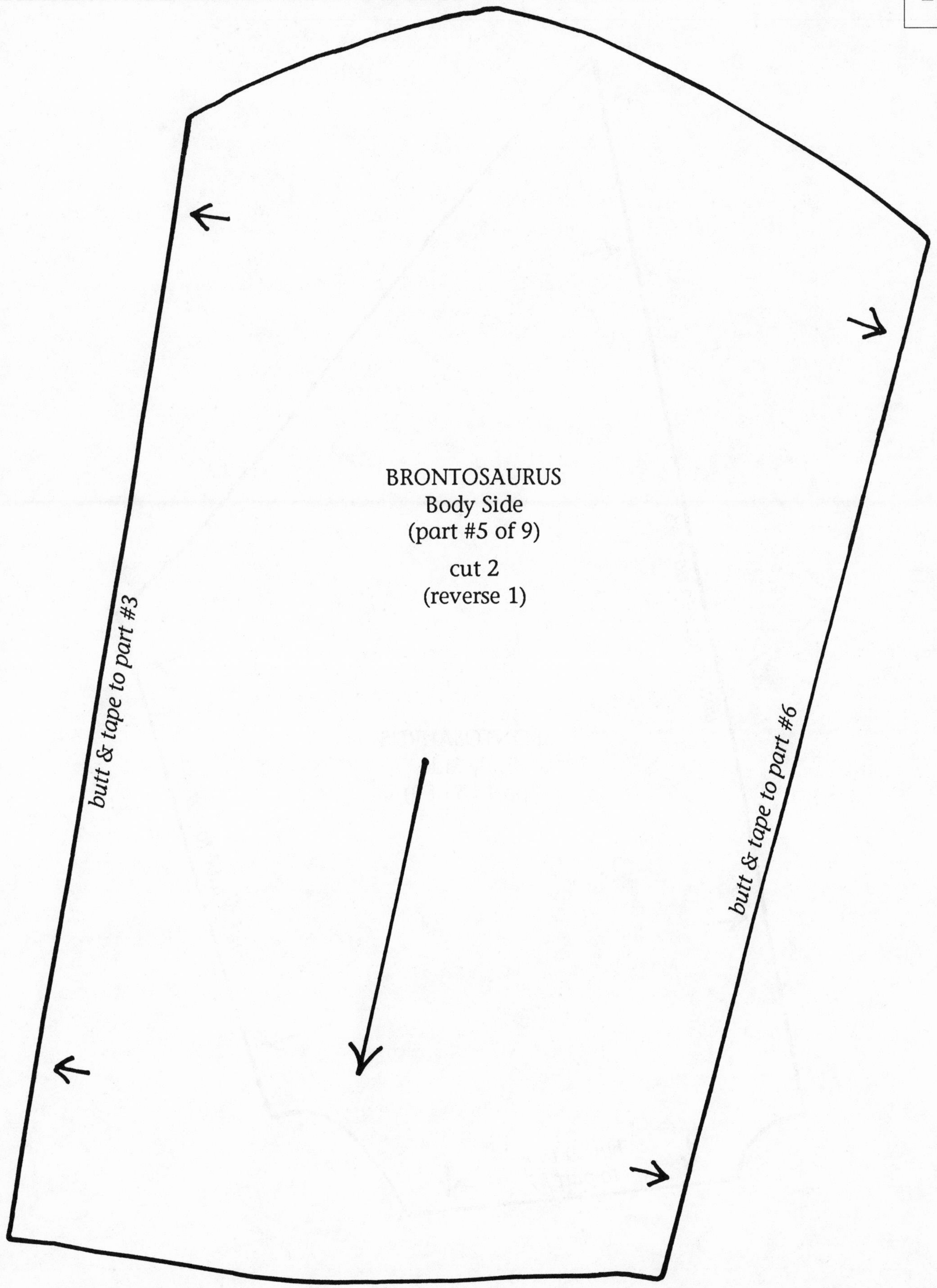

BRONTOSAURUS
Body Side
(part #5 of 9)

cut 2
(reverse 1)

butt & tape to part #3

butt & tape to part #6

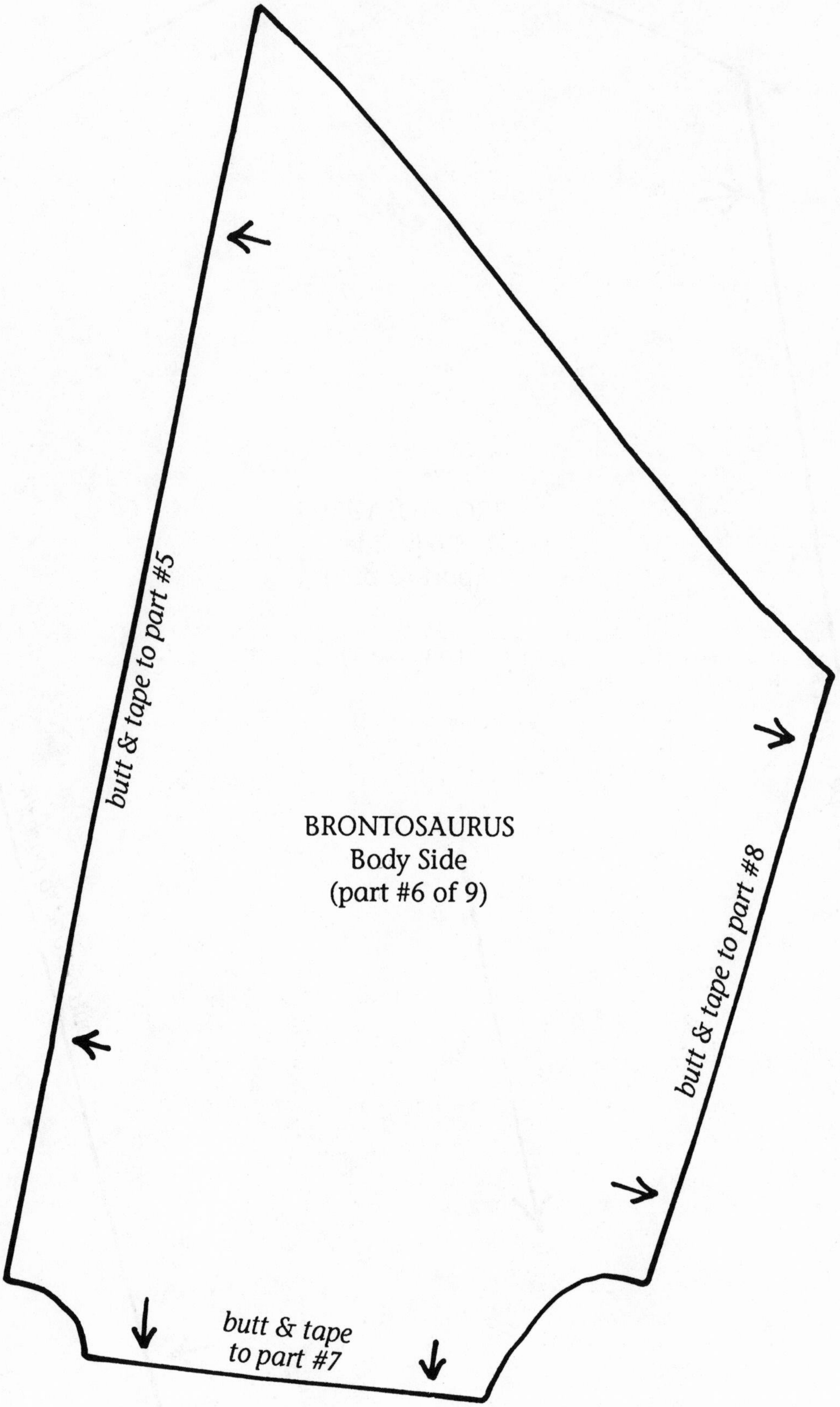

butt & tape to part #5

butt & tape to part #8

BRONTOSAURUS
Body Side
(part #6 of 9)

butt & tape
to part #7

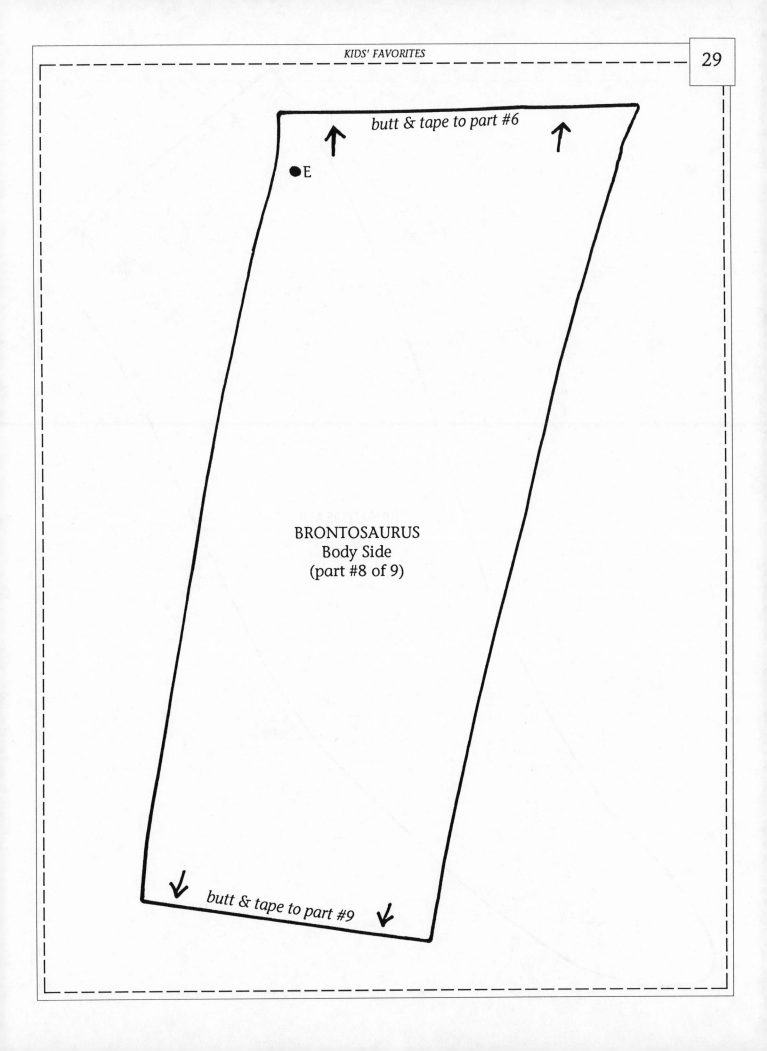

butt & tape to part #6

● E

BRONTOSAURUS
Body Side
(part #8 of 9)

butt & tape to part #9

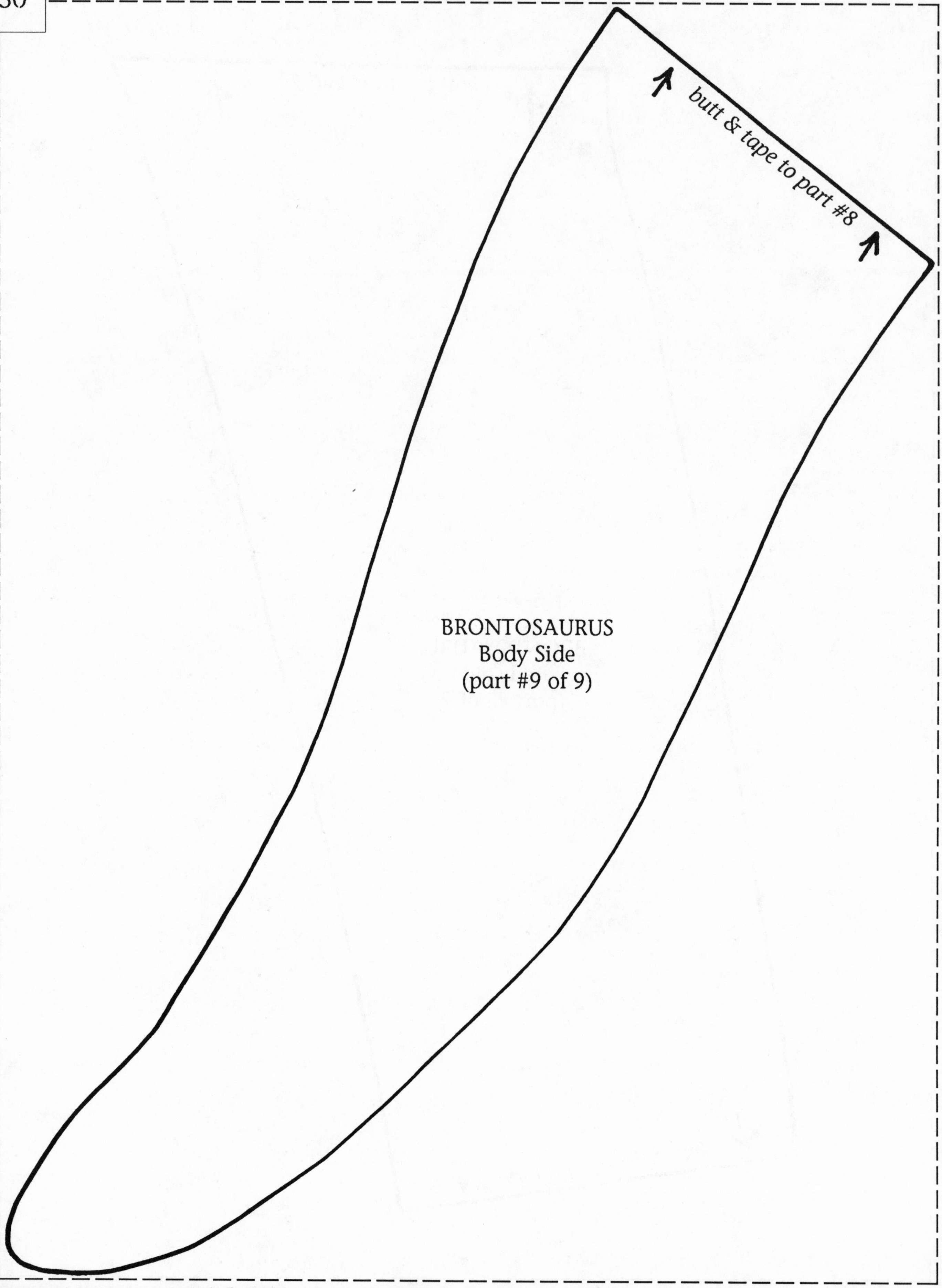

butt & tape to part #8

BRONTOSAURUS
Body Side
(part #9 of 9)

TRICERATOPS

The largest and heaviest of the horned dinosaurs, the triceratops measured 25 feet from snout to the tip of the tail. Standing 9½ feet tall, this vegetarian weighed 5 to 6 tons. The triceratops lived throughout Montana, Wyoming, and Alberta, Canada. This huggable stuffed version stands 10" and is 22" long. He is made from a soft fabric which simulates the look of suede.

MATERIALS

¾ yard doe suede

Matching thread

Two 9 mm eyes

Polyester fiberfill stuffing

Polyester batting

INSTRUCTIONS

Note: All seam allowances are ¼" unless otherwise instructed.

Prepare patterns as instructed on page 10. Pin them to the fabric. Cut out. Transfer all markings to the wrong side of the fabric. Mark horn and eye placements on right side of the fabric of the head sides.

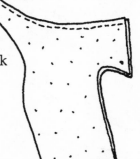

1. Right sides facing, pin and stitch two back legs together along long edge, as shown.

2. Right sides facing, fold and pin dart in underbody gusset. Stitch.

3. With right sides together, pin back legs to underbody gusset as shown, matching dots B and matching dot A on underbody gusset to seam in back legs. Stitch.

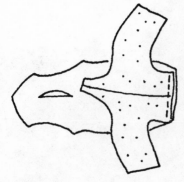

4. Matching dots C and D, pin front legs to underbody gusset. Stitch.

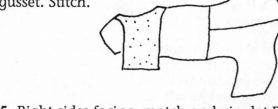

5. Right sides facing, match and pin dot E on front of underbody gusset to dot E on one body side. Continue pinning down the front of the front leg to the bottom of the foot. Stitch from dot E down the front of the leg. Repeat for other body side.

6. On one side, match and pin body side to gusset/inside legs from bottom of back of front leg to bottom of front of back leg. Stitch. Repeat for other side, leaving an opening between the dots on the gusset on one side.

7. On one side, match and pin dots F on inside back leg to dot F on one body side. Pin down to bottom back of back legs. Stitch. Repeat for other side.

8. Pin body sides together from dot E at chest, up neck, over the humps on the back, down the top of the tail, around the tip, and up to dot F behind hind legs. Stitch.

9. Pin foot soles to bottom of legs, right sides facing, matching dots on foot soles to seams of legs. Turn triceratops right side out. Stuff, beginning with the extremities. Ladderstitch the opening closed.

10. Cut two pieces of batting about an inch larger all around than the head side pattern. Lay the batting pieces flat on your work surface. Lay two opposing head sides wrong side down on top of the pieces of batting. Baste the head sides to the batting. Trim extra batting close to stitching.

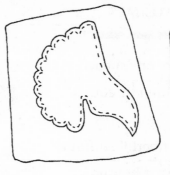

11. Pin and stitch the two head sides together, right sides facing, along forehead seam, as shown. Stitch.

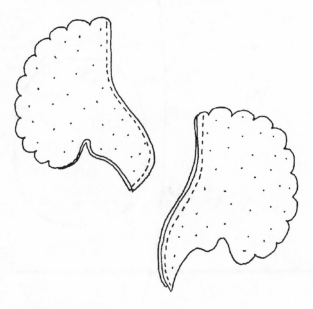

Repeat for two remaining head sides. (Just step 11, no batting needed.)

12. Right sides facing, pin the heads together. Stitch all the way around.

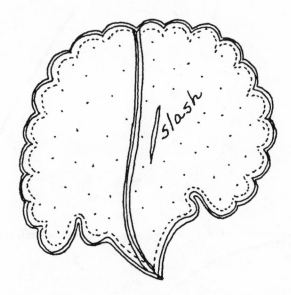

13. Cut a 2" long slash in the head without the batting. Turn head right side out. Press. Handstitch the opening closed. This side will go against the body.

14. Install the eyes following the instructions on page 15.

15. Pin the head to the neck. Consult the photo to determine where to place it. Hand-stitch the head to the neck.

16. Right sides facing, pin two horn pieces together. Stitch, leaving the short, straight edges open. Repeat for the other two sets.

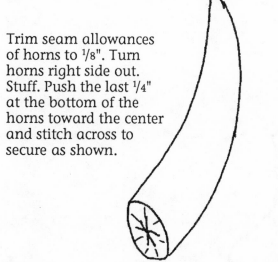

Trim seam allowances of horns to ⅛". Turn horns right side out. Stuff. Push the last ¼" at the bottom of the horns toward the center and stitch across to secure as shown.

Stitch horns to head at markings. Bend the horns toward the center.

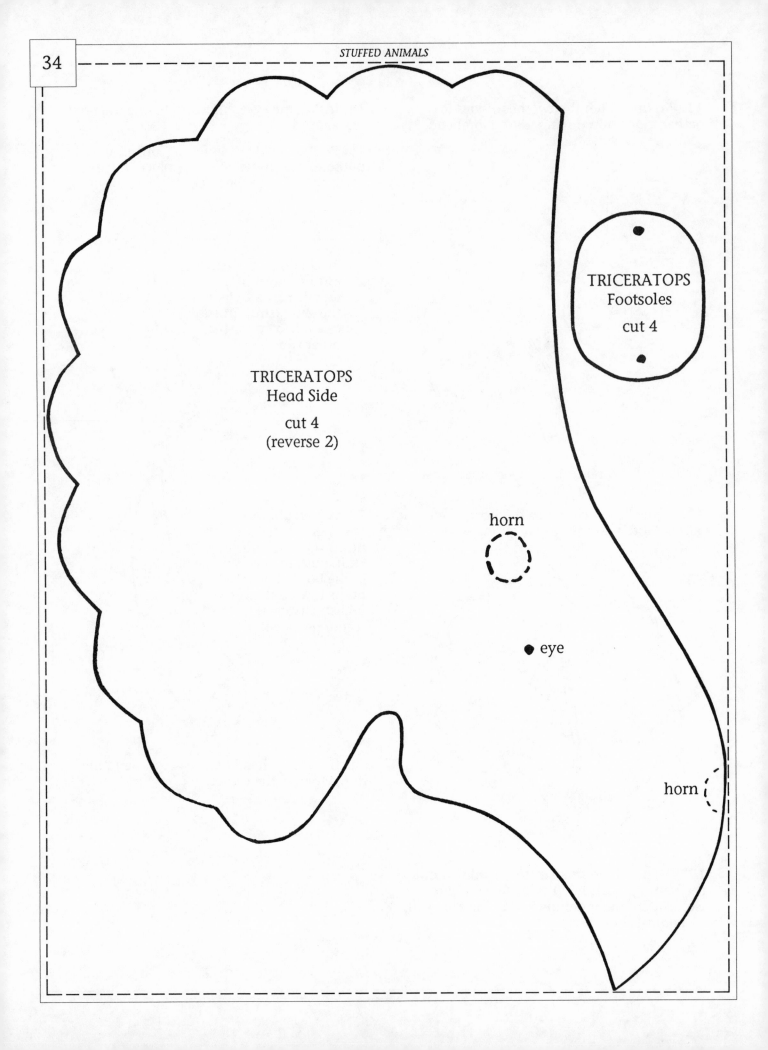

TRICERATOPS
Footsoles

cut 4

TRICERATOPS
Head Side

cut 4
(reverse 2)

horn

● eye

horn

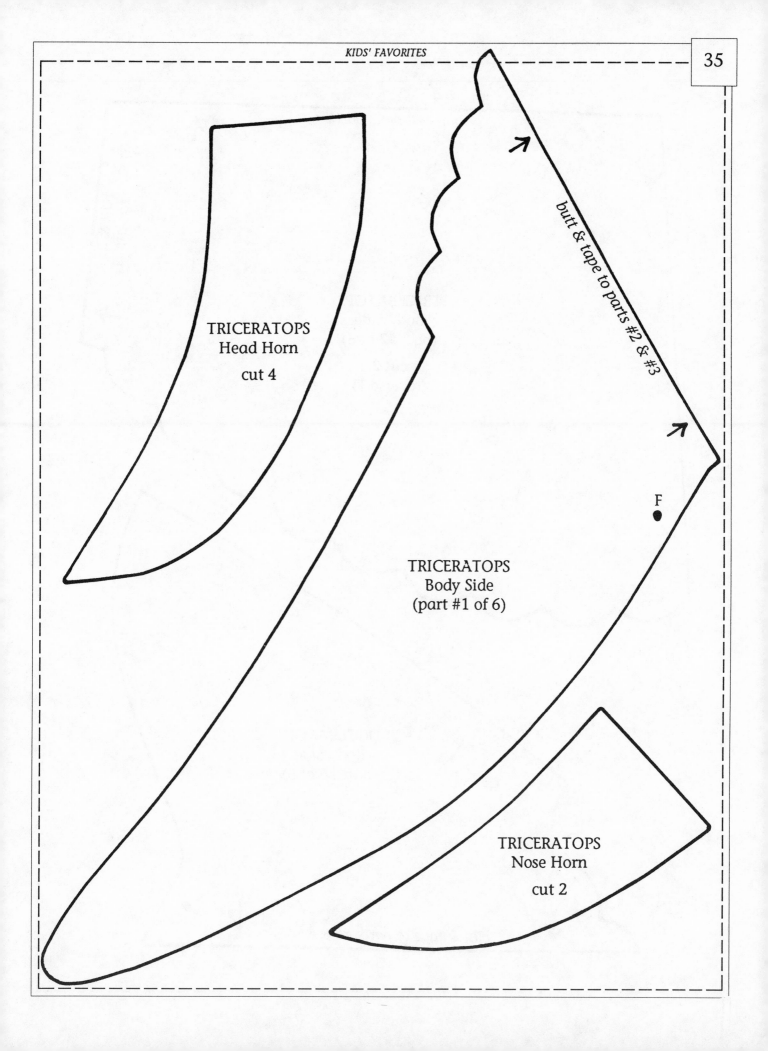

TRICERATOPS
Head Horn

cut 4

butt & tape to parts #2 & #3

F

TRICERATOPS
Body Side
(part #1 of 6)

TRICERATOPS
Nose Horn

cut 2

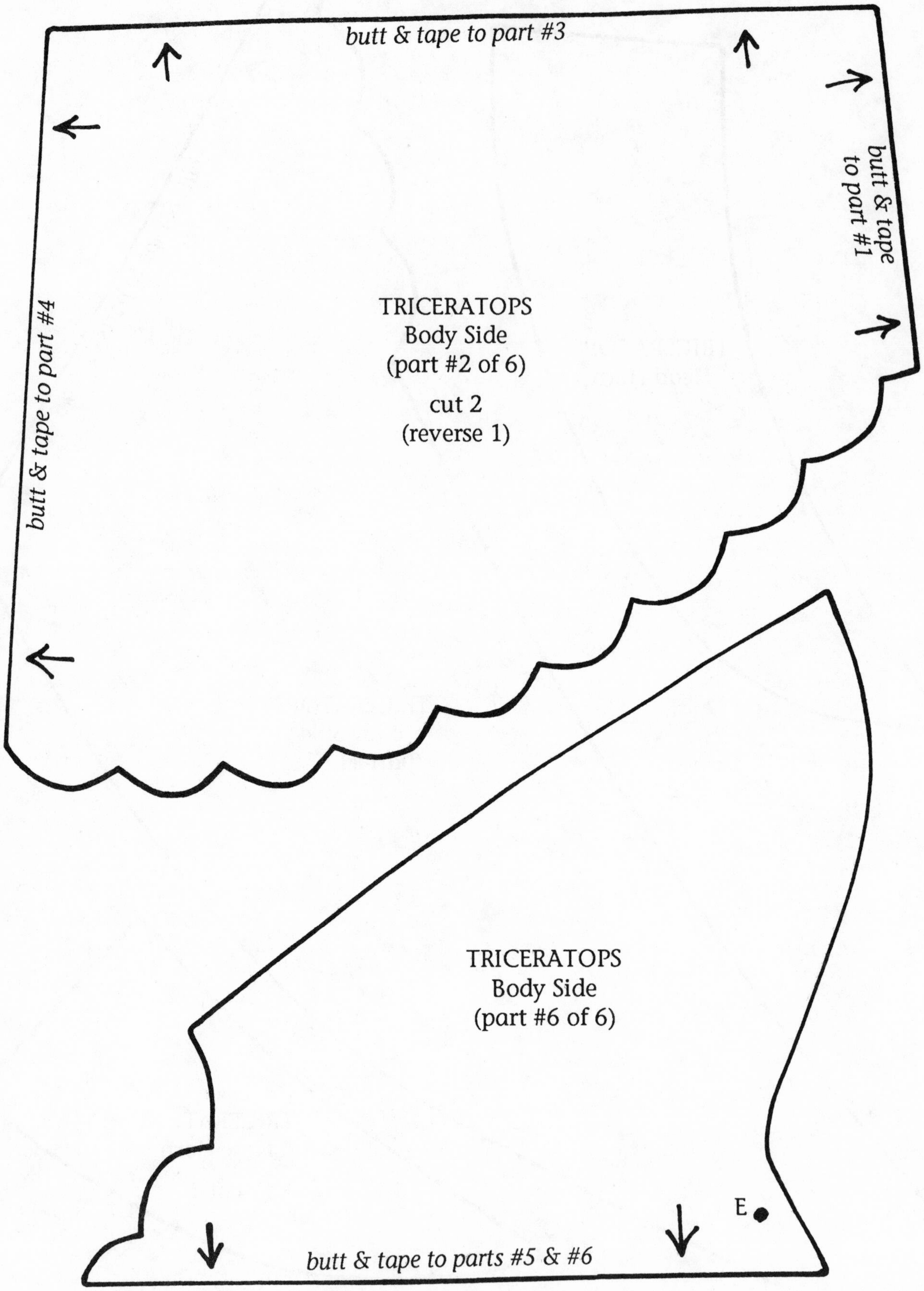

butt & tape to part #3

butt & tape to part #1

butt & tape to part #4

TRICERATOPS
Body Side
(part #2 of 6)

cut 2
(reverse 1)

TRICERATOPS
Body Side
(part #6 of 6)

E

butt & tape to parts #5 & #6

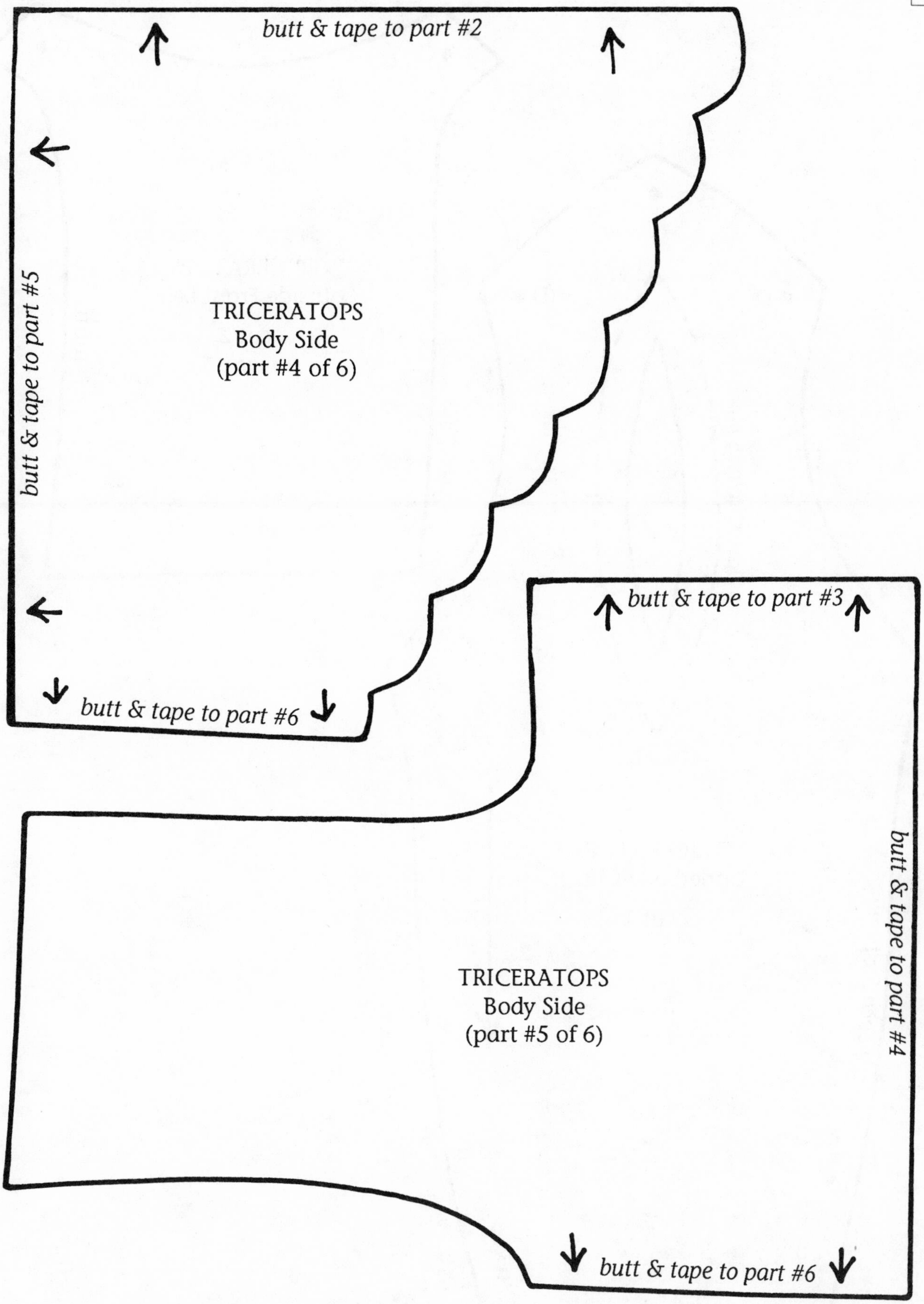

butt & tape to part #2

butt & tape to part #5

TRICERATOPS
Body Side
(part #4 of 6)

butt & tape to part #3

butt & tape to part #6

butt & tape to part #4

TRICERATOPS
Body Side
(part #5 of 6)

butt & tape to part #6

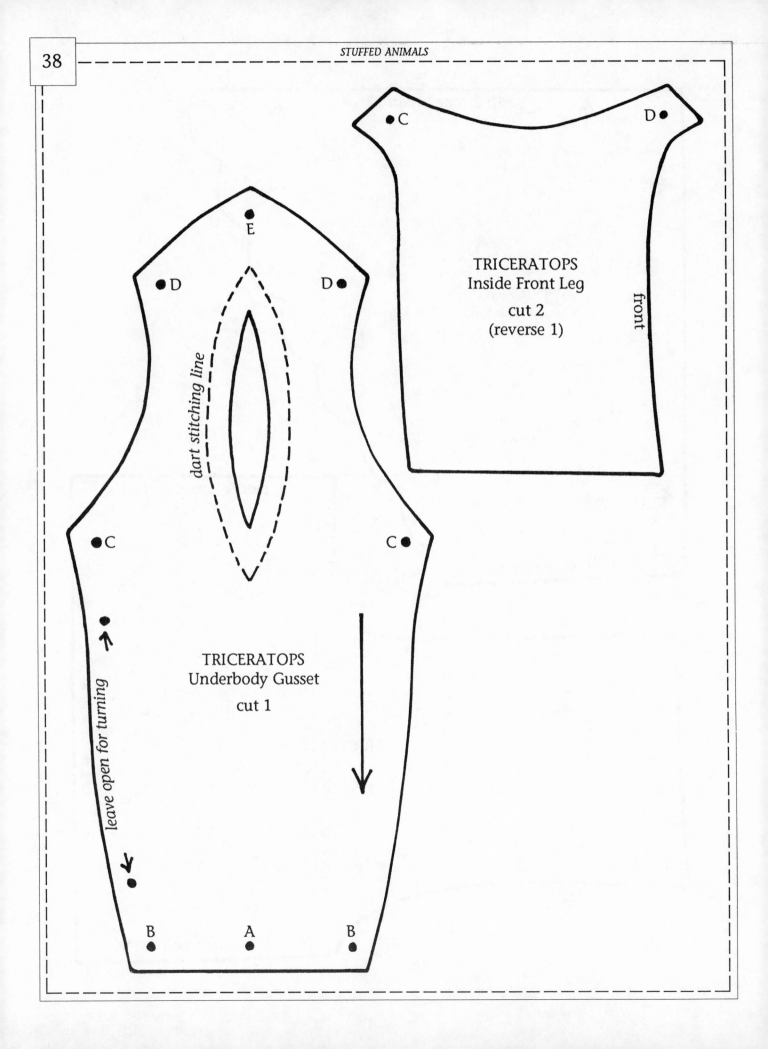

TRICERATOPS
Inside Front Leg

cut 2
(reverse 1)

front

E

D   D

dart stitching line

C   C

leave open for turning

TRICERATOPS
Underbody Gusset

cut 1

B   A   B

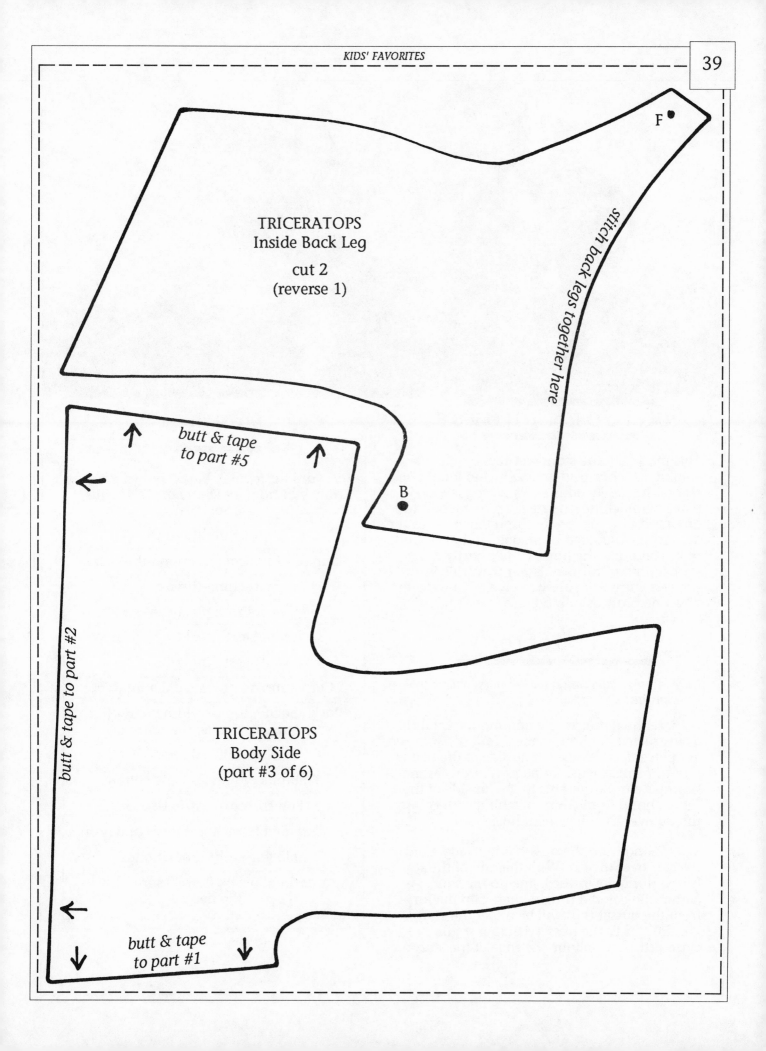

TRICERATOPS
Inside Back Leg

cut 2
(reverse 1)

stitch back legs together here

F

butt & tape
to part #5

B

butt & tape to part #2

TRICERATOPS
Body Side
(part #3 of 6)

butt & tape
to part #1

UNICORN / HORSE

This proud equine stands 14 inches tall, excluding his ears, and is 15½ inches long. The star on his forehead is easily zigzagged in place by machine and his silky mane and tail are hand sewn as the finishing touch. With the addition of a golden horn, golden hooves and mane and tail, the horse can be easily transformed into a unicorn. Either way, this furry little creature will surely receive a big welcome when he prances into a horse lover's heart!

INSTRUCTIONS

Note: All seam allowances are ¼" unless otherwise instructed.

Prepare the patterns, cut and mark the fabric as instructed in chapter one. Mark the star and ear placement on the wrong side of the head gusset. As instructed on page 17, transfer the star and ear placements to the fur side of the fabric, hand or machine stitching with colored thread over the placement lines.

1. Working from the gusset's right side, hold the star over the fur. With the nap of the star fur pointing downward, line up the star within the colored thread lines. Clip the fur from the gusset that will be under the star. Pin the star to the gusset. Using a small zigzag stitch, applique the edge of the star to

MATERIALS

½ yard fur (camel, black, brown, and white seal from by Diane or CR's Crafts, see Sources)

Matching thread

Scrap of white seal fur (optional, for star)

Matching thread

Two 14 mm plastic eyes

Scrap of black wool for hooves

Polyester fiberfill

Carpet thread or waxed dental floss

Black, mocha, tan or white Pretty Hair® (from CR's Crafts, see Sources)

Matching thread

Embroidery floss or perle cotton

For Unicorn, substitute:

¼ yard gold fabric for hooves and horn

Gold yarn for mane and tail

A garland of silk flowers surrounds the neck

the head gusset. Push the white star fur into the center of the star as you stitch, keeping it out of the stitching. When finished, brush the star fur out over the zigzag stitching and blend it in with the colored gusset fur.

2. Right sides facing, pin the dart in the head gusset. Stitch ¼" from the straight, raw edge.

3. Choose two ear pieces, one right pointing and one left pointing. Trim fur as instructed on page 11. Pin to other two ear pieces, right sides facing. Stitch, leaving straight edges open.

At tips of ears, trim seam allowances to ⅛" from stitching. Turn right side out. Set aside.

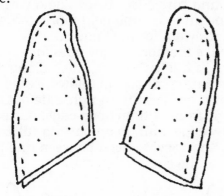

4. Pin and stitch two horse sides together, right sides facing, from dot A at nose to dot B at chest.

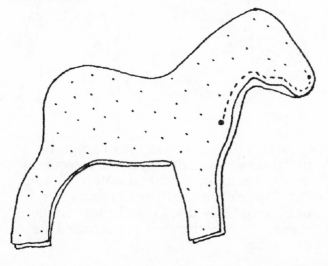

5. Match and pin dot A at nose on head gusset to dot A at junction of seam of head on body sides. Pin dot C on head gusset to dot C on neck of one horse side. Pin along the gusset between the two dots. Stitch. Repeat for second side of gusset and second body side.

6. Matching dots D, E, F and G to their counterparts, pin and stitch inside front and back leg pieces to underbody gusset as shown. Repeat for the other side.

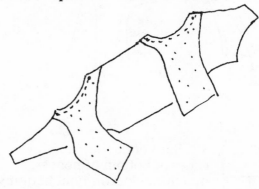

7. Right sides facing, pin and stitch hooves to bottoms of body side legs and inside legs as shown.

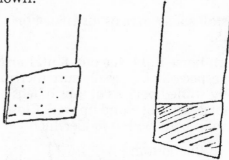

8. Starting with dot B at chest, pin one side of underbody gusset to chest, and front of front leg of one body side, matching dots B, raw edges and hooves. Stitch, leaving bottom of hooves open.

Repeat for other side of chest/front of front leg.

9. On one side of body, pin and stitch back of front legs, tummy, and front of back legs, matching hooves and easing to fit.

Repeat for other side, leaving an opening between the dots for turning.

10. Match and pin dot H at back (under tail) of underbody gusset to dot H on one side of body side. Continue pinning down back of leg and hoof. Stitch.

Repeat for other side.

11. Pin and stitch body sides together along back from dot C to dot H.

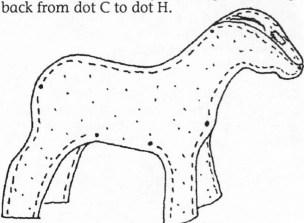

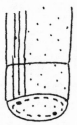

12. Pin hoof bottoms to raw edges at bottom of hooves, matching dots on hoof bottoms to seams in hooves. Stitch.

13. Install safety eyes as instructed on page 15.

14. Turn horse right side out. Stuff horse firmly, especially in legs. Be sure there are no softly stuffed pockets at tops of legs or your horse will not stand up well. Close opening in body with a ladderstitch.

15. Turn the bottom edges of the ears ¼" to the inside. Whipstitch closed. Handstitch to head at markings, having points of ears facing center and trimmed ears facing forward.

16. Cut a length of Pretty Hair® 10" long. Find the middle of the hair and stitch it to the dart seam at the top of the horse's neck, about a half inch behind the ears. One half of the hair will fall forward for the forelock and the other half will fall to one side of the neck to begin the mane. Cut five more lengths of Pretty Hair®, each 10". Fold them in half and stitch the folds down the neck, on the seam, each about an inch below the preceding one. Brush all mane hair to one side of the neck.

Cut two lengths of Pretty Hair®, each 16". Treating them as one, find the middle and stitch to the horse at the top of the rear of the underbody gusset. (Point H on horse's body side.)

17. For nose and mouth embroidery, turn to the instructions on page 15.

Unicorn

Make a white horse as instructed above, substituting curled (see below) gold yarn for the mane and tail, and gold fabric rather than black wool for the hooves.

To make the horn: Right sides facing fold the horn in half as shown. Stitch along the stitching lines. Trim seam allowances to ⅛" at top of horn. Turn horn right side out. Stuff to 1" from bottom open edge. Baste ½" from raw edge. Pull up on basting stitches tightly. Knot. Sew to head between and just in front of the ears.

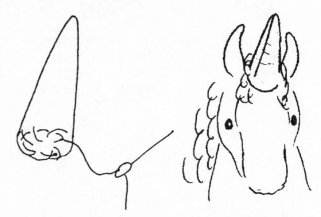

To curl the yarn: Wrap yarn around metal skewers or knitting needles, securing the ends with tape. Soak in water. Place in 200-degree oven for 10 or 15 minutes or until completely dry. Cool. Remove from skewers. Apply the yarn as instructed for the mane.

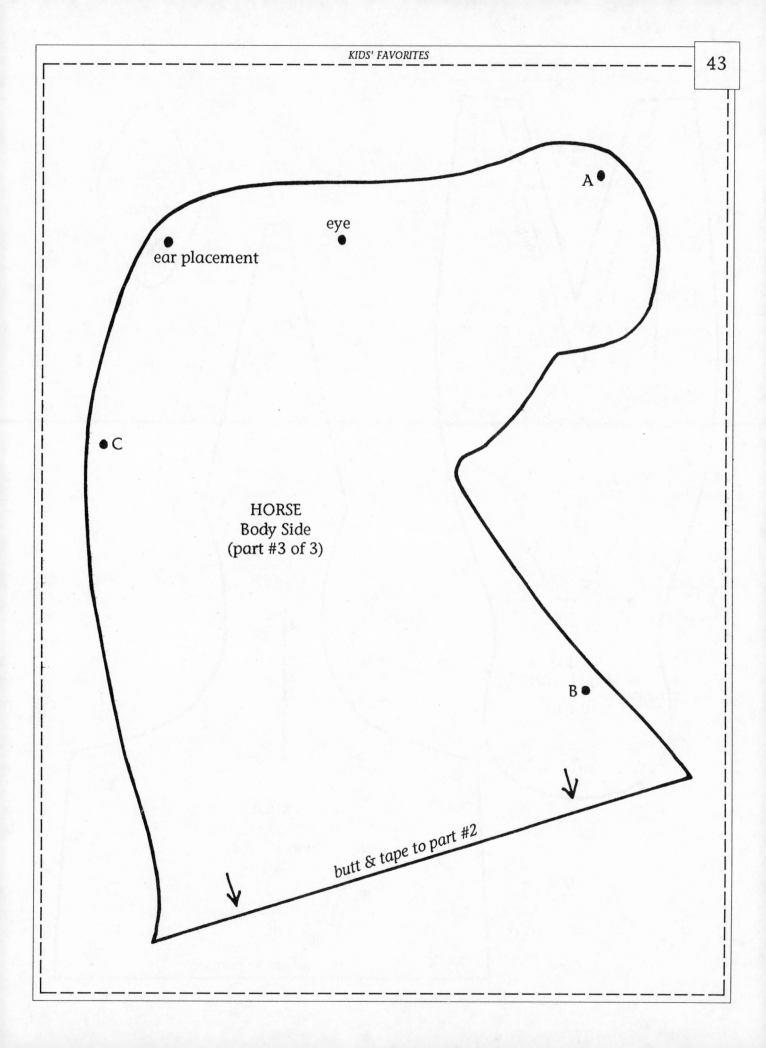

A

eye

ear placement

C

HORSE
Body Side
(part #3 of 3)

B

butt & tape to part #2

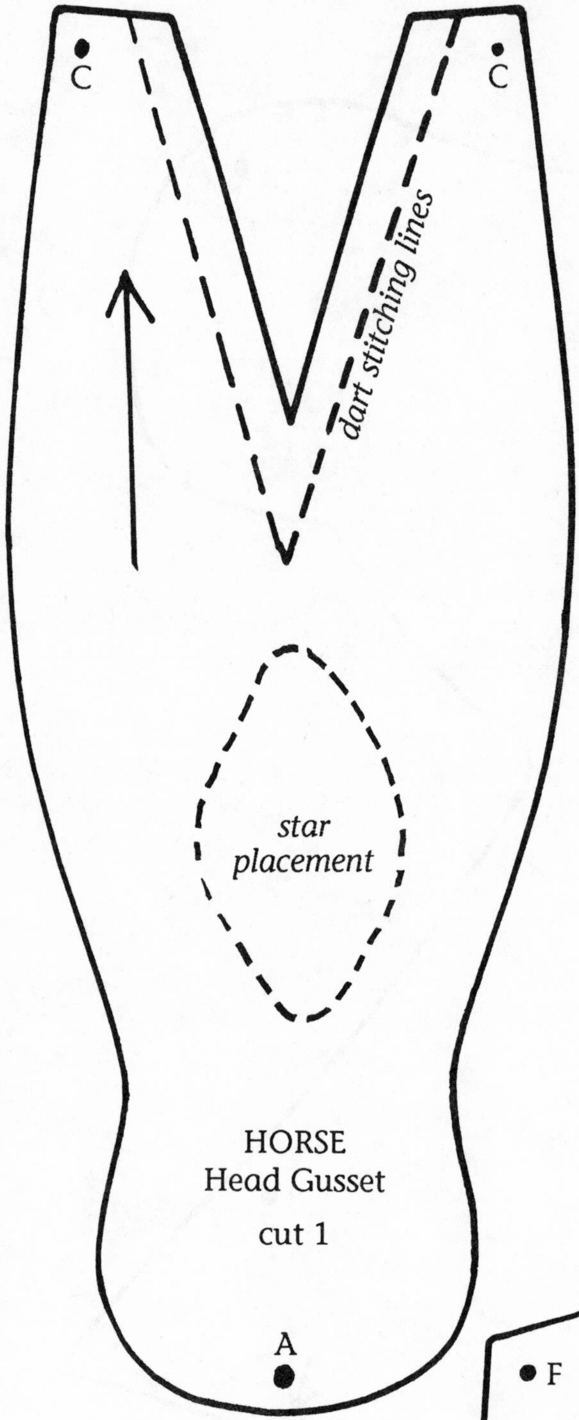

C

C

dart stitching lines

star placement

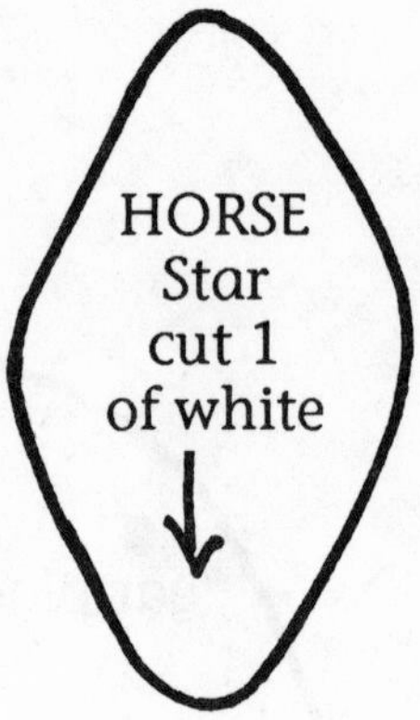

HORSE
Star
cut 1
of white

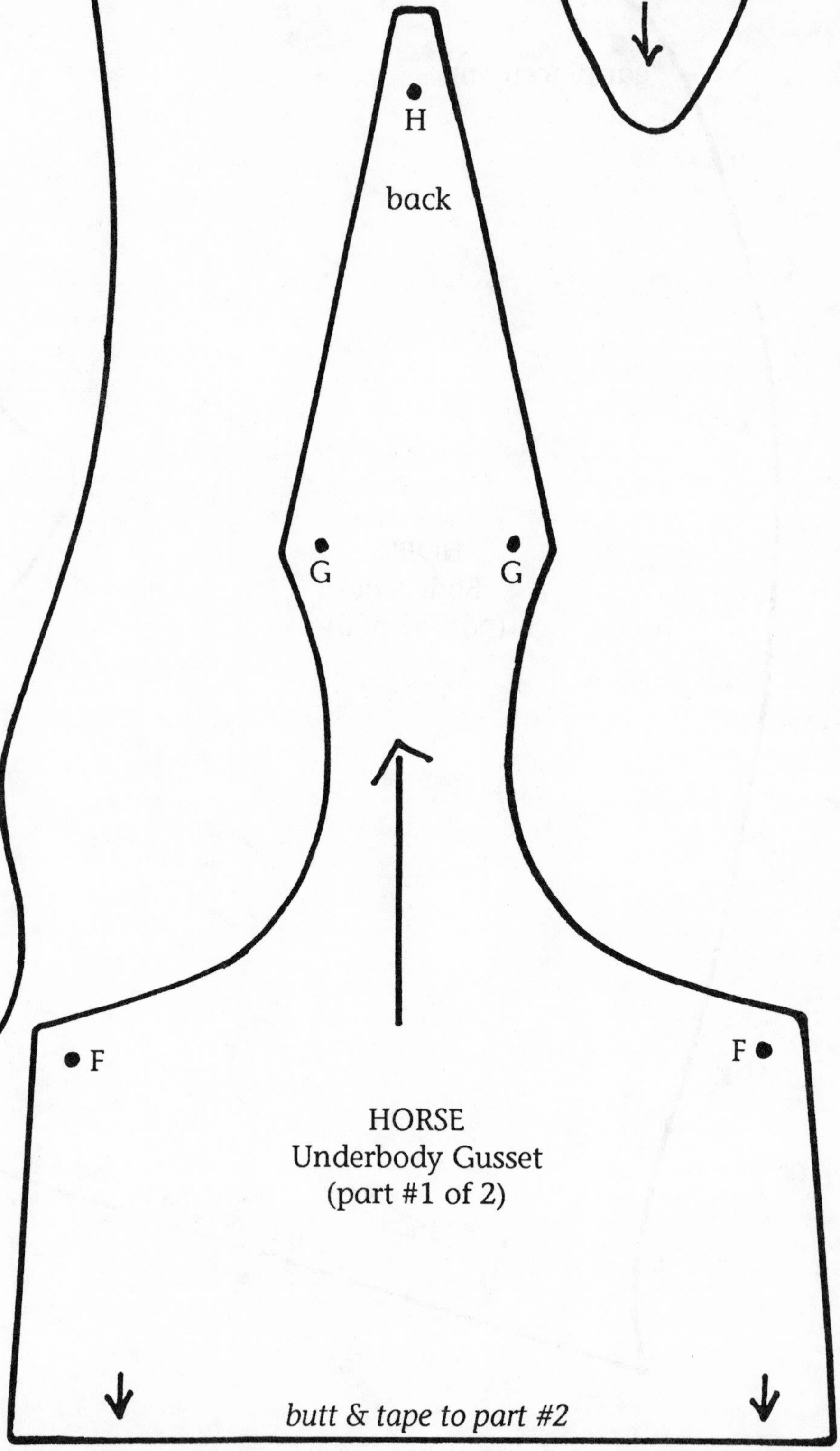

H

back

G

G

HORSE
Head Gusset
cut 1

A

F

F

HORSE
Underbody Gusset
(part #1 of 2)

butt & tape to part #2

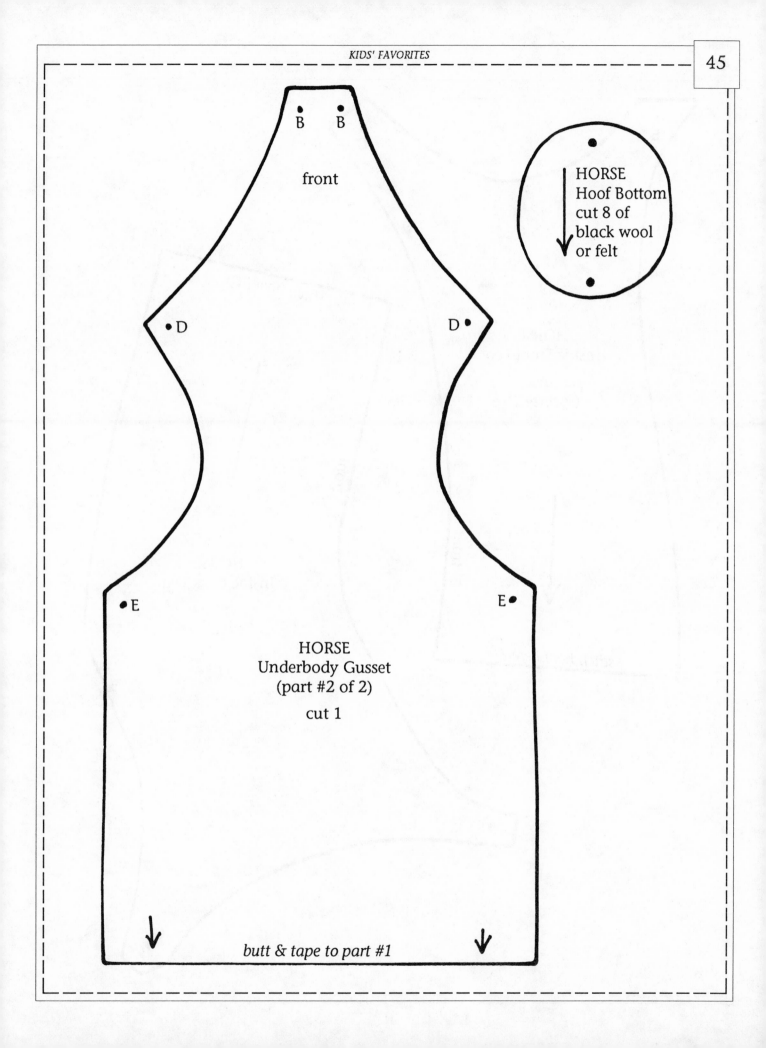

B   B

front

• D   D •

HORSE
Hoof Bottom
cut 8 of
black wool
or felt

• E   E •

HORSE
Underbody Gusset
(part #2 of 2)

cut 1

butt & tape to part #1

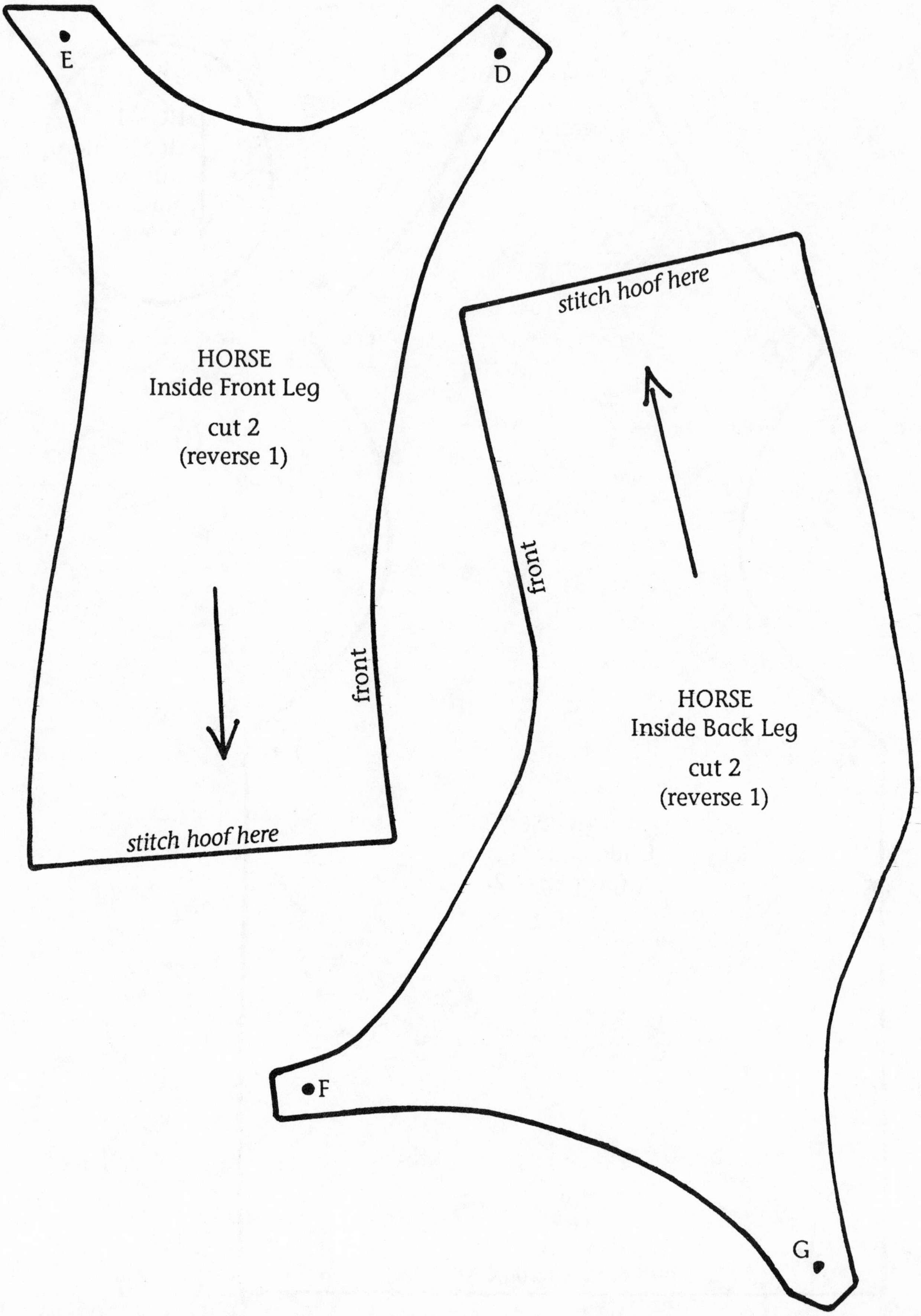

E

D

HORSE
Inside Front Leg

cut 2
(reverse 1)

front

stitch hoof here

stitch hoof here

front

HORSE
Inside Back Leg

cut 2
(reverse 1)

F

G

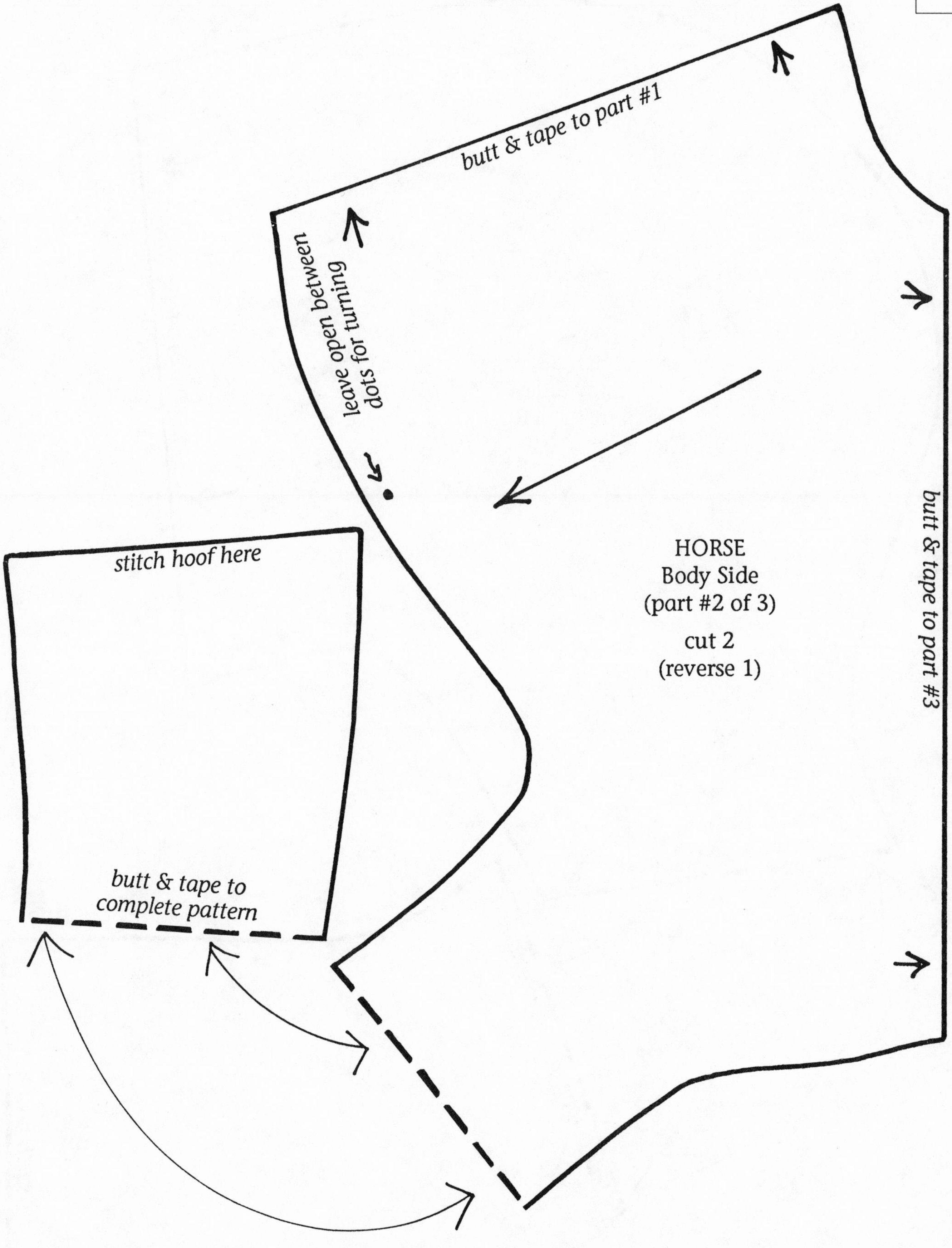

butt & tape to part #1

leave open between
dots for turning

stitch hoof here

butt & tape to part #3

HORSE
Body Side
(part #2 of 3)

cut 2
(reverse 1)

butt & tape to
complete pattern

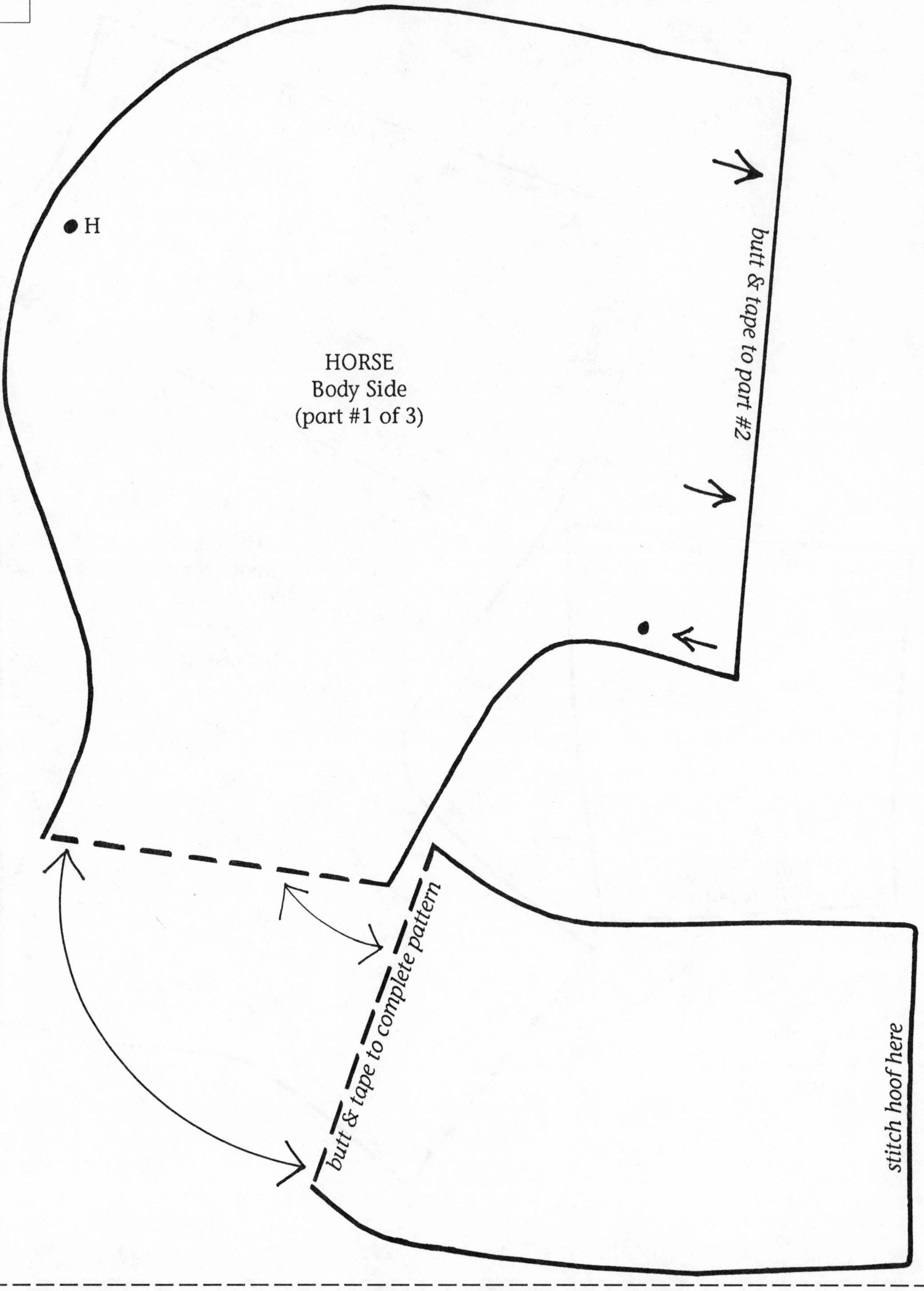

● H

HORSE
Body Side
(part #1 of 3)

butt & tape to part #2

butt & tape to complete pattern

stitch hoof here

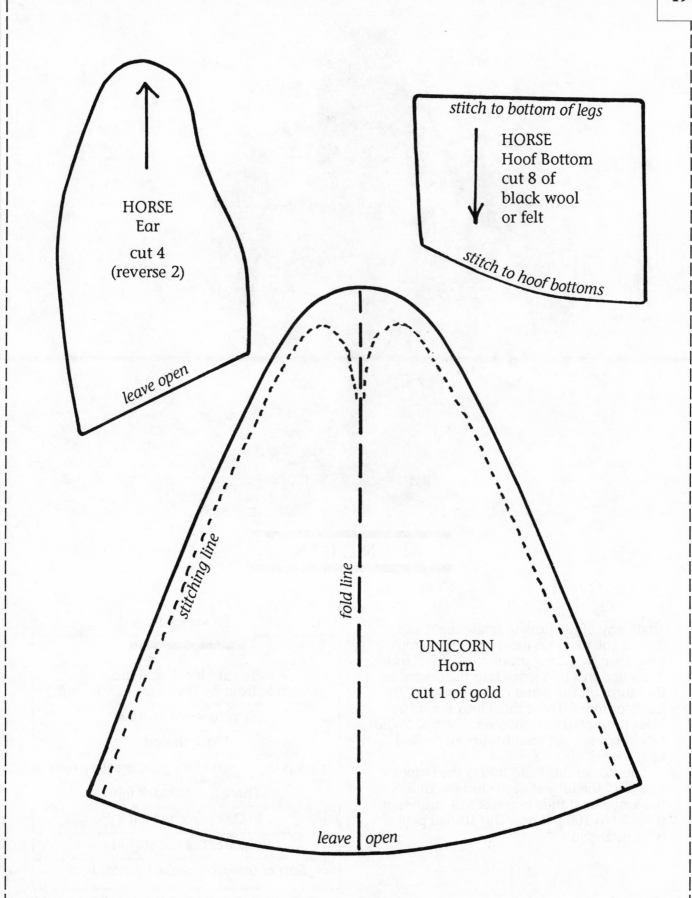

HORSE
Ear

cut 4
(reverse 2)

leave open

stitch to bottom of legs

HORSE
Hoof Bottom
cut 8 of
black wool
or felt

stitch to hoof bottoms

stitching line

fold line

UNICORN
Horn

cut 1 of gold

leave open

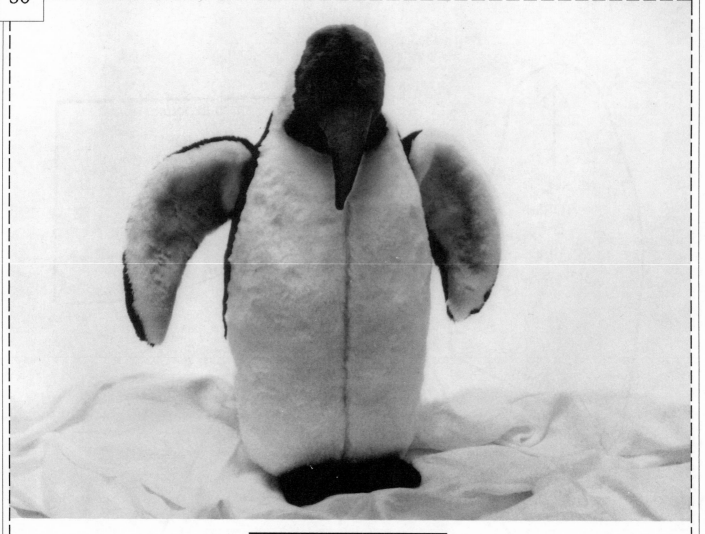

PENGUIN

Their way of life having made flight super-fluous, the penguin looks like a ludicrous little man waddling around in formal attire. But when this bird leaps into the ocean, he flies through the water at good speed, 10 knots or more. These ridiculous seafaring birds prompted one observer to write, "Who would believe in penguins unless he had seen them?"

The star of this collection is the Emperor penguin, the largest of the family. In life, the Emperor stands four feet tall and weighs from 50 to 100 pounds. Our stuffed penguin is 22 inches tall.

MATERIALS

¾ yard black seal fur
(available from by Diane and CR's Crafts)

¾ yard white seal fur

Black thread

One pair 14 mm black plastic safety eyes

Three pieces black felt

One piece red felt

Polyester fiberfill stuffing

Carpet thread or waxed dental floss

INSTRUCTIONS

Note: All seam allowances are ¼" unless otherwise instructed.

As instructed on page 10, prepare and cut out patterns pieces. Transfer markings for the eye, foot, and wing placement to the wrong side of the fur. Mark the wing placement on the fur side of the black body backs and the foot placement on the body bottom by hand or machine basting over the markings with colored thread.

1. Pin and stitch white body front pieces to black body back pieces, matching notches.

2. Match and pin dots A and B on one black head side to one white body front. Stitch from dot A to the front raw edge.

   Matching dots C, pin head side to body front from dot A to dot C. Stitch

Repeat for other head side/body front.

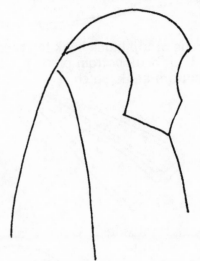

3. Pin the two body/head assemblies together, right sides facing. Stitch from dot D under the tail, around the tail, up the back and to the top of the beak opening. Stitch from under the beak opening and down the tummy.

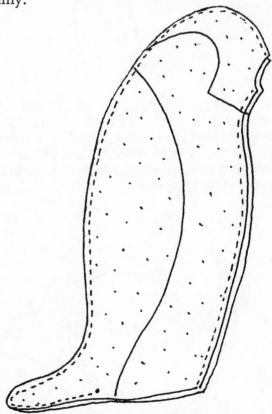

4. Pin two black top beak pieces together along top edges as indicated on pattern. Stitch.

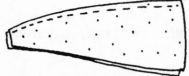

Right side of top black beak top piece facing red felt beak bottom piece, pin top beak to bottom beak. Stitch.

Turn beak right side out. Insert beak into opening in head. Pin, matching seam at black beak tops with seam at top of beak opening in fur head. Stitch.

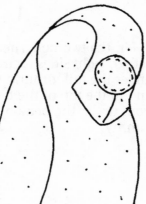

5. Pin body bottom to penguin, matching small dot to dot D under tail in black fabric and the large dot to the bottom of the penguin's center front seam. Stitch, leaving an opening as marked on the body bottom for turning and stuffing.

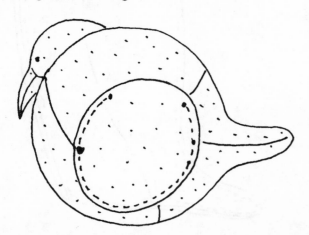

6. Install eyes as instructed on page 15.

7. Starting with small bits of stuffing, carefully stuff the beak. Stuff the remainder of the penguin with larger handfuls of stuffing. Close the opening in the body bottom as instructed on page 14.

8. Pin a white and a black wing piece together, right sides facing. Stitch, leaving an opening as indicated on the pattern.

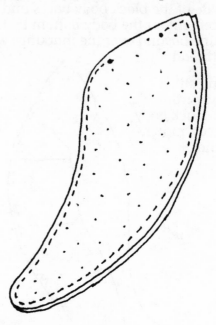

Repeat for other wing.
Turn both wings right side out. Turn openings to inside and ladderstitch closed. Handstitch to side of penguin at colored thread markings. Remove thread markings.

9. Using a 1/8" seam allowance, stitch two felt feet pieces together. On one thickness of felt cut the cross marked on the foot. Turn the foot right side out. Stuff lightly, just enough to give the foot shape. Handstitch the slashed cross closed. Handstitch foot to bottom of body at colored markings, having the cross against the bottom of the body. Repeat for second foot.

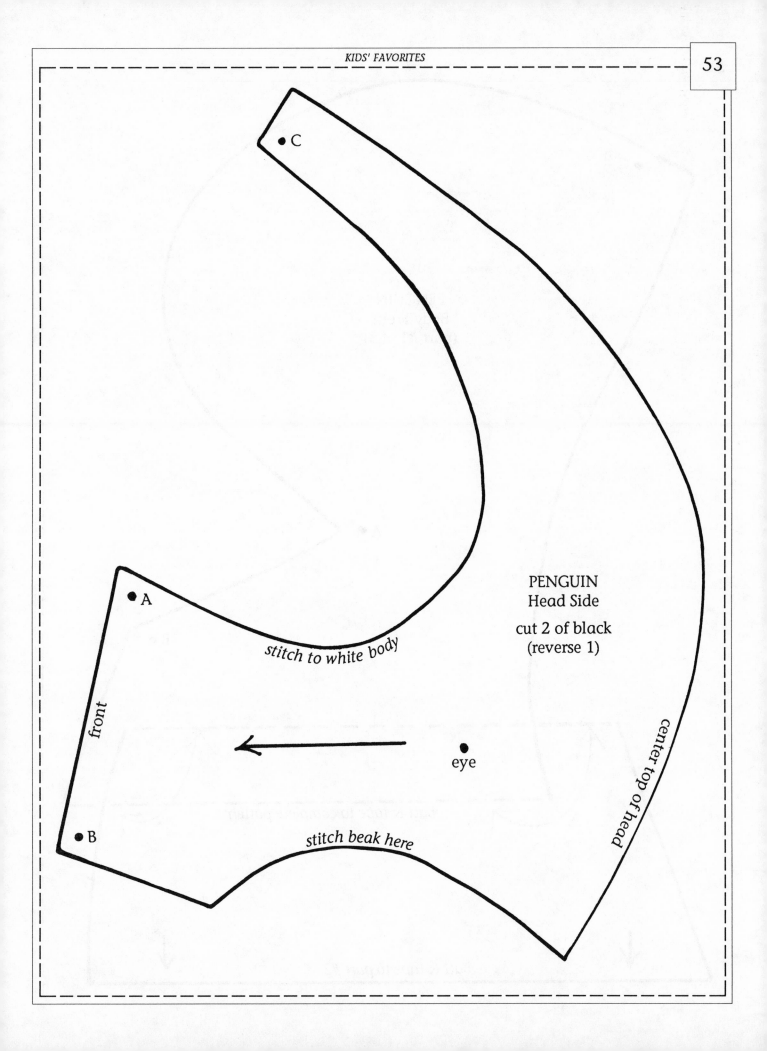

• C

• A

stitch to white body

PENGUIN
Head Side

cut 2 of black
(reverse 1)

front

eye

center top of head

• B

stitch beak here

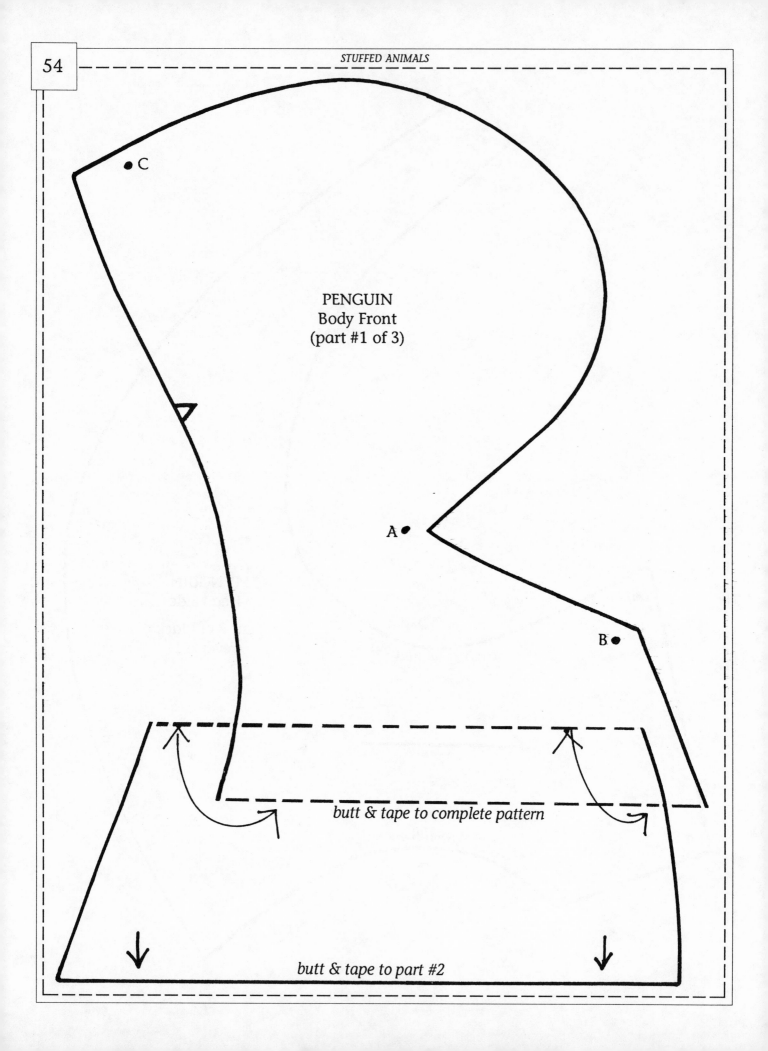

• C

PENGUIN
Body Front
(part #1 of 3)

A •

B •

butt & tape to complete pattern

butt & tape to part #2

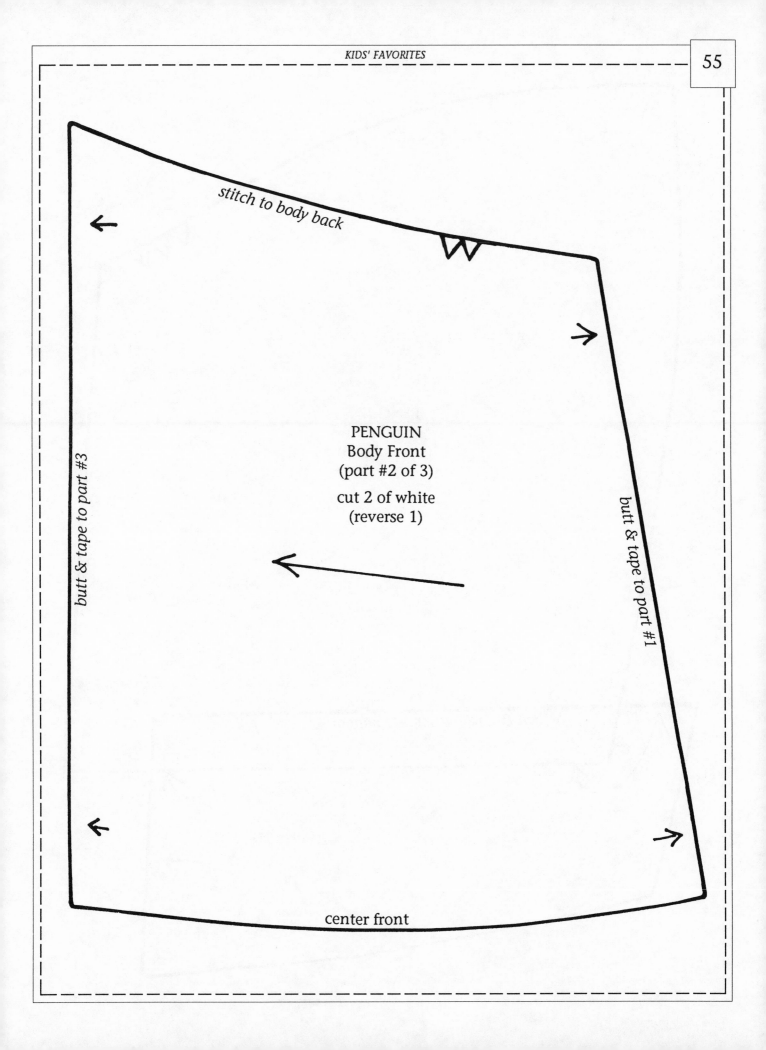

stitch to body back

butt & tape to part #3

PENGUIN
Body Front
(part #2 of 3)

cut 2 of white
(reverse 1)

butt & tape to part #1

center front

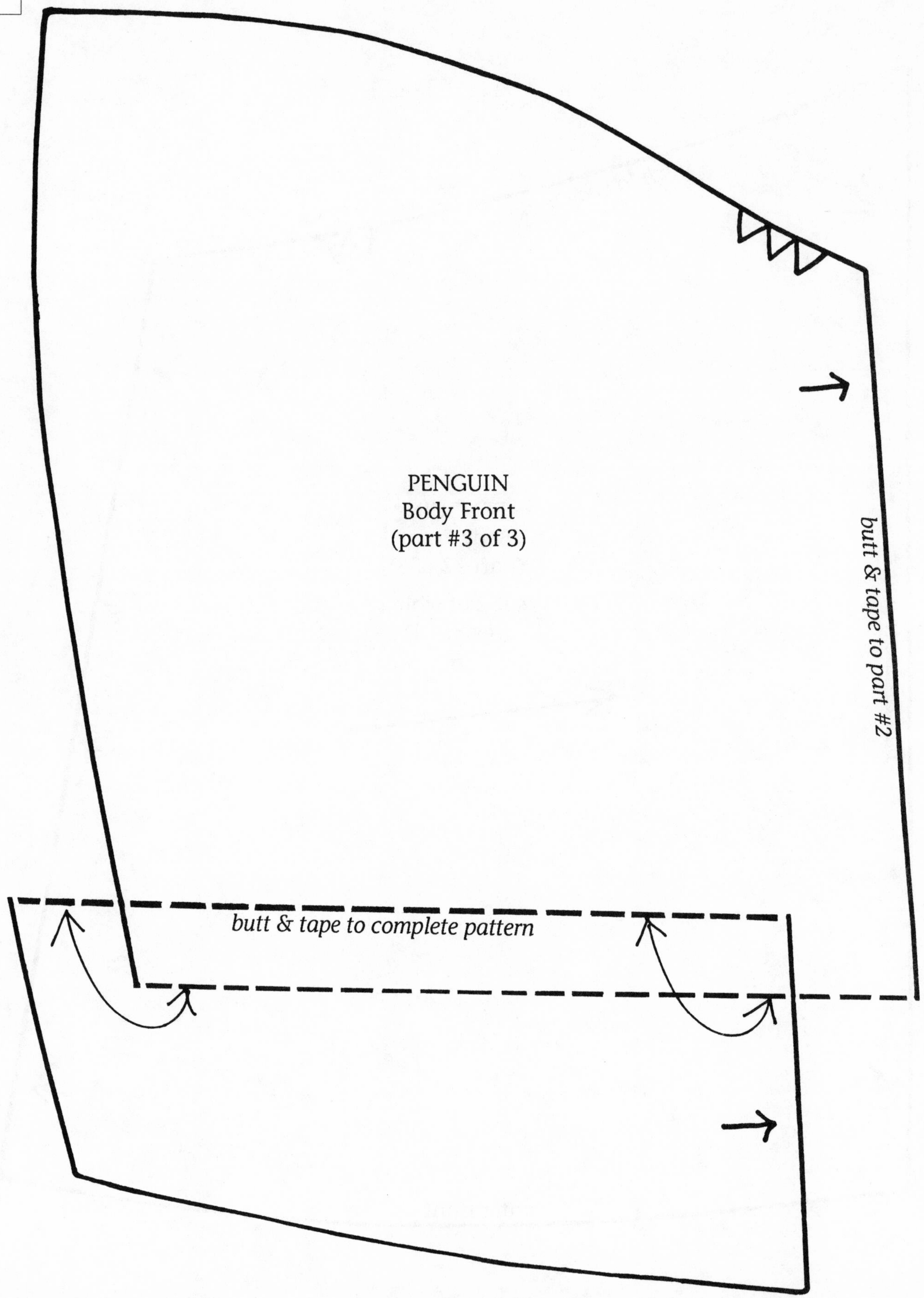

PENGUIN
Body Front
(part #3 of 3)

butt & tape to part #2

butt & tape to complete pattern

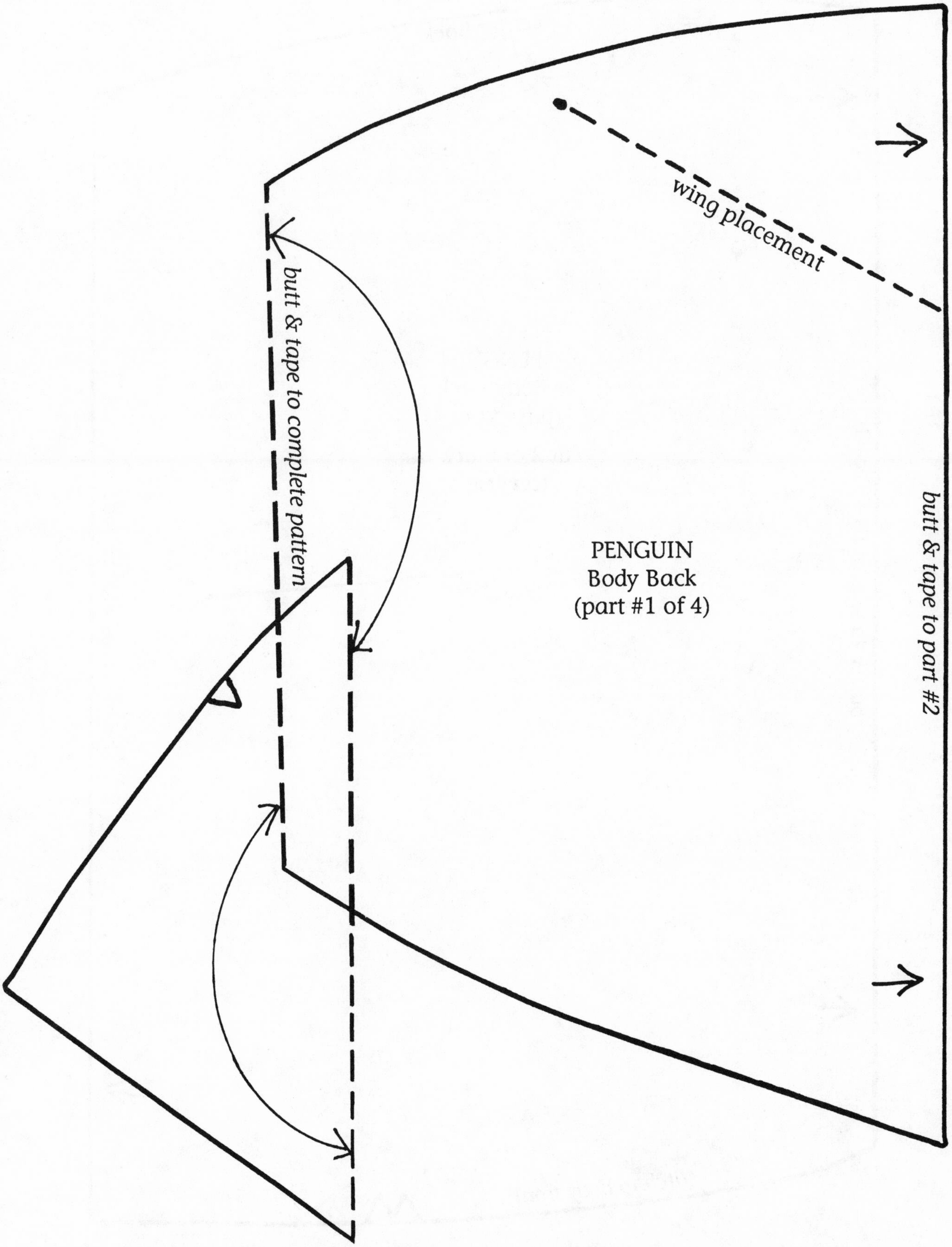

wing placement

butt & tape to part #2

butt & tape to complete pattern

PENGUIN
Body Back
(part #1 of 4)

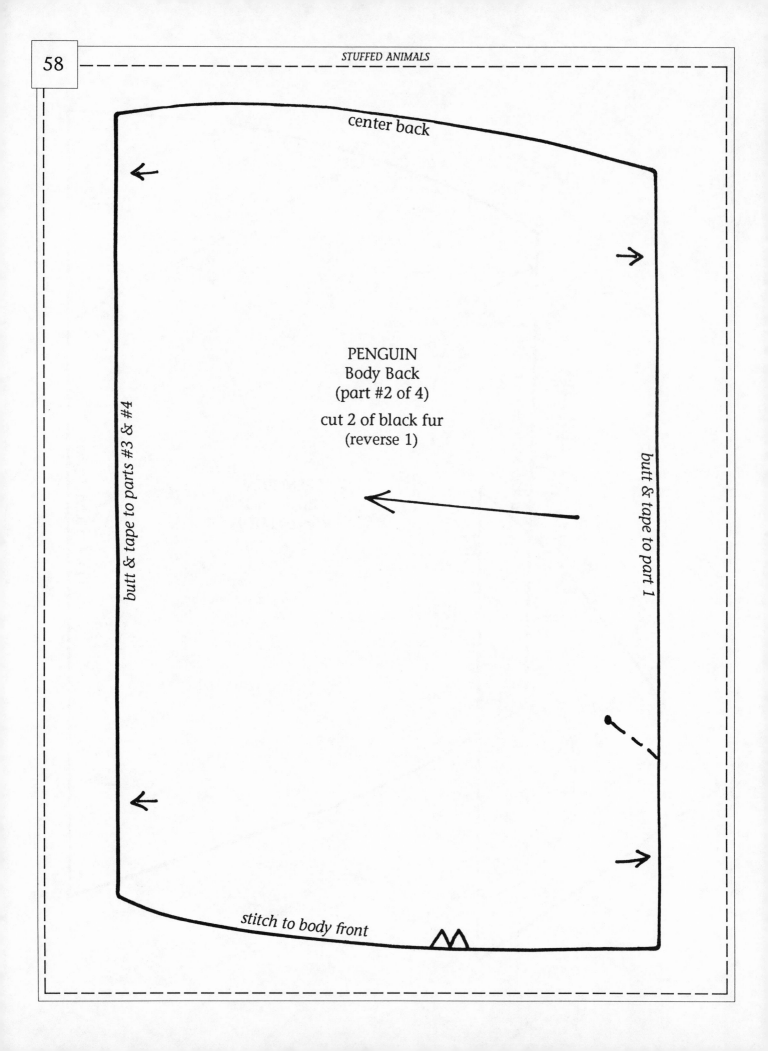

center back

PENGUIN
Body Back
(part #2 of 4)

cut 2 of black fur
(reverse 1)

butt & tape to parts #3 & #4

butt & tape to part 1

stitch to body front

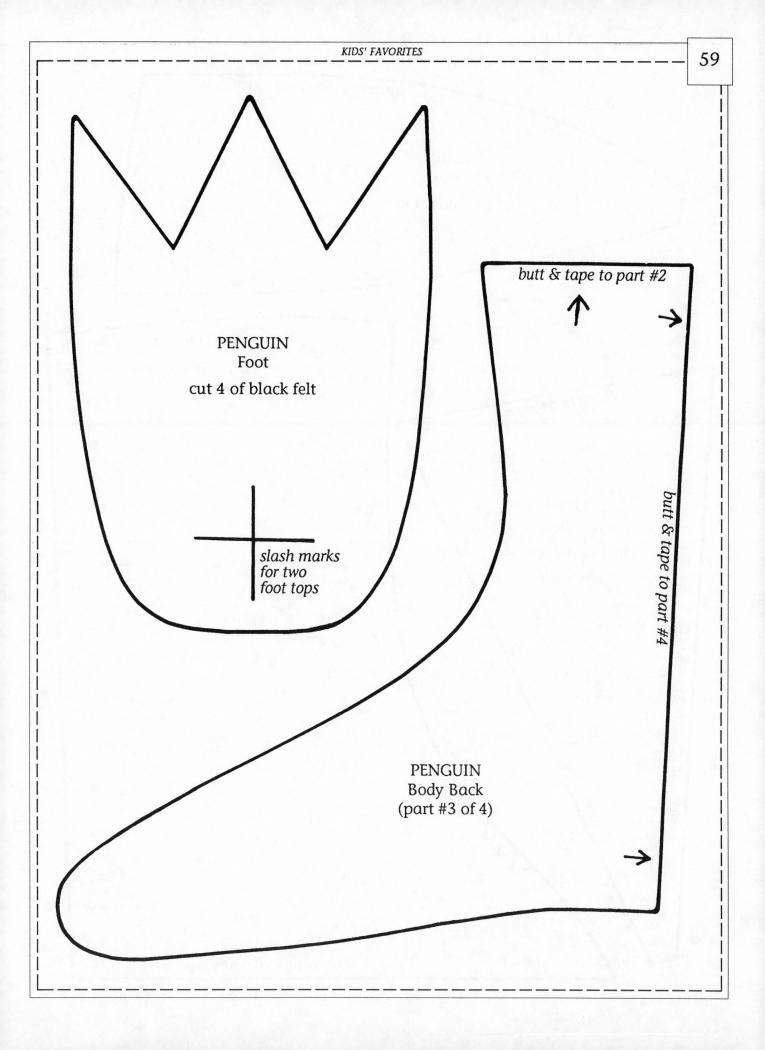

PENGUIN
Foot

cut 4 of black felt

*slash marks
for two
foot tops*

butt & tape to part #2

butt & tape to part #4

PENGUIN
Body Back
(part #3 of 4)

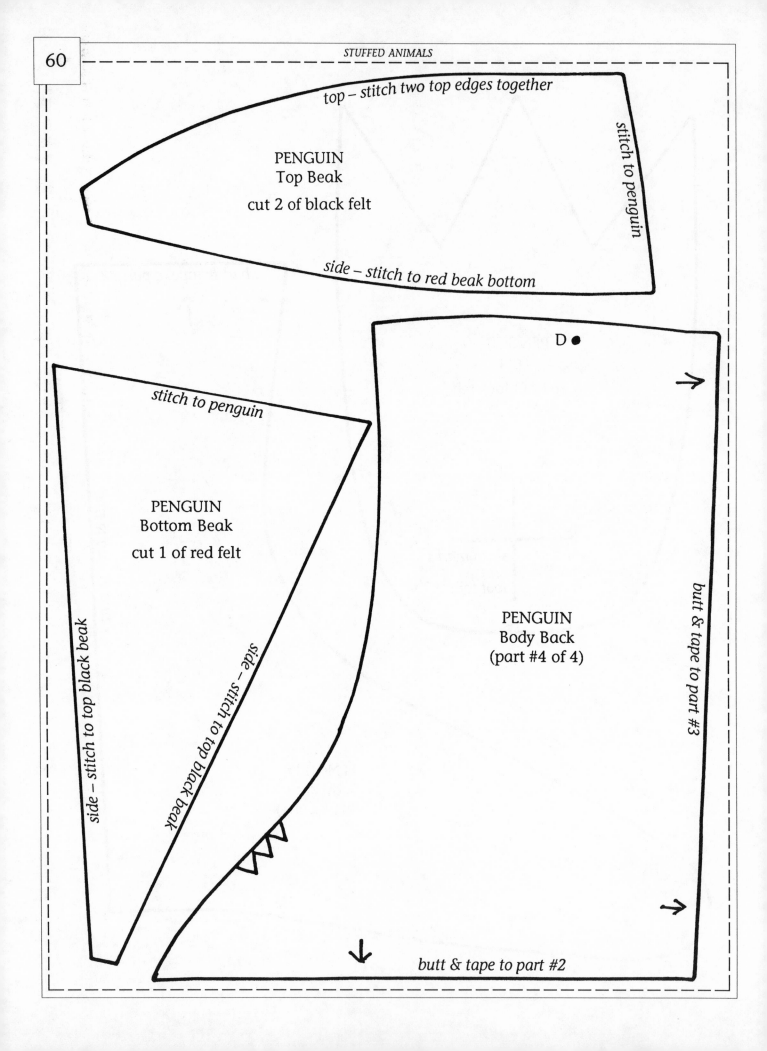

top – stitch two top edges together

PENGUIN
Top Beak

cut 2 of black felt

stitch to penguin

side – stitch to red beak bottom

D •

stitch to penguin

PENGUIN
Bottom Beak

cut 1 of red felt

side – stitch to top black beak

side – stitch to top black beak

PENGUIN
Body Back
(part #4 of 4)

butt & tape to part #3

butt & tape to part #2

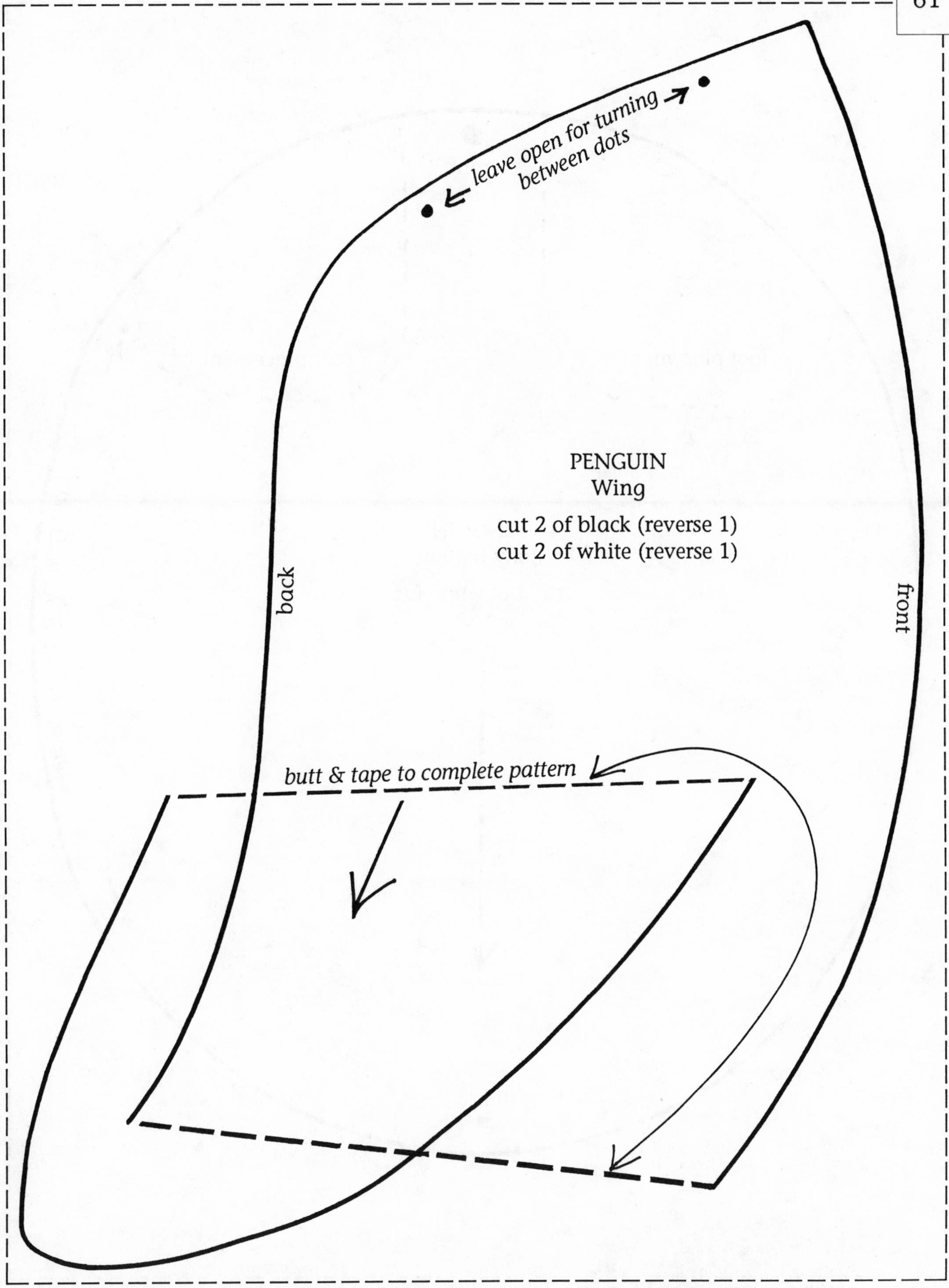

leave open for turning
between dots

PENGUIN
Wing

cut 2 of black (reverse 1)
cut 2 of white (reverse 1)

back

front

butt & tape to complete pattern

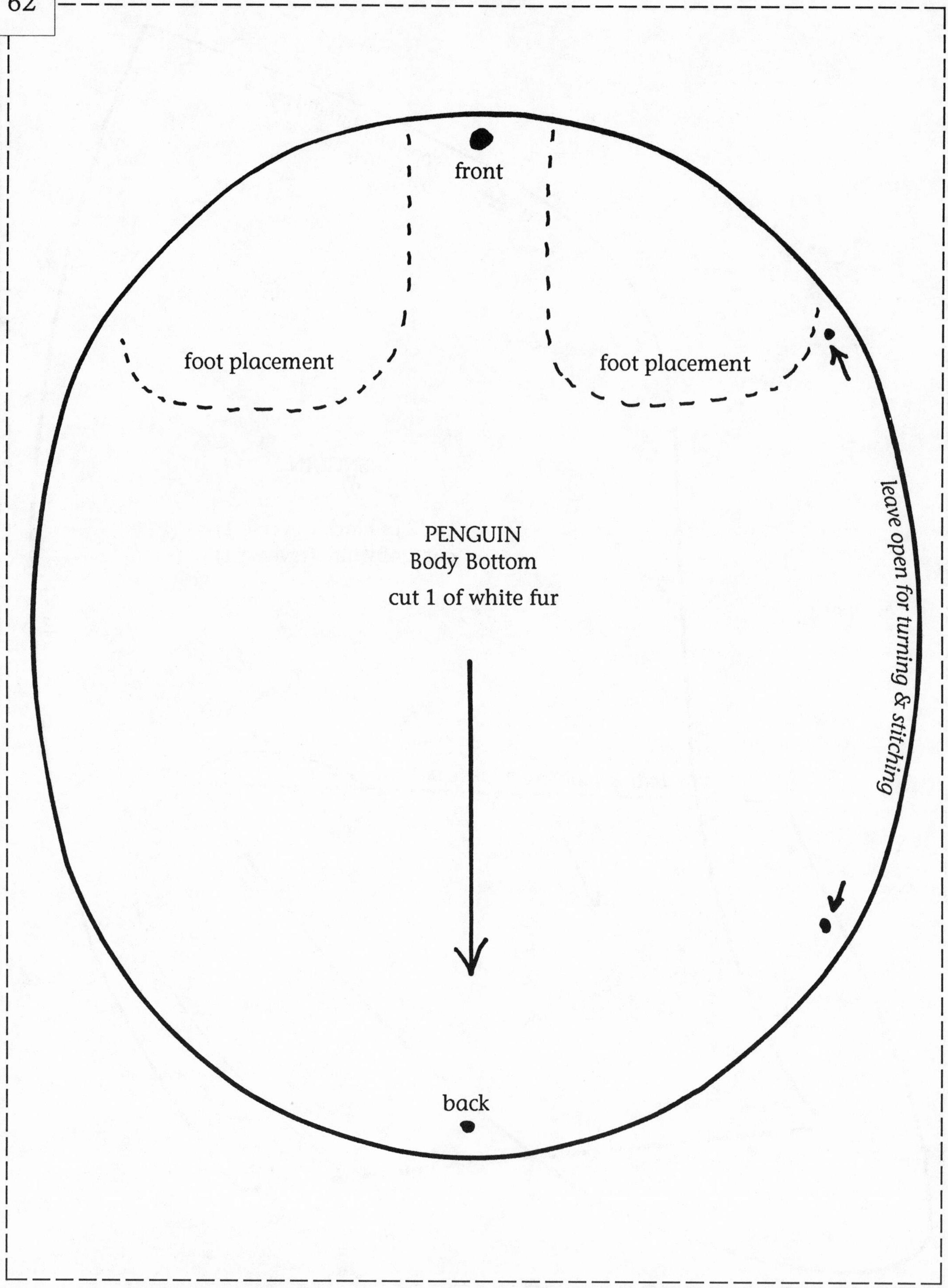

front

foot placement

foot placement

leave open for turning & stitching

PENGUIN
Body Bottom

cut 1 of white fur

back

LAMB

Standing 16 inches tall, this sweet little lamb is just right for hugging. Tie a baby blue or light pink ribbon — perhaps with a bell on it — around the lamb's neck to turn this winsome fellow into the perfect baby gift.

MATERIALS

½ yard shearling

Matching thread

Two 12 mm eyes

Polyester fiberfill

Carpet thread or waxed dental floss

Pink embroidery floss or perle cotton

Ribbon and bell
(see CR's Crafts in Sources)

INSTRUCTIONS

Note: All seam allowances are ¼" unless otherwise instructed.

Prepare the patterns, cut and mark the fabric as instructed on page 10.

1. Using a long machine stitch, gather the short, curved edge of the back head gusset, as indicated on the pattern piece.

Pin to front head gusset, matching dots A. Adjust gathers to fit. Stitch.

2. Pin two ear pieces together, right sides facing. Stitch, leaving straight edges open.

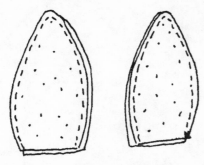

Turn right side out. Repeat for second ear.

3. Fold tail in half along lines as marked on pattern. Pin. Stitch, leaving edges open as marked. Turn right side out.

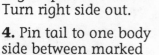

4. Pin tail to one body side between marked dots as shown. Baste.

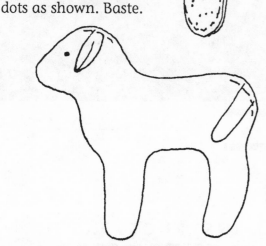

Fold ears in half lengthwise. Pin ears to body sides at dot, fold facing to the back. Baste.

5. Pin body sides together from dot B at nose to dot C at chest. Stitch.

6. Pin dot B at nose on front head gusset to dot B at nose in body sides. Pin dot D on back head gusset to dot D at back neck of one body side. Pin along the side of the gusset between the two dots. Stitch, including the ear in the seam. Repeat for second side of gusset.

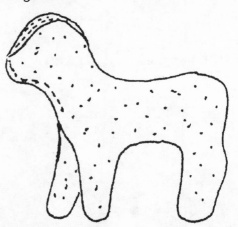

7. Pin and stitch inner front and inner back leg pieces to underbody gusset as shown, matching dots.

8. Starting with dot C at chest, pin one side of underbody gusset to one body side at chest, front leg, tummy, and back leg, ending at dot I under tail. Repeat for second side, this time leaving an opening between dots for turning as marked.

9. Pin body sides together from dot D at back of neck to dot I under tail. Stitch, including the tail in the seam.

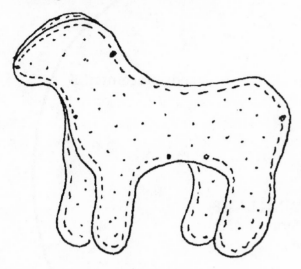

10. Install eyes as instructed on page 15.

11. Stuff. Ladderstitch opening in body closed.

12. To embroider the nose: Using a long needle, start the embroidery floss as instructed on page 15. Come up in the fabric at point A as illustrated. Go back in at point B and out at point C, leaving the thread loose.

Push the needle back into the fur at point D and out at E, leaving the thread loop loose.

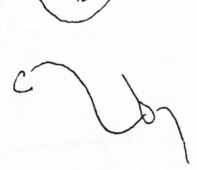

Go under and then over the first loop between A and B and back into the fur on the bottom side of loop C and D at F. Emerge anywhere in the fur. Pull up on the thread, taking up slack in the two loops until they are even. Finish off the thread as instructed on page 17.

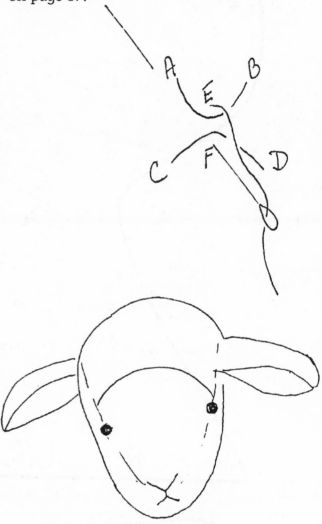

13. Thread the bell on the ribbon and tie the ribbon around the lamb's neck.

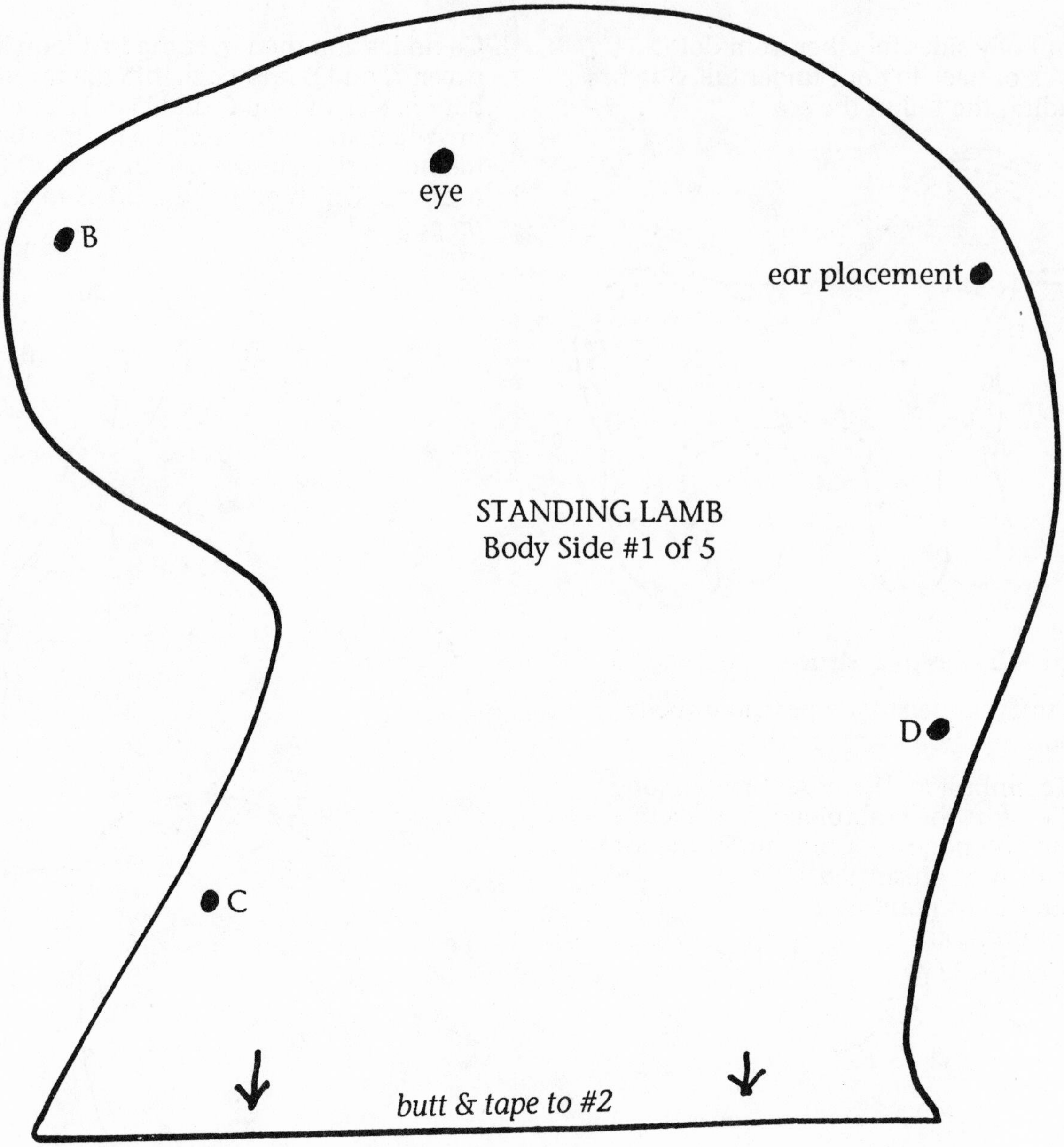

eye

B

ear placement

STANDING LAMB
Body Side #1 of 5

D

C

↓   ↓

butt & tape to #2

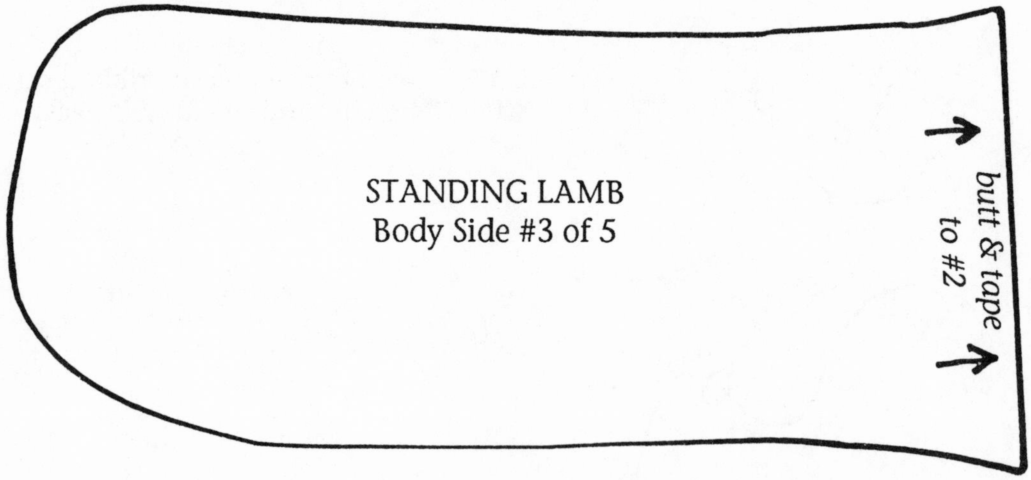

STANDING LAMB
Body Side #3 of 5

→

butt & tape to #2

→

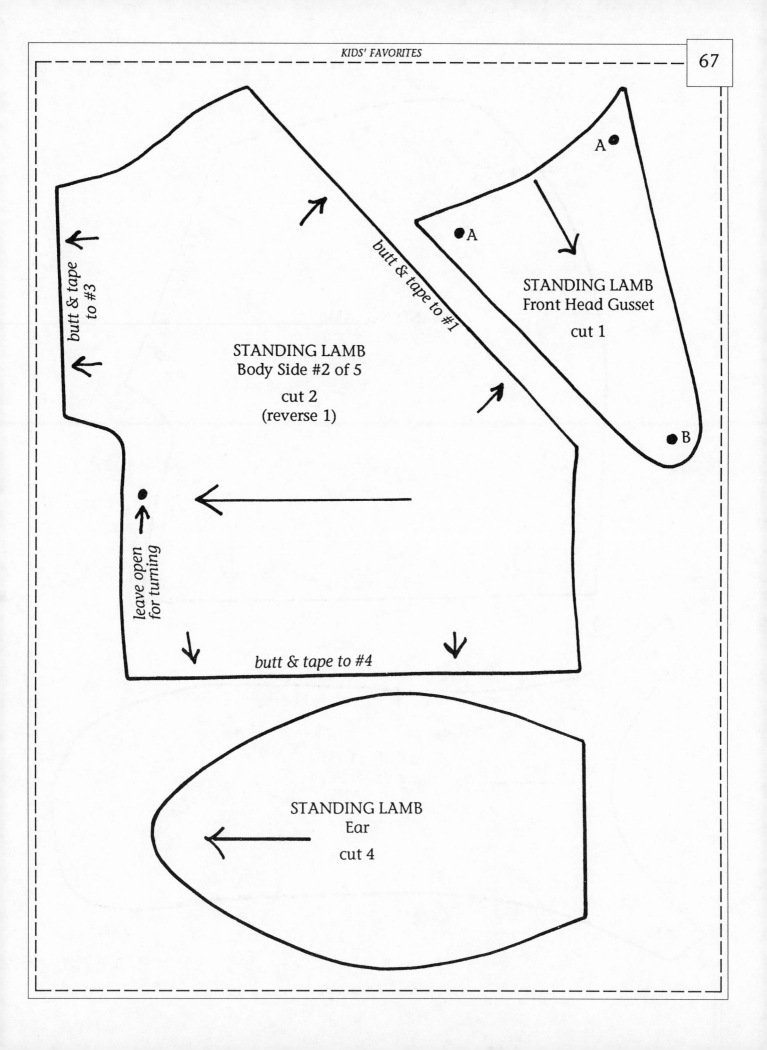

butt & tape to #1

A

A

B

STANDING LAMB
Front Head Gusset

cut 1

butt & tape
to #3

STANDING LAMB
Body Side #2 of 5

cut 2
(reverse 1)

leave open
for turning

butt & tape to #4

STANDING LAMB
Ear

cut 4

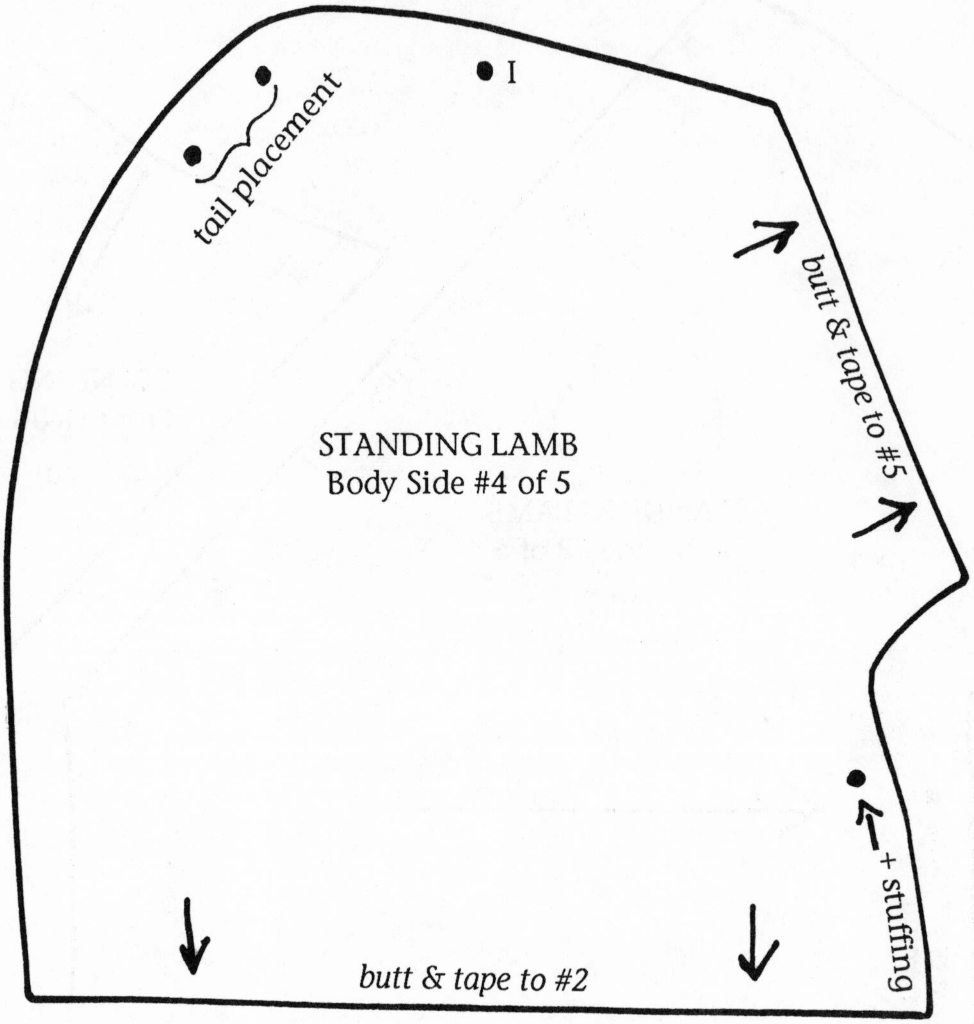

tail placement

● I

butt & tape to #5

STANDING LAMB
Body Side #4 of 5

+ stuffing

butt & tape to #2

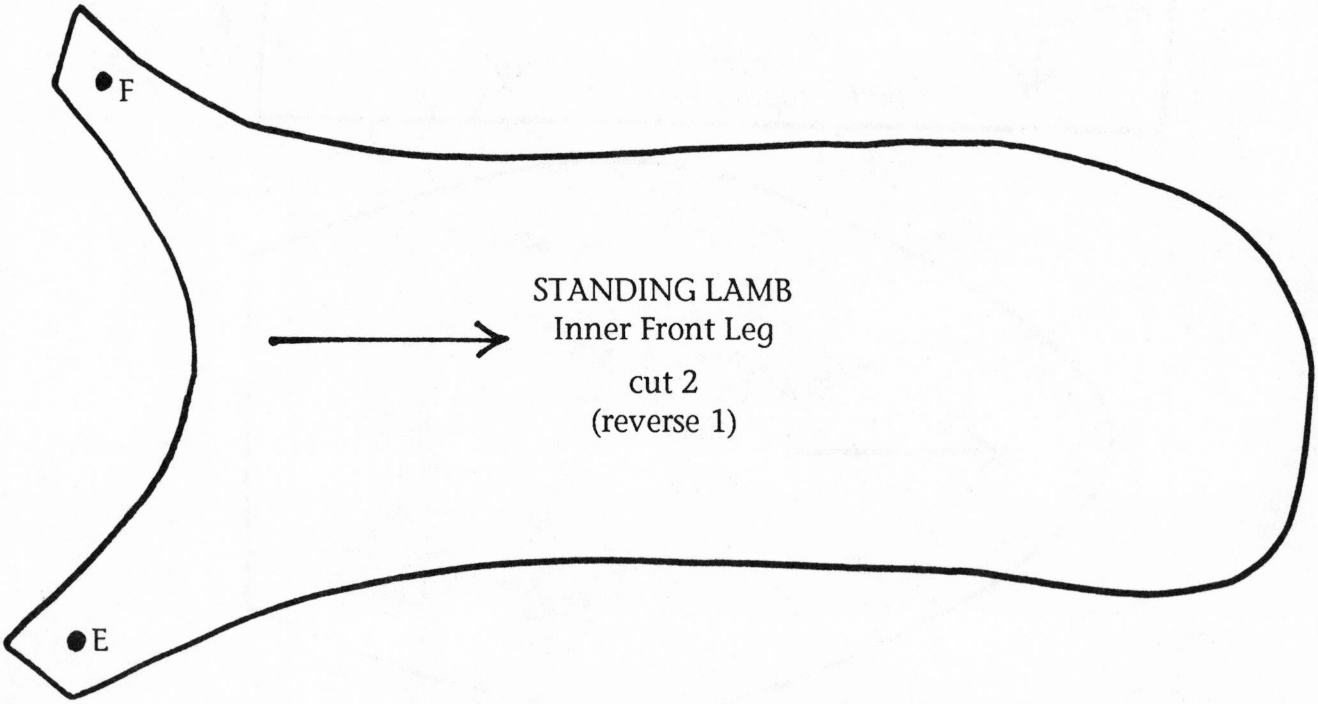

● F

STANDING LAMB
Inner Front Leg

cut 2
(reverse 1)

● E

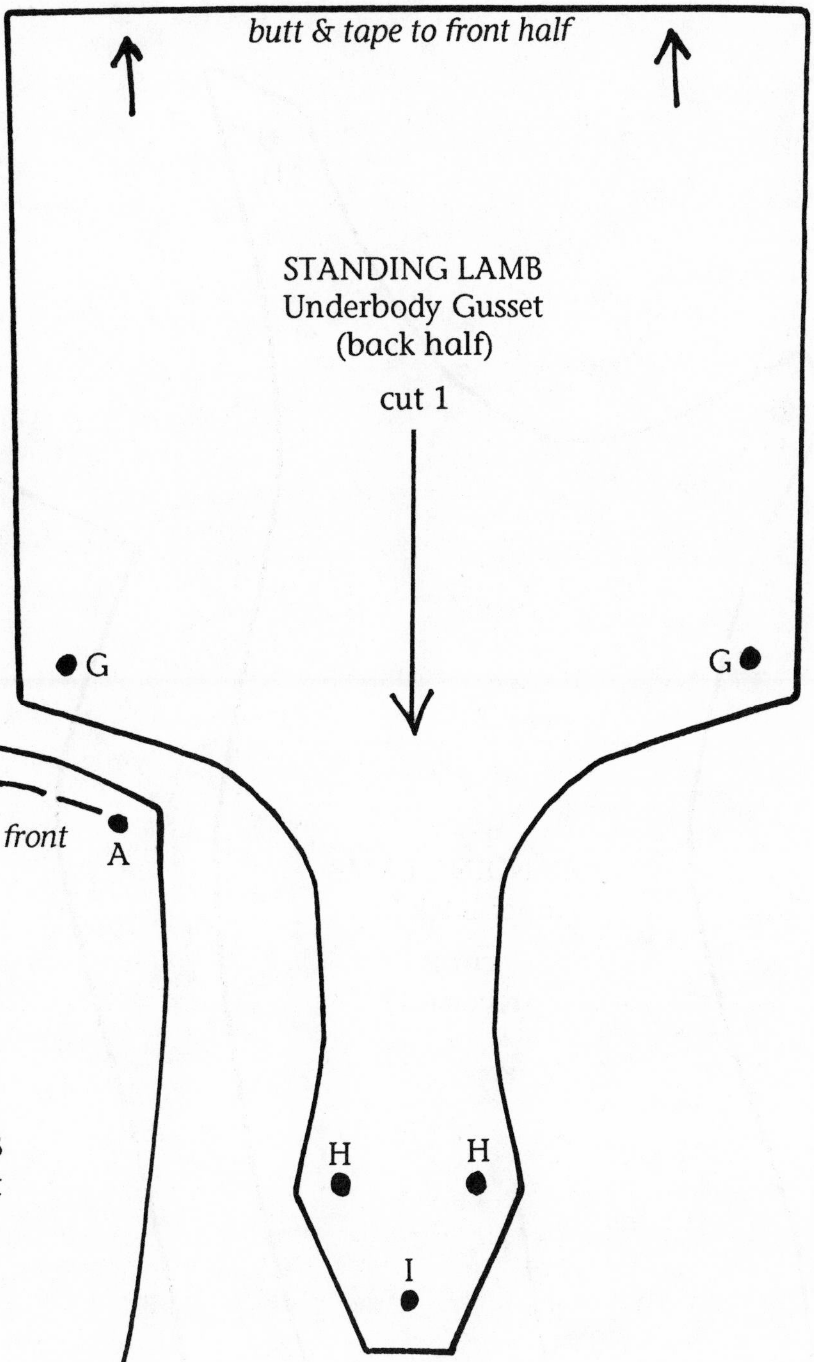

butt & tape to front half

STANDING LAMB
Underbody Gusset
(back half)

cut 1

● G

G ●

H   H

I

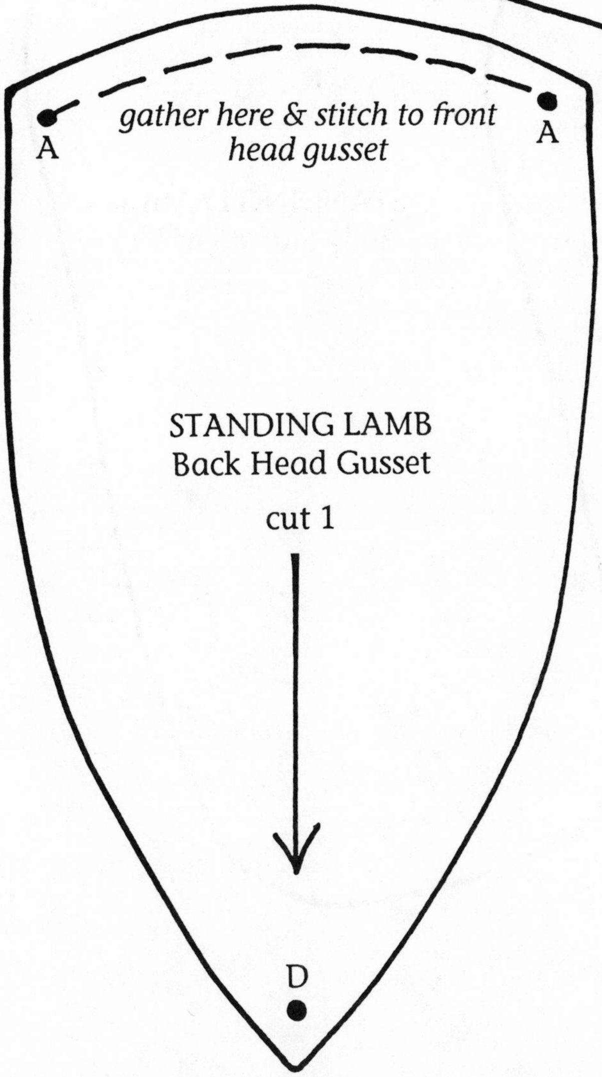

STANDING LAMB
Back Head Gusset

cut 1

● A

*gather here & stitch to front
head gusset*

A ●

D
●

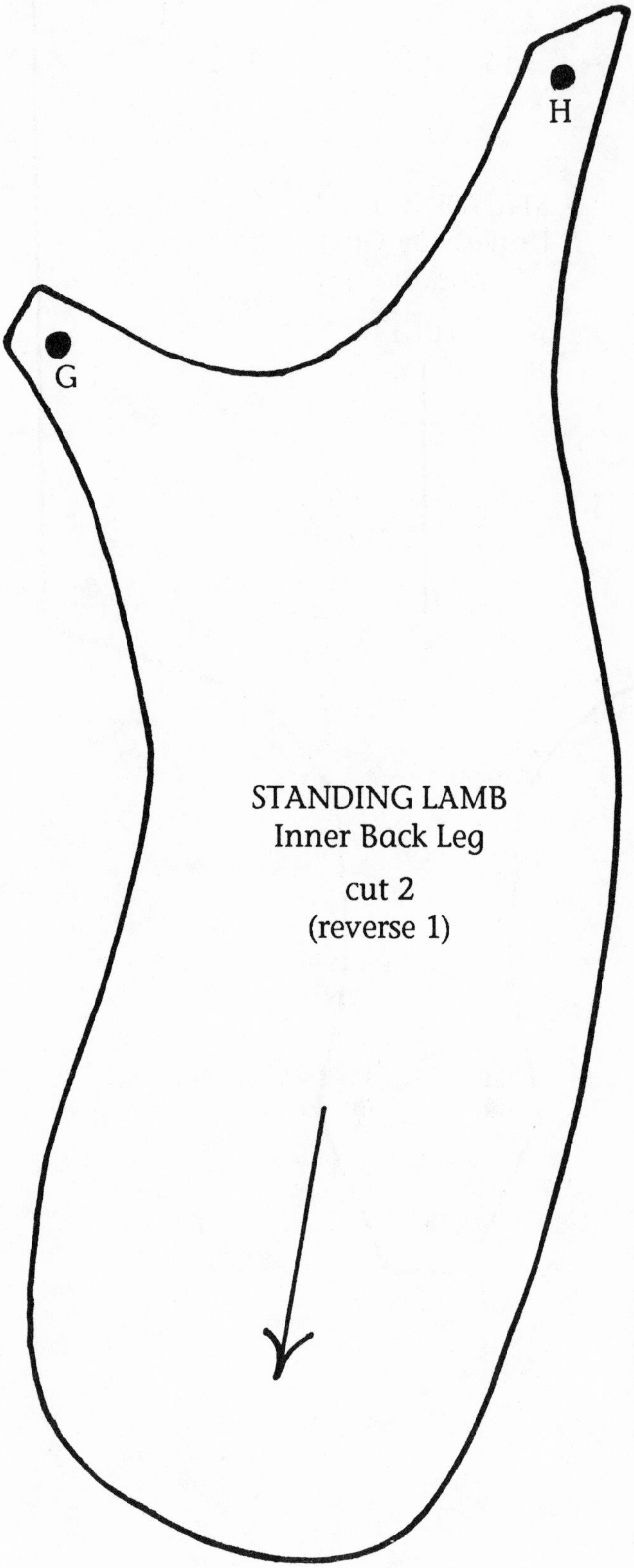

H

G

STANDING LAMB
Inner Back Leg

cut 2
(reverse 1)

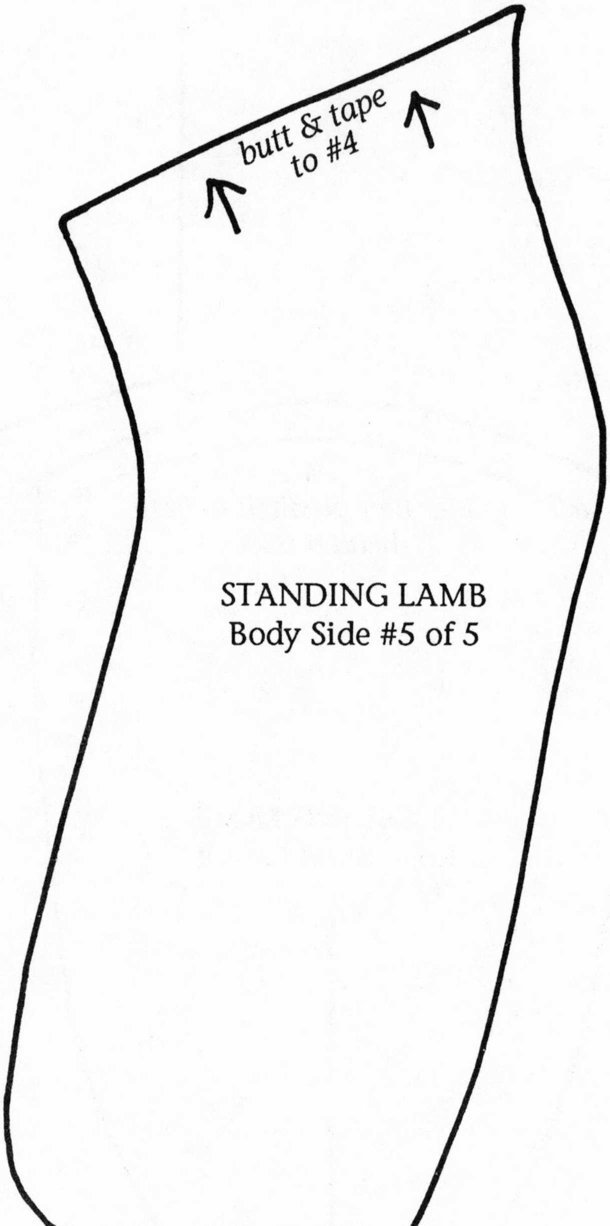

butt & tape
to #4

STANDING LAMB
Body Side #5 of 5

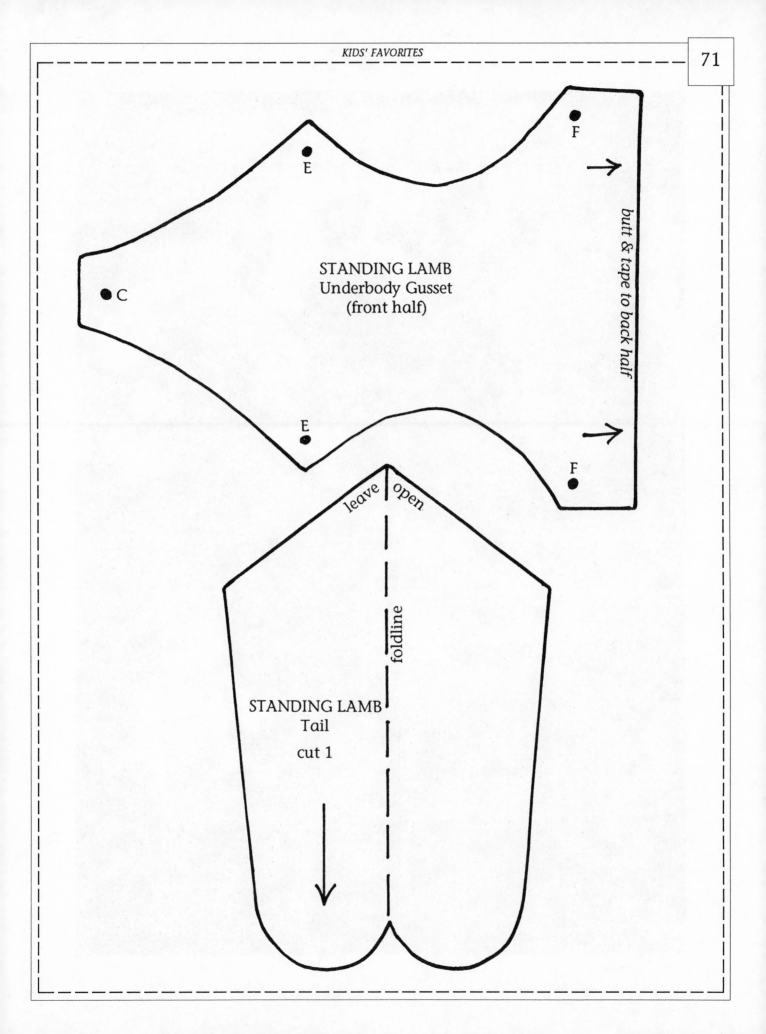

STANDING LAMB
Underbody Gusset
(front half)

E

F

C

E

F

butt & tape to back half

leave open

foldline

STANDING LAMB
Tail
cut 1

♥ ♥ ♥

For the Kid In Us All

♥ ♥ ♥

ROOSTER

Standing a proud 16 inches tall, this chanticleer is full of cheer. His body is strip-pieced from wool. His tail feathers are out-of-date neckties stiffened with wire. For the body and tail, I purchased wool skirts and old neck ties inexpensively from the Salvation Army and recycled them into this stately creature. The rooster stands sturdily thanks to a cardboard tube secured with stuffing deep inside his body. Wire is wound around the cardboard and extends outside his body through gaps in the lower body, becoming legs and feet which are then wrapped with fiberfill and wool strips.

MATERIALS

Various wools recycled from old clothing – I used six wool skirts to make several roosters

Matching thread

½ yard muslin

Six old neckties

20-gauge wire

One cardboard tube
from a roll of paper towels

Pipe cleaners

Masking tape

Two black ¼" buttons for eyes

Carpet thread or waxed dental floss

Polyester fiberfill stuffing

INSTRUCTIONS

Note: All seam allowances are ¼" unless otherwise instructed.

1. Cut wool fabric into 39 1½" wide strips each approximately 20" long. Sew 14 of them together either randomly or in a chosen order. Then sew another 14 strips. Stitch five strips together. This narrower piece will be used for the body gusset. Reserve the remaining six strips for wrapping the legs. Press all seam allowances in one direction. Place wrong side up on a table. Cut two body and one body gusset pattern pieces out of muslin. Place the muslin body pattern pieces on top of the wrong side of the pieced wool as shown. Remember to flip one muslin body piece so you have a right and a left. Pin. Baste the muslin to the wool all around the edges, just inside the ¼" seam allowance. Cut wool by following the raw edge of the muslin pattern pieces.

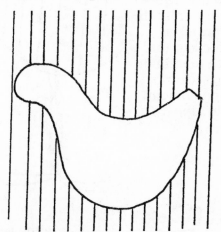

Transfer dots and eye placement markings. Using the thread method described on page 15, transfer the eye markings and dots A, B, C, D, E, and F to the right side of the wool body sides.

2. Pin the underbody gusset to one body side matching dots A and B and easing to fit. Stitch, leaving open between dots M and N as indicated on pattern.

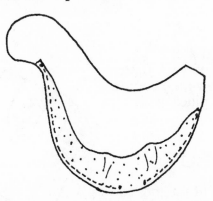

3. Pin underbody gusset to second body side as above. This time leave open between dots L and N.

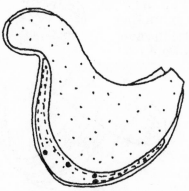

4. Pin body sides together from dot A under chin to tail and from tail to dot B as shown.

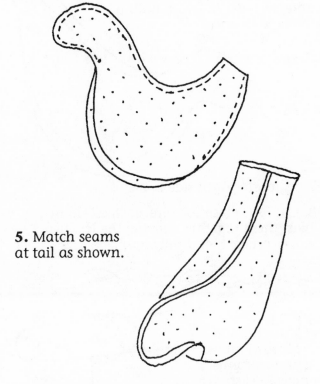

5. Match seams at tail as shown.

6. Measuring from pointed tips of neck ties cut each tie in varying lengths anywhere from 9" to 14". For each tie, twist the ends of two pipe cleaners together. Fold the pipe cleaner in half at the twist and insert folded end into tie. Trim the ends of the pipe cleaners sticking out of the tie to about 1". Stitch across the cut end of the tie between the pipe cleaners.

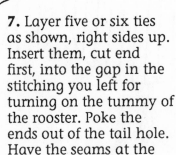

7. Layer five or six ties as shown, right sides up. Insert them, cut end first, into the gap in the stitching you left for turning on the tummy of the rooster. Poke the ends out of the tail hole. Have the seams at the

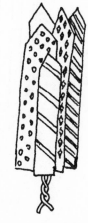

tail meet, as shown. Stitch very carefully, one stitch at a time, in order to avoid hitting the pipe cleaners.

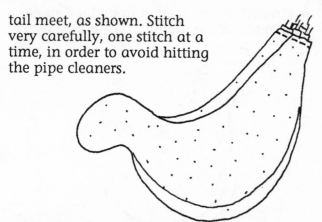

Turn rooster right side out.

8. Cut four pieces of wire, each 22" long. Twist them together, leaving the last two inches on each end untwisted.

Wrap middle of wires around cardboard tube as shown (only one wire is shown for clarity).

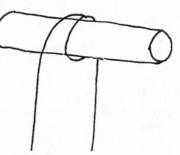

Insert tube end first into large opening on tummy until the cut ends of the wires are inside the body. Carefully push the cut ends out of the openings. Stuff the rooster, starting with the head and then the tail end, centering the cardboard tube in the body.

9. Bend two wires forward and two wires back on each leg to form feet. Wrap the legs and feet with fiberfill or batting, securing by wrapping with masking tape as you go.

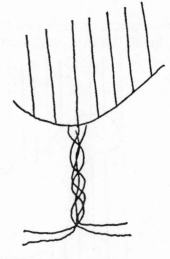

Wrap the feet with a thin covering of fiberfill or batting. Use a lot of tape to secure the fiberfill in place. It will look like the rooster's leg is bandaged.

Cut eight 2" x 2" squares of wool. Cover each toe with a square. Tape in place as shown.

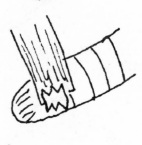

Starting at the toes as shown tape one end of a strip of wool at one toe, wind the wool strip up the toe and over to another toe. Be sure to cover tape with wool.

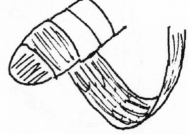

Cover as much as you can with one strip, tape the end in place, and continue with another strip. Once the toes are wrapped, wind the wool up the leg. Tape the wool securely at the top of the leg. If the foot looks too lumpy, try again. It takes a little practice to get a feel for the wrapping.

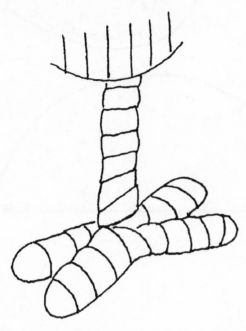

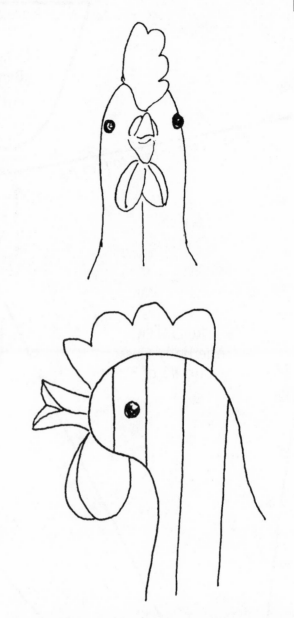

Pull the body down over the tops of the legs. Ladderstitch the openings closed, stitching the body to the leg wool.

10. Cut the wattle pieces, comb and beak from tie fabric, red for the wattles and comb, gold or brown for the beak. Stitch two wattle pieces together, right sides facing. Repeat for other two. Pink or clip the seam allowances. Turn right side out.

11. Stitch two beak pieces together, right sides facing. Repeat for other two. Pink or clip the seam allowances. Turn right side out.

12. Right sides facing, pin and stitch the two comb pieces together. Pink or trim the seam allowances. Clip into the angles. Turn right side out.

13. Lightly stuff the comb and wattles. Turn raw edges of wattles, beaks, and comb to inside at openings and whipstitch closed.

14. Pin and stitch comb to the head between dots C and D, beaks between D and E, and wattles between E and F. Stitch the beaks into U shapes, the open ends of the U's touching, and stitch the two wattles side by side.

15. Sew buttons for eyes at dots. Remove all thread markings.

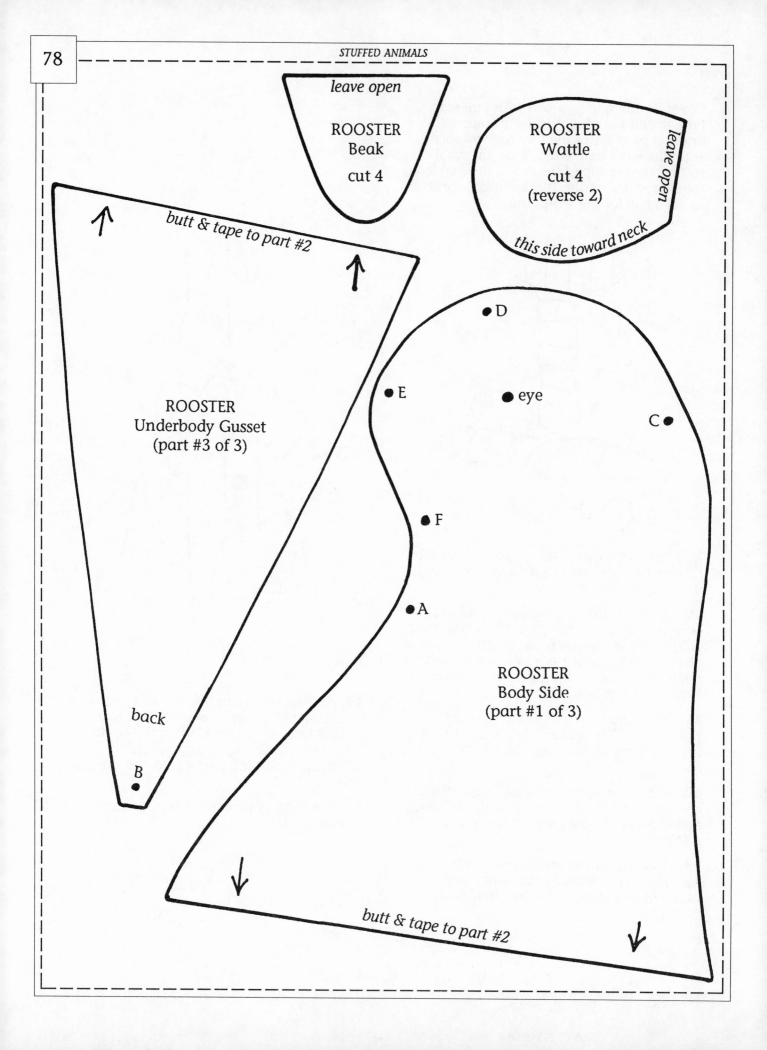

leave open

ROOSTER
Beak
cut 4

ROOSTER
Wattle
cut 4
(reverse 2)

leave open

this side toward neck

butt & tape to part #2

ROOSTER
Underbody Gusset
(part #3 of 3)

• D

• E

• eye

• C

• F

back

• A

• B

ROOSTER
Body Side
(part #1 of 3)

butt & tape to part #2

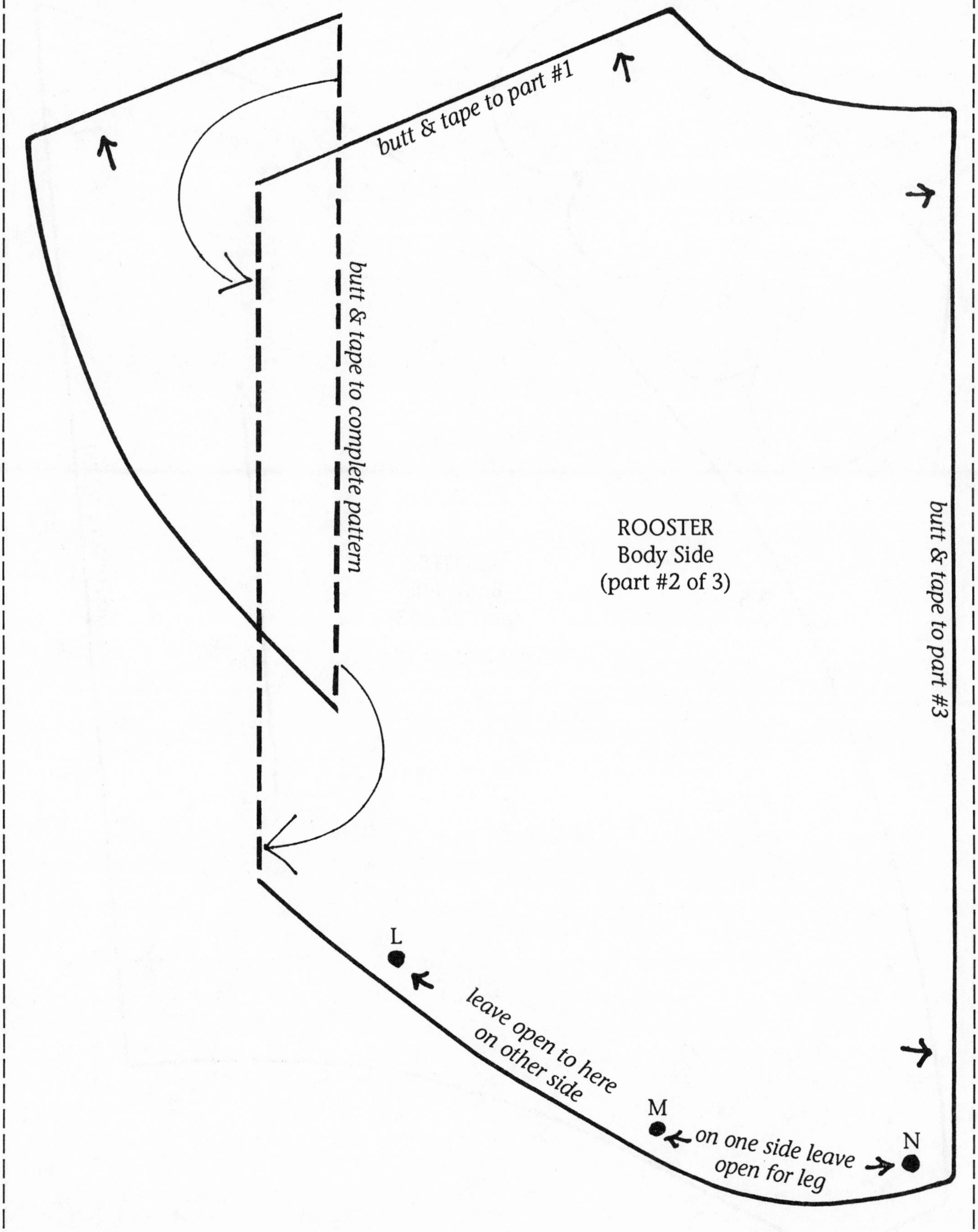

butt & tape to part #1

butt & tape to complete pattern

ROOSTER
Body Side
(part #2 of 3)

butt & tape to part #3

L

leave open to here
on other side

M

on one side leave
open for leg

N

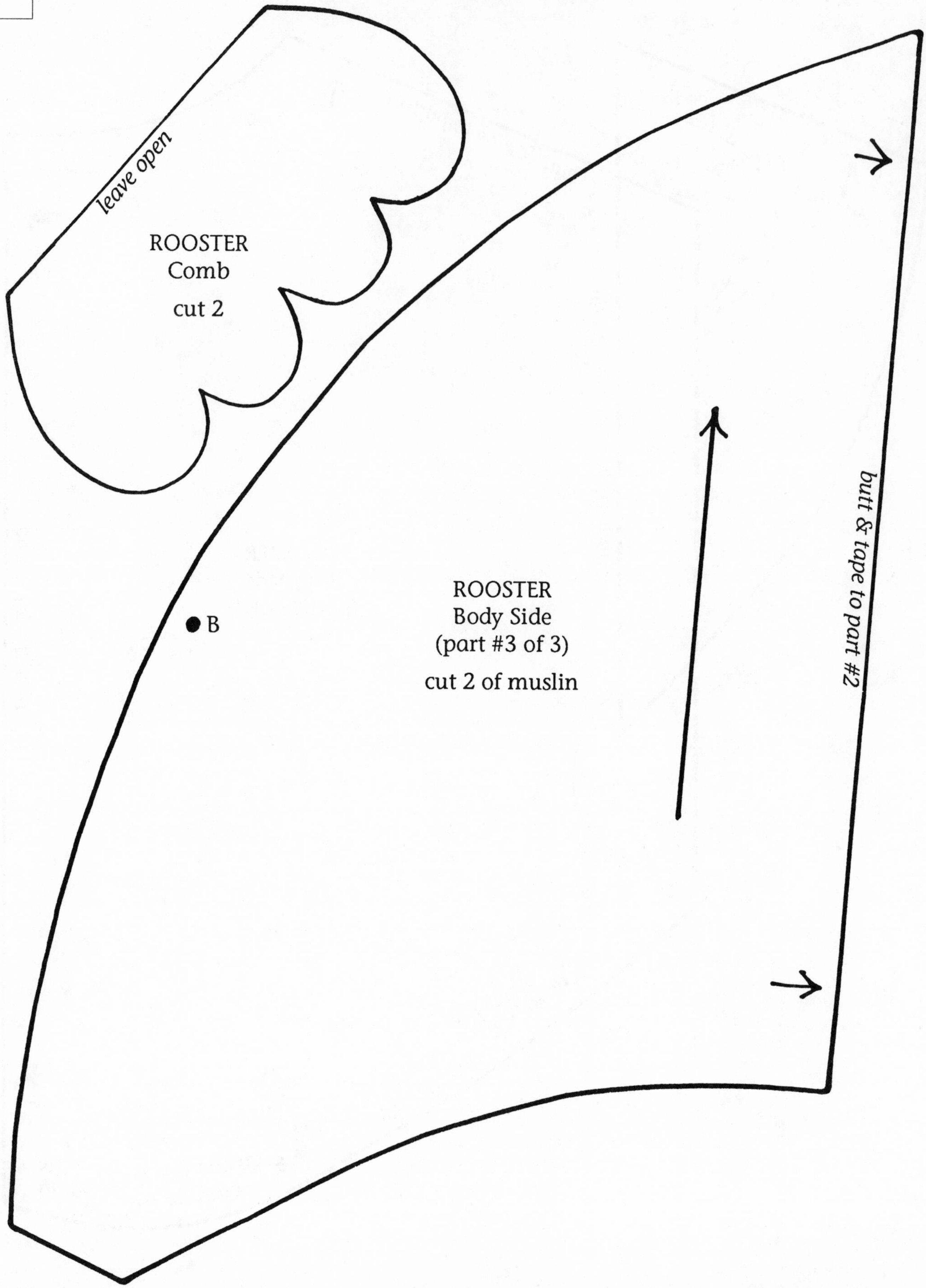

leave open

ROOSTER
Comb

cut 2

ROOSTER
Body Side
(part #3 of 3)

cut 2 of muslin

● B

butt & tape to part #2

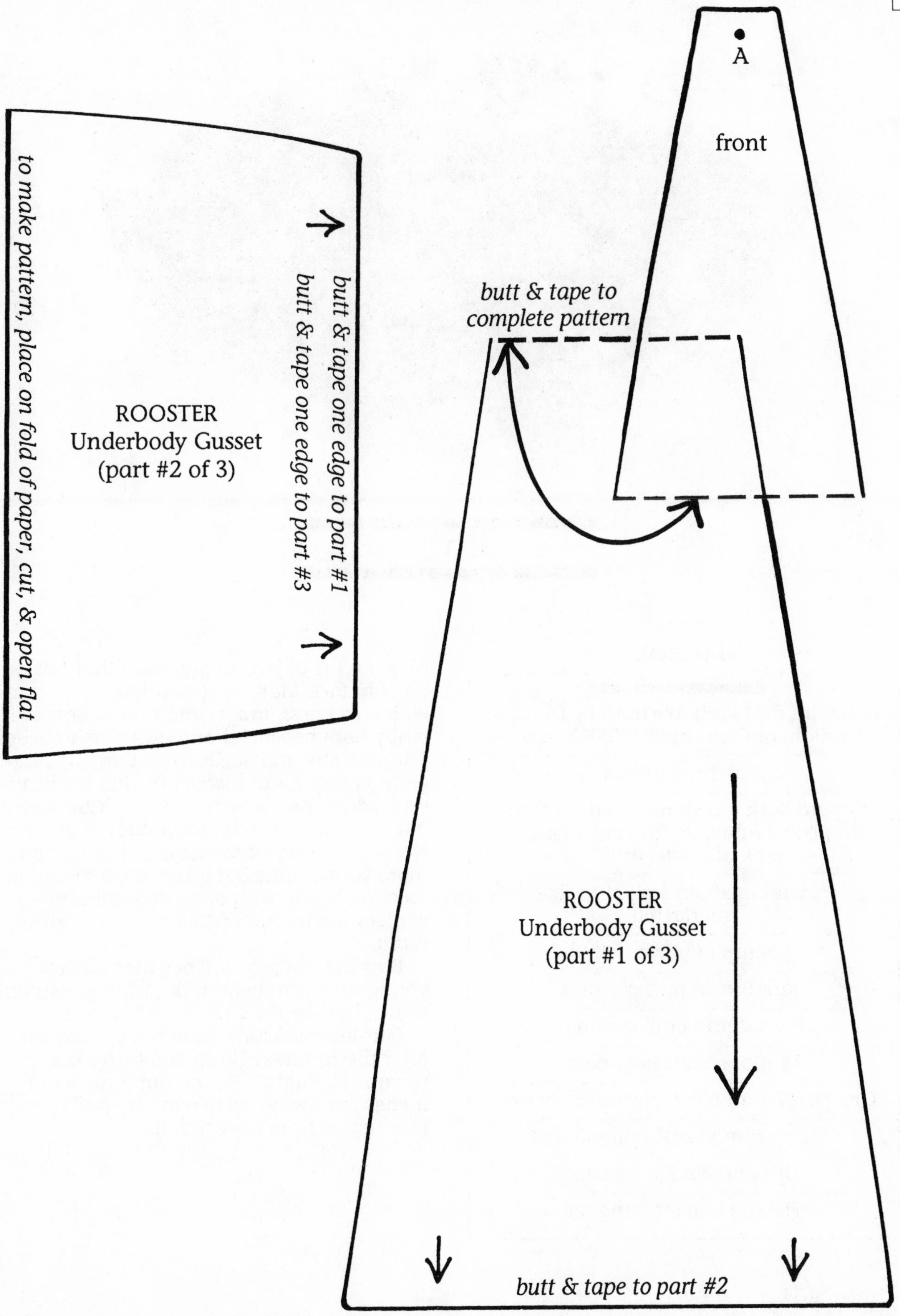

A

front

*butt & tape to
complete pattern*

ROOSTER
Underbody Gusset
(part #2 of 3)

to make pattern, place on fold of paper, cut, & open flat

butt & tape one edge to part #1
butt & tape one edge to part #3

ROOSTER
Underbody Gusset
(part #1 of 3)

butt & tape to part #2

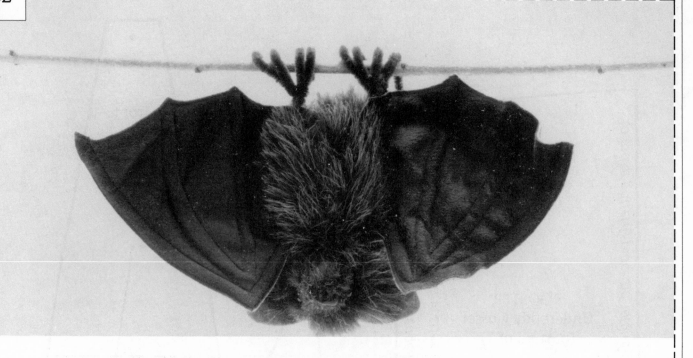

B A T

MATERIALS

¼ yard fur (available from by Diane (kodiak) or CR's Crafts (905K Koala))
Matching thread
¼ yard dark brown doe suede (a thin, drapeable fabric which simulates the look of suede) or felt
¼ yard medium weight fusible interfacing
Scrap of brown felt
Dark brown pipe cleaners
Polyester fiberfill stuffing
14 mm plastic bear nose
One pair 7 mm black plastic safety eyes
One 30 mm plastic animal joint
Dark brown felt for ears
Fishing line for hanging

Bats are the objects of prejudice that has no basis in fact. Many Americans equate "bat" with creepiness, fangs, and rabies. Bats are really both beneficial and harmless to people. They are shy and docile. And they eat staggering amounts of insects. During his heaviest feeding, just after sunset, the little brown bat may capture 600 mosquitoes in one hour! No wonder they are welcome in more and more yards. Some bat lovers erect special bat roosting boxes, with open bottoms and vertical baffles from which the furry friends hang.

Bats are mammals. They give birth to live young and feed them milk. A full grown little brown bat weighs a mere half ounce!

Our life-sized furry little bat is designed after the common North American bat (Myotis lucifugus). He measures about 11 inches from wing tip to wing tip and about four inches from nose to tail.

INSTRUCTIONS

Note: All seam allowances are ¼" unless otherwise instructed.

1. Prepare patterns and cut and mark fabric as instructed on page 10. Cut a piece of suede and one of interfacing 14" by 24".

2. For wings: Fuse the interfacing to the wrong side of the suede following manufacturer's instructions. Fold interfaced fabric in half, wrong sides facing so it measures 14" by 12". Place wing pattern over one half of fabric and pin in place. Trace around the wing pattern, onto the fabric. Transfer the topstitching lines to the fabric as marked on the pattern. Flip the pattern over, pin and trace for second wing. Remove pattern. Pin layers of wings together.

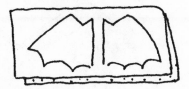

3. Set your sewing machine to a small zigzag stitch. Zigzag all around each wing, leaving openings along the body edge and between the dots where the legs will poke out as marked.

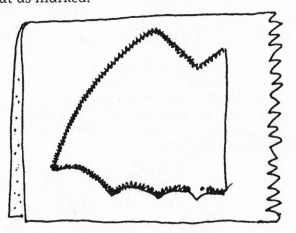

Trim all layers of fabric close to stitching and cut along long, straight, unstitched line (body edge).

4. Cut a piece of pipe cleaner 7" long. Attach the zipper foot to your sewing machine. Bend the pipe cleaner to fit the top of the wing. Put the pipe cleaner into the wing and push it against the zigzag stitching at the top edge of the wing. The extra length of the pipe cleaner will point out of the straight edge (body side) of the wing. With a regular machine stitch, topstitch close to the pipe cleaner as shown in "x-ray" illustration.

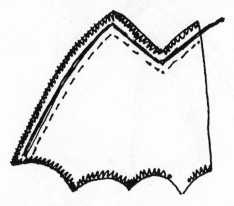

5. Stitch along the outermost topstitching line, as indicated on the pattern.

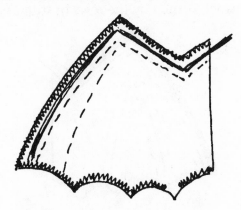

Cut a second piece of pipe cleaner 7" long. Fold in half and insert into wing as shown in the "X-ray" illustration.

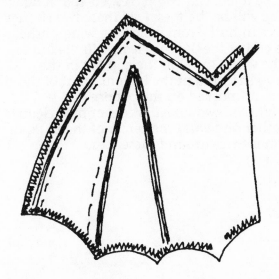

Stitch along next two topstitching lines, starting at the bottom of the wing, pivoting at the top of the "V", and continuing down to the bottom of the wing.

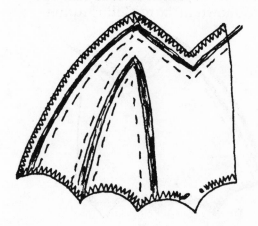

Sew the last marked row of topstitching and the inner "V", pushing the pipe cleaner into the channel formed by the rows of stitching.

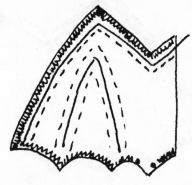

Repeat steps 3, 4, and 5 for the second wing.

6. Cut one piece of pipe cleaner 8" long. This will be a leg. Cut two pieces, each 3" long. These will be the toes. Fold these two shorter pieces in half. From inside the wing push one end of the 8" pipe cleaner to the outside of the wing, through the gap left in the zigzag stitching at the bottom point of the wing, as marked on the pattern.

Hold the two folded pieces of pipe cleaner together and wind the center of the 8" pipe cleaner twice around these toes.

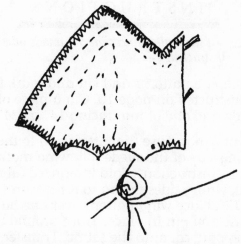

Push the free end of the 8" long pipe cleaner back through the hole in the bottom of the wing, back into the wing and out the body side edge of the wing.

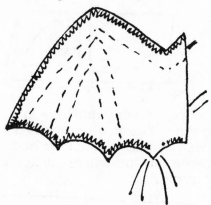

Repeat step 6 for the second wing and leg.

7. Pin two body pieces together at edges marked center front and back. Stitch. This will be the body center back seam. Pin remaining two bodies together as above. Stitch, leaving an opening between the dots. This is the body front.

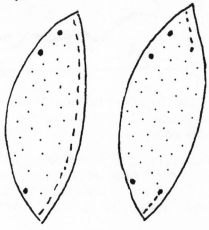

8. Open body front. From the right side of body front insert the outer, pointed end of one wing into the body front opening. Match top and bottom body side edges of wings to dots at body side. (Check direction of fur nap to determine top of body.) Pin. Baste.

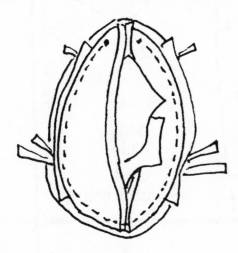

Repeat for second wing.

9. Pin body back over body front, scrunching up wings and legs in between so they won't be in the way. Yes, this is a tight fit! The ends of the pipe cleaners protruding out of the wings will end up inside the body of the bat, as they should, if they protrude outside of the body at this point. Starting at one dot 1/4" from the body top, stitch all the way around the body, including the wings in the seam. Stop at the other dot 1/4" from the top. This will form a gap in the stitching for installing the head joint. To avoid broken needles, be careful not to stitch through the pipe cleaners. Rather, stop and push the body past the pipe cleaner so the needle will not hit it.

Turn body right side out.

10. Clip fur on face of head sides and head gusset as marked and instructed on page 11. Pin and stitch two head sides together at bottom necks, matching dots A at nose.

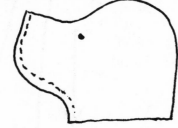

11. Pin dot A on gusset to dot A at junction of head sides seam at nose. On one side of head and gusset, pin dot C on head side to dot C on respective side of gusset. Pin between the dots. Stitch from dot B to neck edge, as shown. The gap between dots B provides space for the post of the nose.
  Repeat for other head side and head gusset.

12. As instructed on page 15, install eyes at dots on head.

13. As instructed on page 15, install nose between dots B.

14. Starting at the nose, stuff the head. Fill the head almost even with the bottom raw edge. Insert the flat side of the stationary disk into the opening, post pointing out. Using heavy thread, baste once around the raw edge of the bottom opening of the neck, 1/4" from the edge. Pull up on the thread. Sew around once or twice again if needed, pulling as you go, until the fabric is closed around the disk as shown. Knot the thread.

15. Install the head in the body as instructed on page 14.

16. Stuff the body and ladderstitch the opening at center front closed.

17. Cut the ears from the felt. Using the photos as a guide, sew the ears to the head.

18. Smooth and bend the wings into a natural, arched shape.

19. To hang the bat, thread a needle with fishing line or thread. Take a small stitch on the bat's back just behind the bat's head. Tie the ends of the threads.

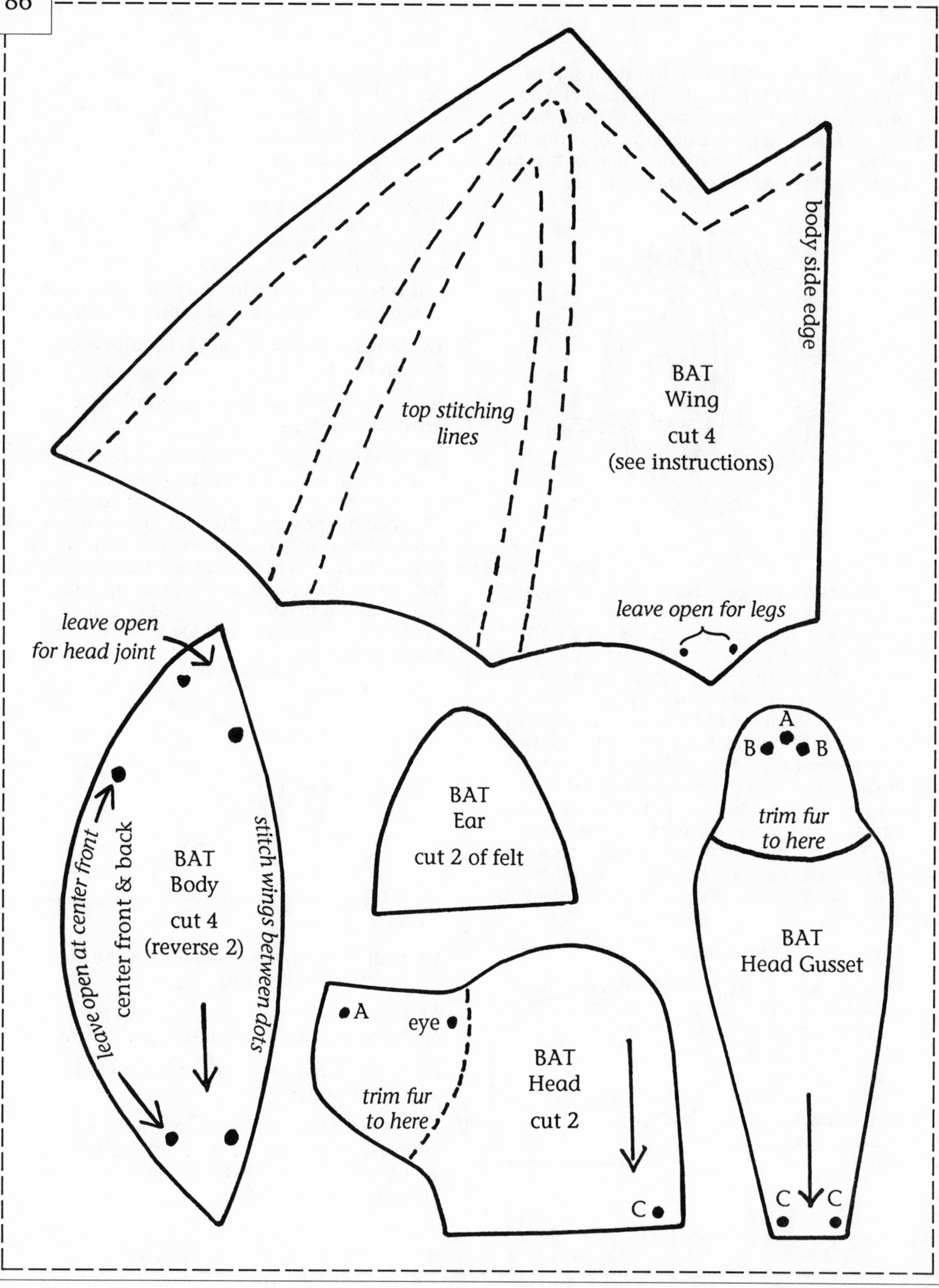

top stitching lines

body side edge

BAT
Wing

cut 4

(see instructions)

leave open for legs

leave open for head joint

center front & back

stitch wings between dots

leave open at center front

BAT
Body

cut 4

(reverse 2)

BAT
Ear

cut 2 of felt

A

B   B

trim fur to here

BAT
Head Gusset

A

eye

trim fur to here

BAT
Head

cut 2

C

C   C

COW

All 12 inches of this sweet creature, from her udders to her horns, are 100 percent pure bovine. As pictured, the cow is spotted like a Holstein, but can easily be made in any number of other breeds. Substitute brown for the black to make a Hereford (and skip the horns), or forget the spots and make the cow from a camel colored seal fur for a Guernsey. You may wish to add a voice box during the stuffing step. The "moo-ers" sound quite life-like and are easy to install. Just follow the instructions on page 14.

MATERIALS

½ yard black or brown seal fur fabric (see by Diane and CR's Crafts, Sources)

Matching thread

¼ yard white seal fur fabric

Pink flannel, fleece or felt for udders

Matching thread

Black wool or felt for hooves

Two 15 mm eyes

Polyester fiberfill

Carpet thread or waxed dental floss

Black or brown Pretty Hair® or folk wool

Cow bell (see CR's Crafts in Sources)

½ yard 1" wide ribbon

Embroidery floss or perle cotton

INSTRUCTIONS

Note: All seam allowances are ¼" unless otherwise instructed.

Prepare the patterns, cut and mark the fabric as instructed on page 10. To transfer the spot markings: Mark the spots on the wrong side of the fur. Using colored thread, baste over the markings.

1. Trim fur from the center of inside white ear pieces to within ¾" of raw edge. Make darts in white ears. Pin white, inside ears to black ears, right sides facing. Stitch, leaving straight edges open. Turn right side out. Fold as illustrated and baste bottom, raw edges together.

2. Pin ears to head sides between dot A and dot C, with white sides of ears facing fur on head sides. Baste in place.

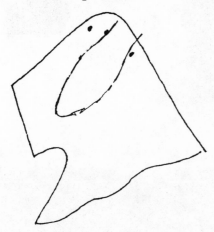

3. Pin dots C on back head gusset to dots C on front head gusset/muzzle. Stitch.

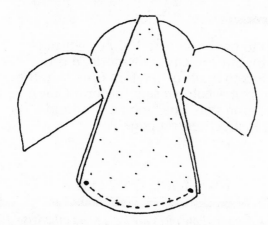

4. Working on one side of the head, match and pin dot D on head side to dot D on front head gusset/muzzle. Match and pin dots F on head side to dot F on back head gusset. Pin gussets to head side between dots, matching dots C. Stitch from dot B to dot D. Stitch from dot C down to bottom of neck, including the ear in the seam. The gap in the stitching is for the horn.

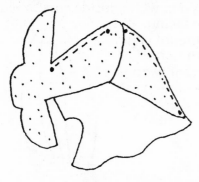

5. On the same side, match and pin dot H on front head gusset/muzzle to dot H on cow head side. Stitch from dot D to raw edge past dot H. Repeat for other side.

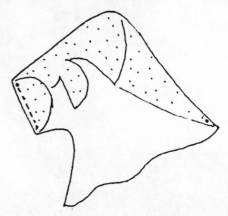

Repeat steps 4 and 5 for the other side of the gussets and remaining head side.

6. On one side of front head gusset/muzzle, fold along foldline, right sides facing, matching dots E. Pin from dot G to dot E. Stitch.

Repeat for other side.

7. Pin and stitch under chin seam from dot E, through H and to bottom raw edge of neck.

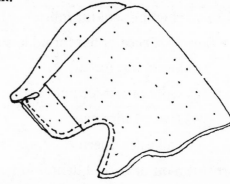

8. As instructed on page 15, install eyes at markings.

9. Trim fur on body sides inside spot markings. Pin spots to body sides. Using a narrow zigzag and black thread, applique the spots to the right side of the cow sides, right sides up. Remove colored basting stitches.

10. Pin black tail piece to white tail piece with black nap pointing toward white, and white nap pointing away from black, as illustrated.

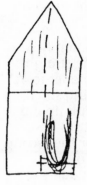

Measure 7" of Pretty Hair®. To cut, rub the wool against the blade of a scissors. This will form a jagged, uneven cut. Fold the wool in half and place on white end of tail as shown, fold of wool toward bottom of tail. Baste.

Fold tail along foldline. Pin. Stitch along long side, and across short white bottom edge, including the hair in the seam and leaving short angled, black edge open. Turn right side out.

Pin tail to one body side at dot J as shown. Baste in place.

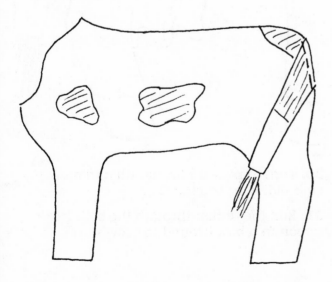

11.. Stitch hooves to bottoms of all legs.

12. Right sides facing, pin inside hind leg pieces together from dot K to dot J. Stitch from K to top raw edge above J.

13. Pin and stitch inside front legs to underbody gusset as shown, matching dots. Pin inside hind legs to underbody gusset from dot K down to dot L. Stitch from dot K down to raw edge past L. Repeat for other side.

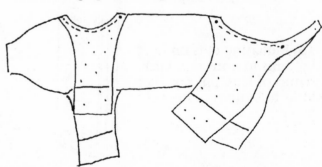

14. Pin and stitch two body sides together, right sides facing, along top of back from top neck edge to dot J.

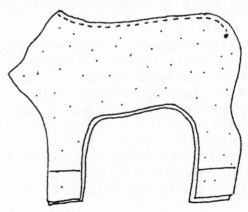

Starting with dot H at chest, pin one side of underbody gusset to chest, front leg, tummy, and back leg, ending at dot J. Stitch from front neck edge at H down front leg to bottom front of hoof. Stitch up the back of front leg, under tummy, and down the front of the back leg. Stitch from dot J down the back of the hind leg. Repeat for second side, this time leaving an opening between dots at the tummy for turning.

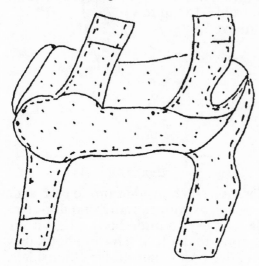

15. Matching dots on hoof bottoms to front and back seams of legs, pin hoof bottoms to bottom of hooves. Stitch.

16. With body still inside out, put head, which is right side out, inside the body. Pin raw edges together, matching top seams and matching dot I to underchin seam on head. Stitch. Turn cow right side out.

17. Pin the two horn pieces together. Stitch, leaving an opening between the dots as marked. Trim the seam allowances across the horn tips. Turn right side out. Stuff, making sure the tips are fully stuffed. Ladderstitch the opening closed. Insert one end of the horn into the opening in the head in front of the ears. Adjust the horn until it fits evenly. Have the tips of the horns point forward. Sew the opening in the head to the horn.

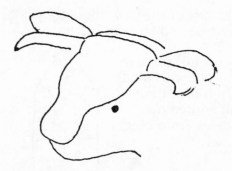

18. Stuff the cow. Ladderstitch the opening in the body closed.

19. Right sides facing, pin and stitch two udder pieces together, leaving the straight edge open, as marked. Stuff the udder to 1/2" from the top. Using a long running stitch, hand gather the straight edge. Pull up on the thread until the udder measures approximately 2" x 1¹/2". Repeat for the second udder. Handstitch one long side of the udders together. Handstitch the udders to the cow's underside turning 1/4" to the inside.

20. Turn to page 15 for mouth and nose embroidery instructions.

21. Run the ribbon through the bell. Tie ribbon in a bow around the cow's neck.

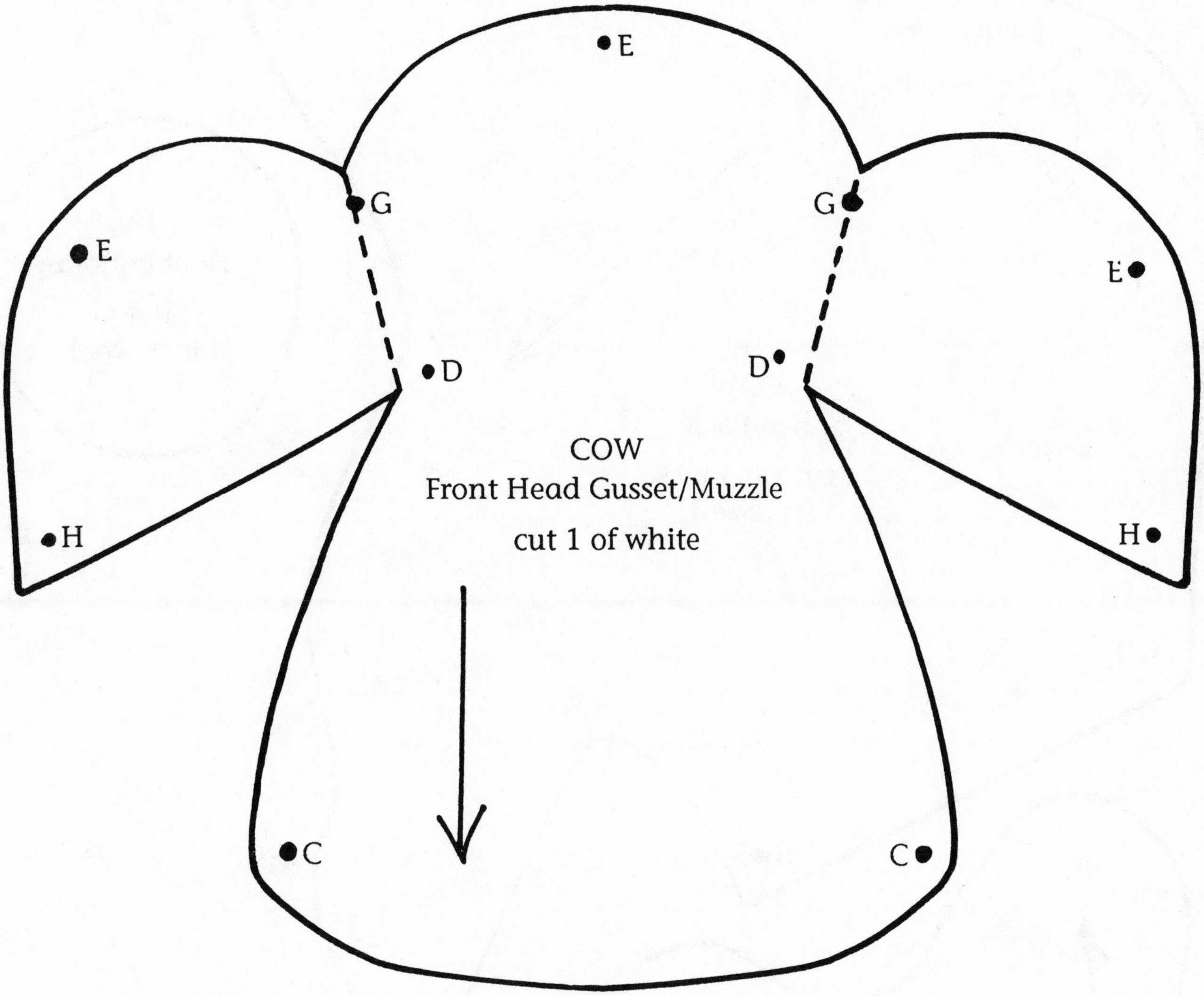

• E

• E

• G

• G

• E

• D

• D

• E

• H

• H

COW
Front Head Gusset/Muzzle
cut 1 of white

• C

• C

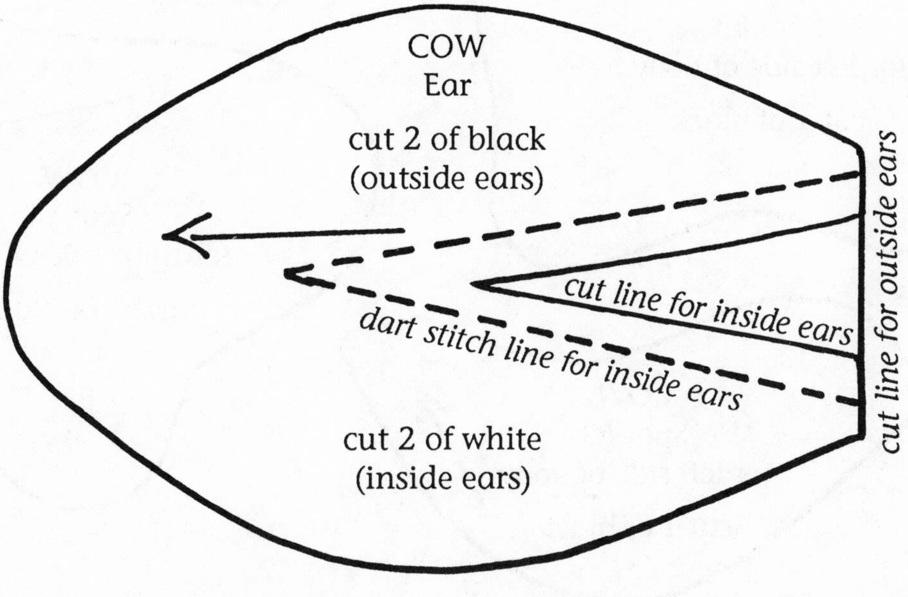

COW
Ear

cut 2 of black
(outside ears)

cut line for outside ears

cut line for inside ears

dart stitch line for inside ears

cut 2 of white
(inside ears)

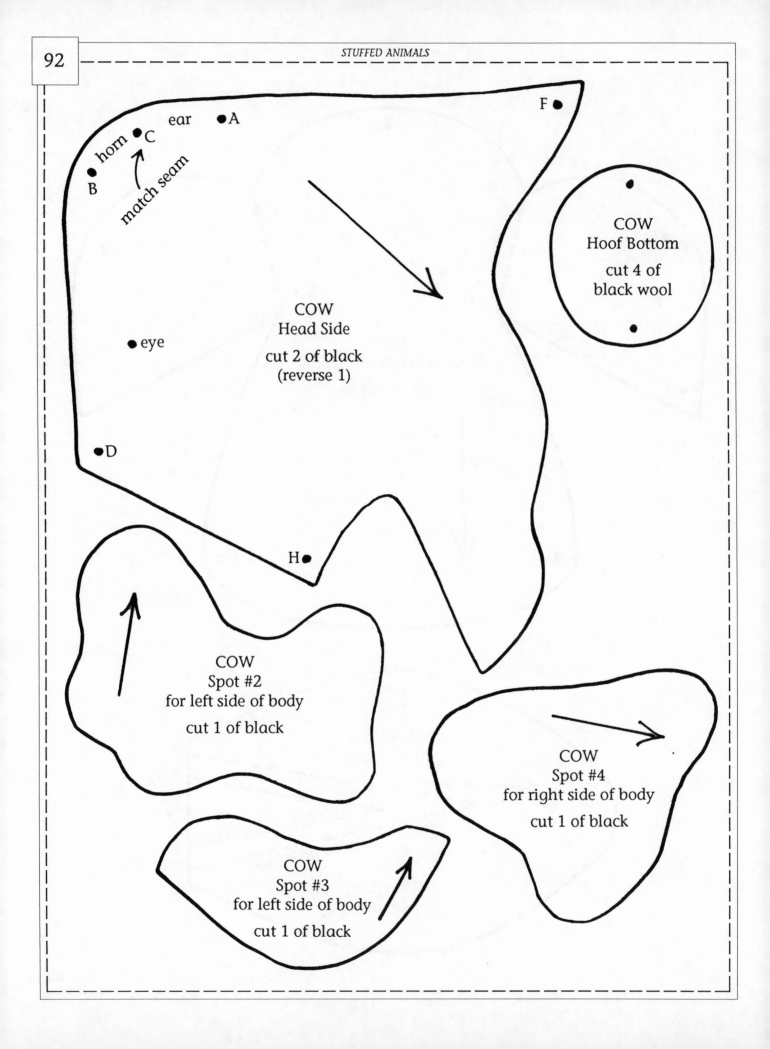

ear   ●A

horn   ●C

●B

match seam

●eye

●D

COW
Head Side

cut 2 of black
(reverse 1)

F ●

COW
Hoof Bottom

cut 4 of
black wool

H●

COW
Spot #2
for left side of body

cut 1 of black

COW
Spot #4
for right side of body

cut 1 of black

COW
Spot #3
for left side of body

cut 1 of black

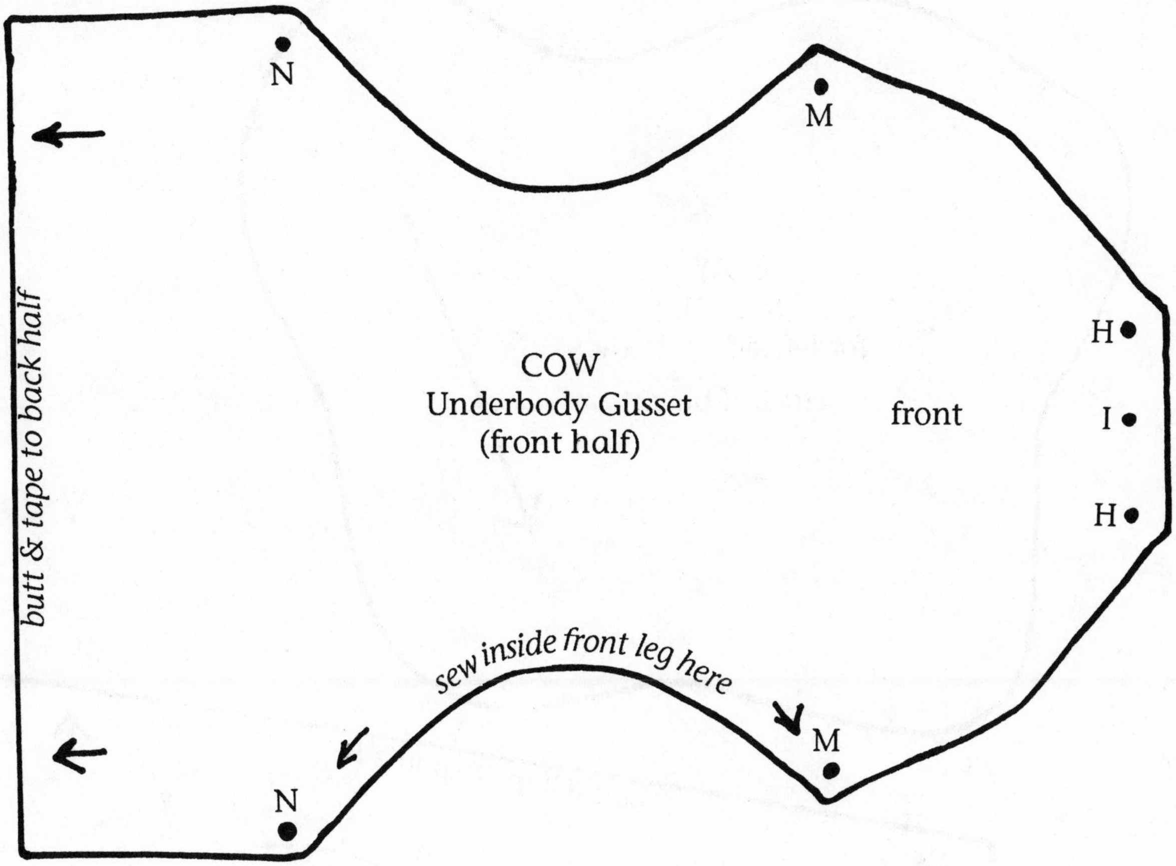

COW
Underbody Gusset
(front half)

front

N

M

H

I

H

butt & tape to back half

sew inside front leg here

N

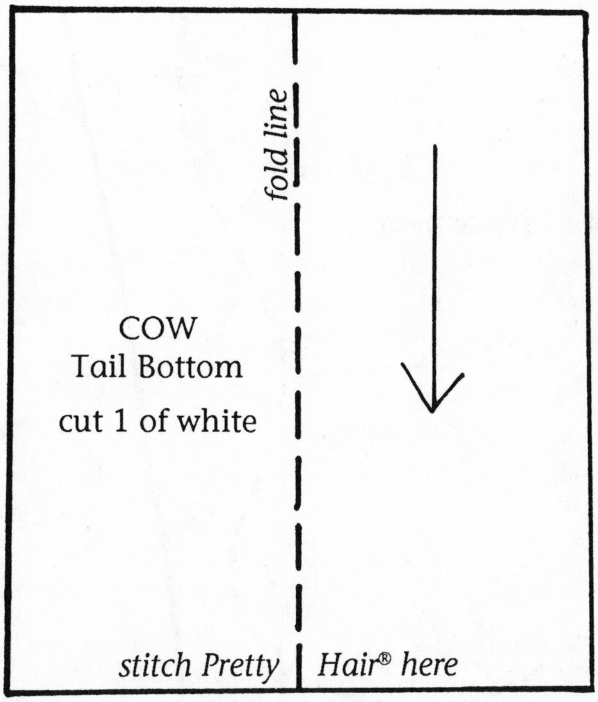

M

COW
Tail Bottom
cut 1 of white

fold line

stitch Pretty Hair® here

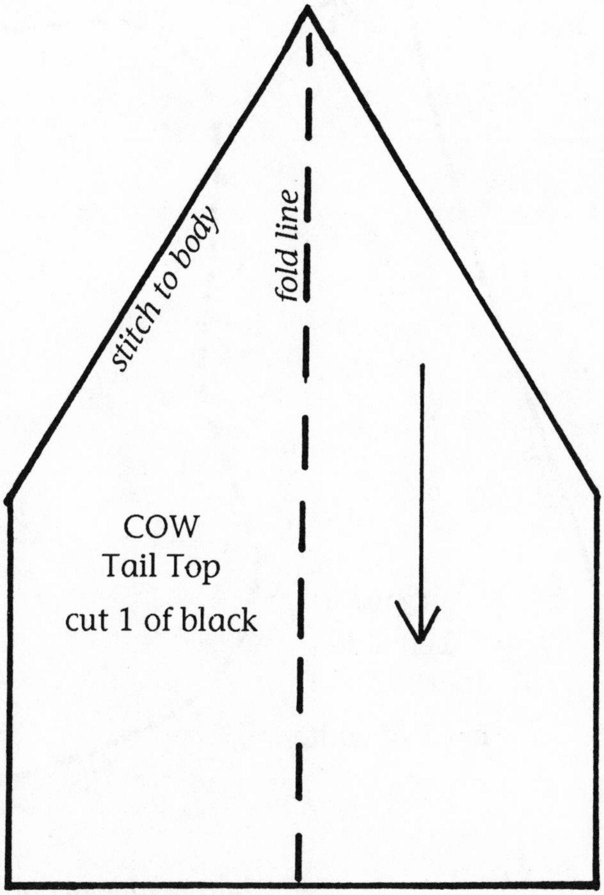

COW
Tail Top
cut 1 of black

fold line

stitch to body

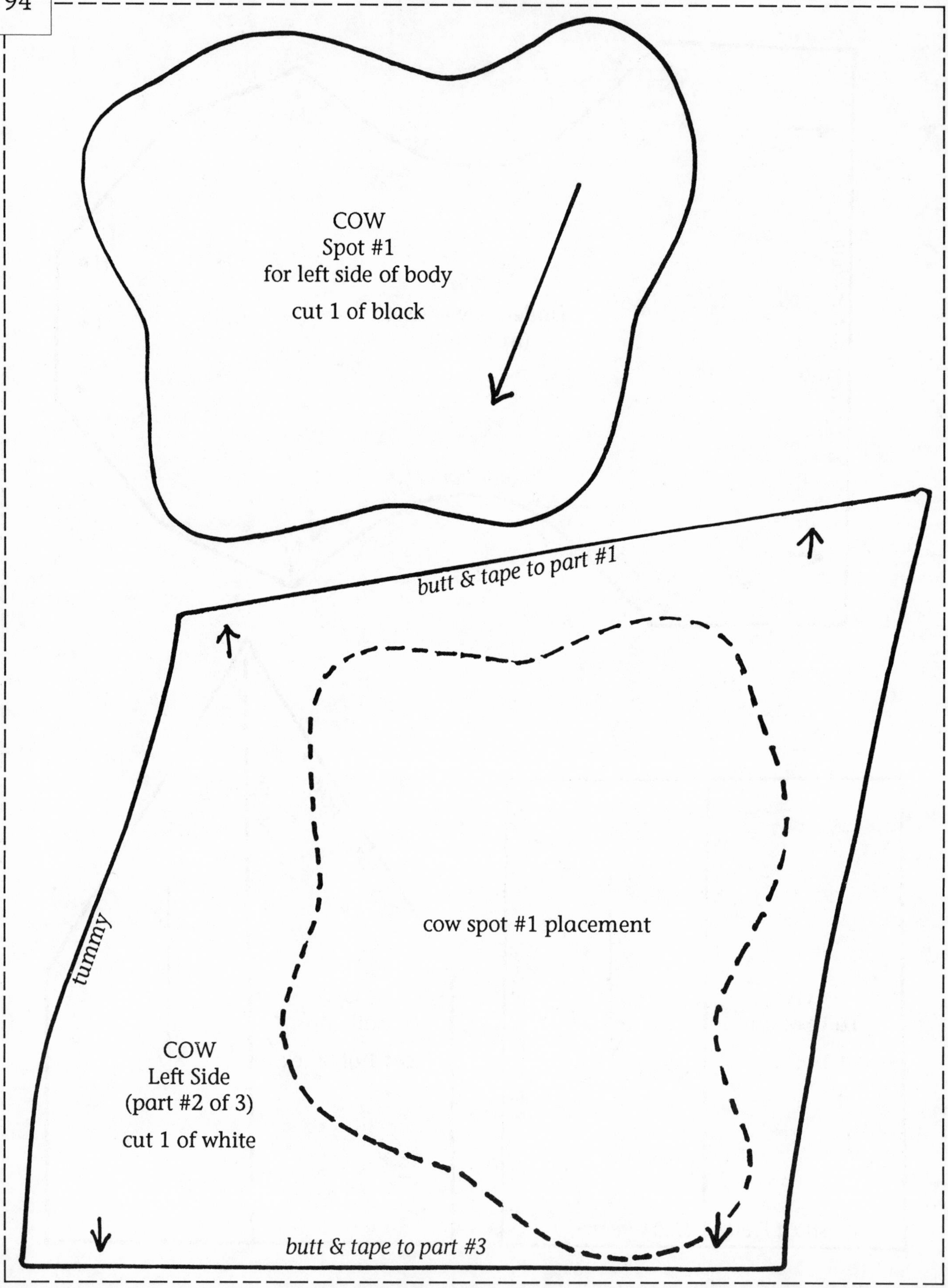

COW
Spot #1
for left side of body

cut 1 of black

butt & tape to part #1

cow spot #1 placement

tummy

COW
Left Side
(part #2 of 3)

cut 1 of white

butt & tape to part #3

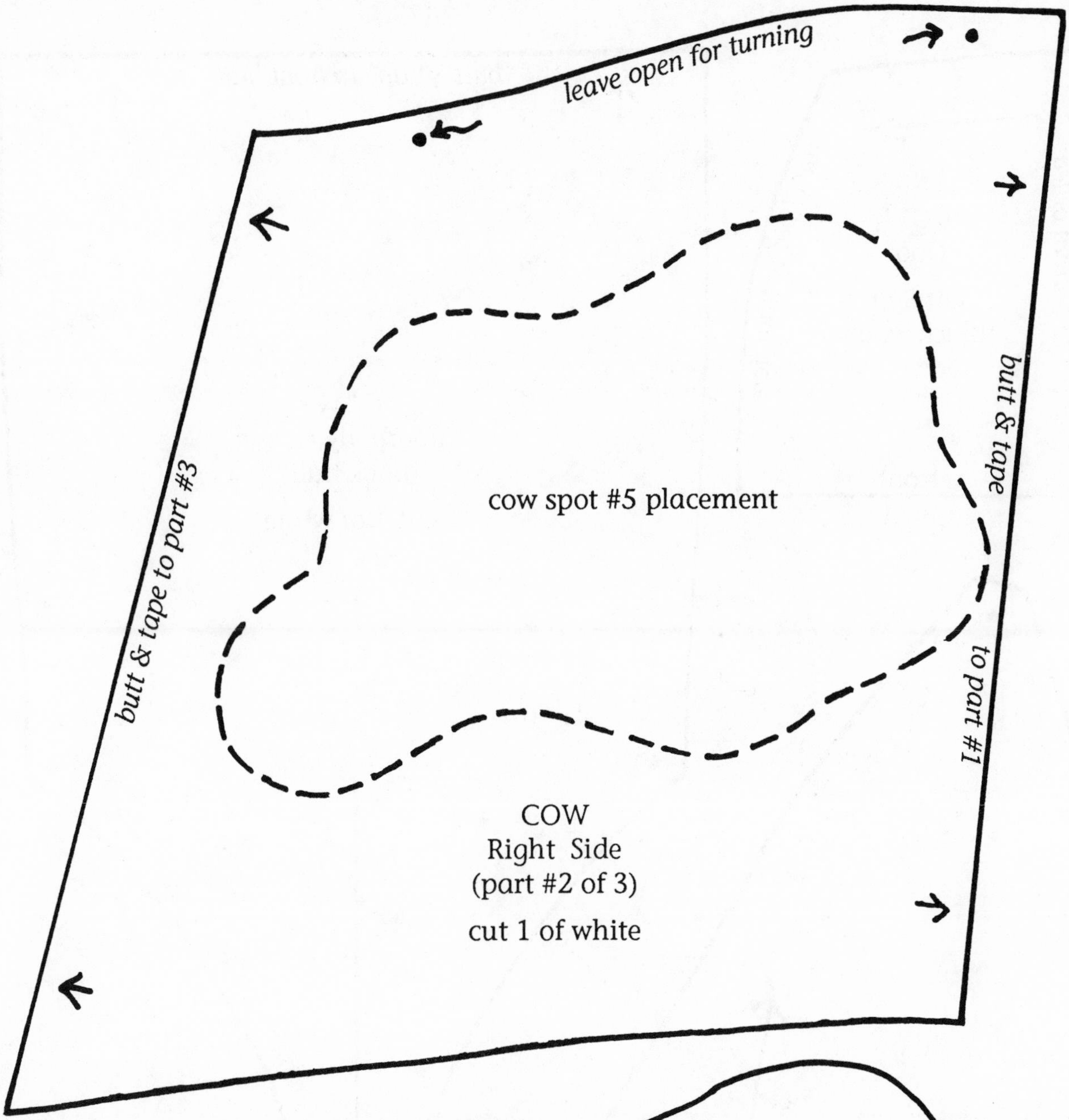

leave open for turning

butt & tape to part #3

butt & tape

to part #1

cow spot #5 placement

COW
Right Side
(part #2 of 3)

cut 1 of white

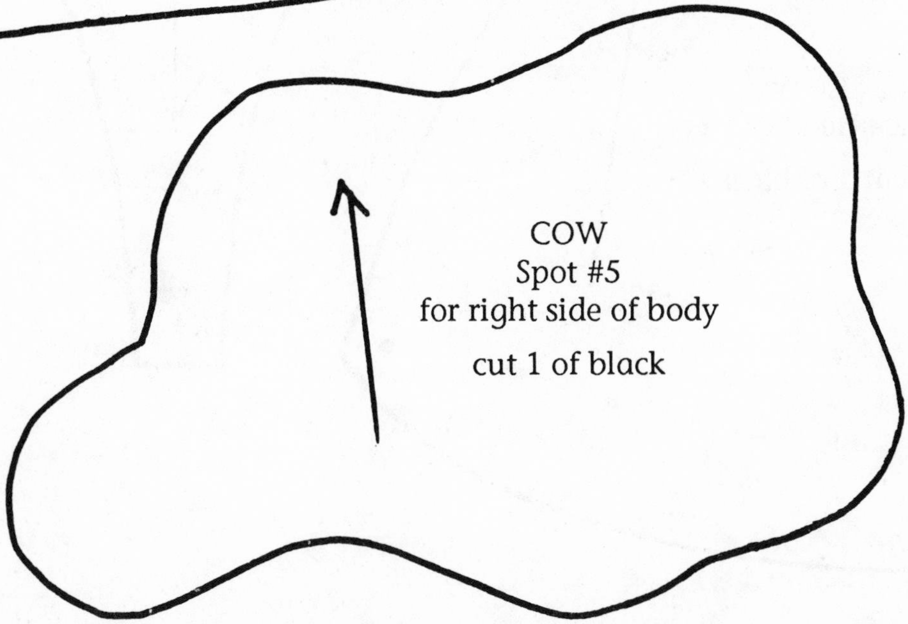

COW
Spot #5
for right side of body

cut 1 of black

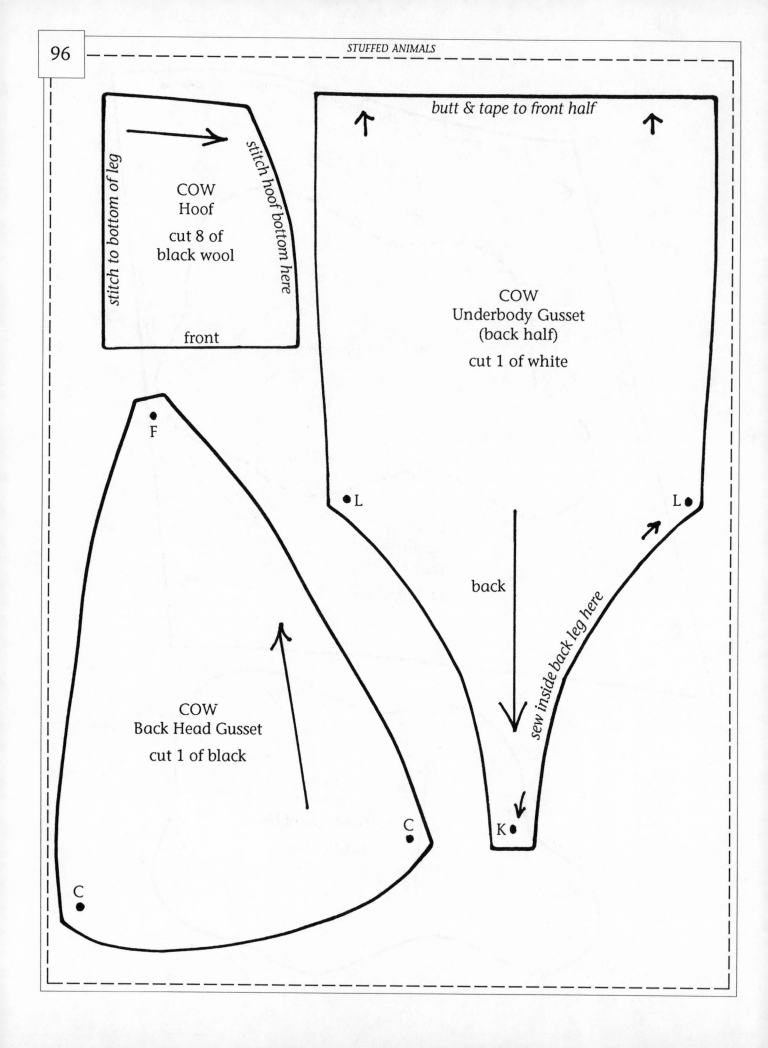

COW
Hoof

cut 8 of
black wool

front

stitch to bottom of leg

stitch hoof bottom here

butt & tape to front half

COW
Underbody Gusset
(back half)

cut 1 of white

• L

L •

back

sew inside back leg here

K •

• F

COW
Back Head Gusset

cut 1 of black

C •

C
•

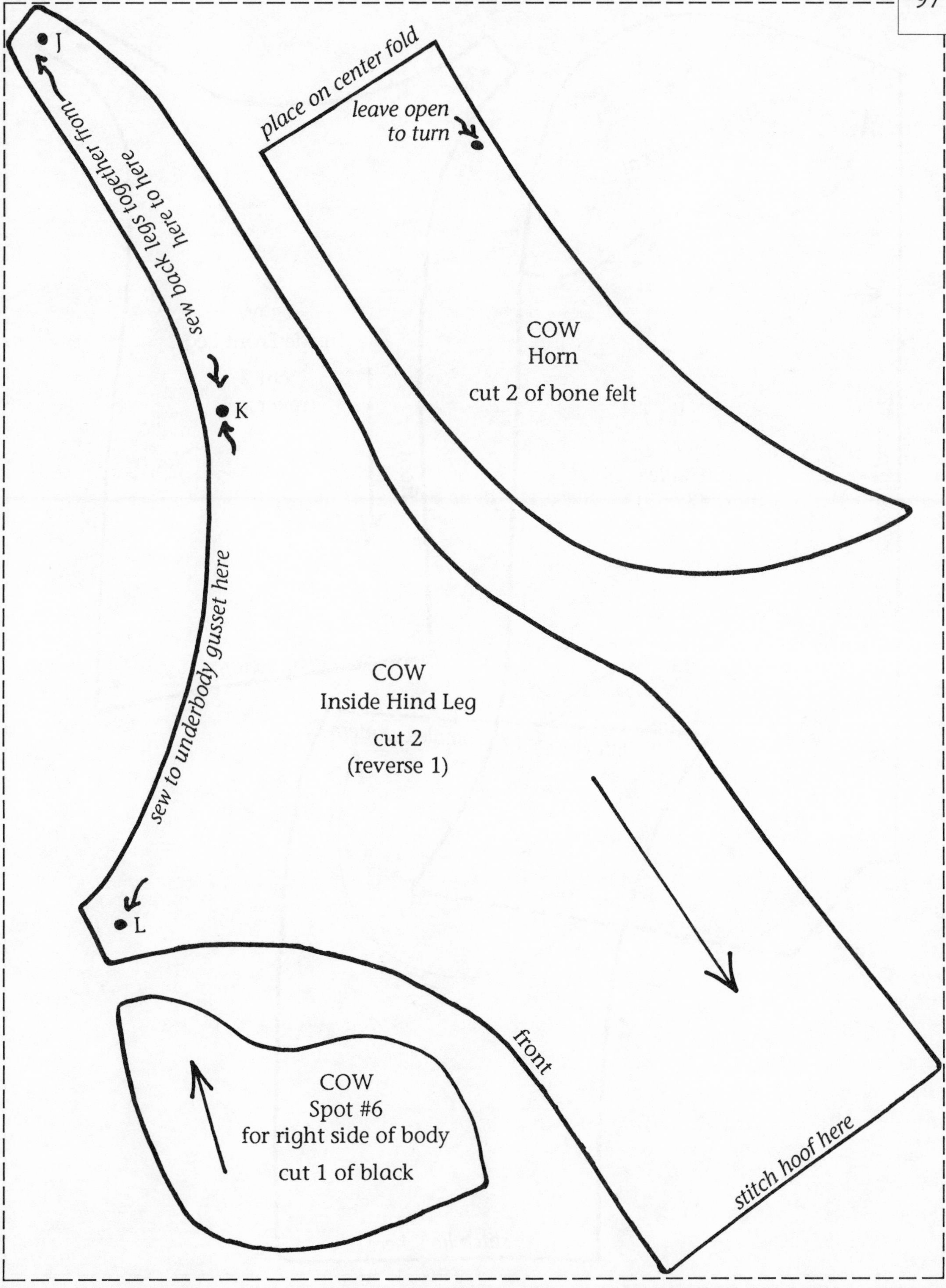

• J

sew back legs together from

sew back legs together to here

place on center fold

leave open
to turn

COW
Horn

cut 2 of bone felt

• K

sew to underbody gusset here

COW
Inside Hind Leg

cut 2
(reverse 1)

• L

front

COW
Spot #6
for right side of body

cut 1 of black

stitch hoof here

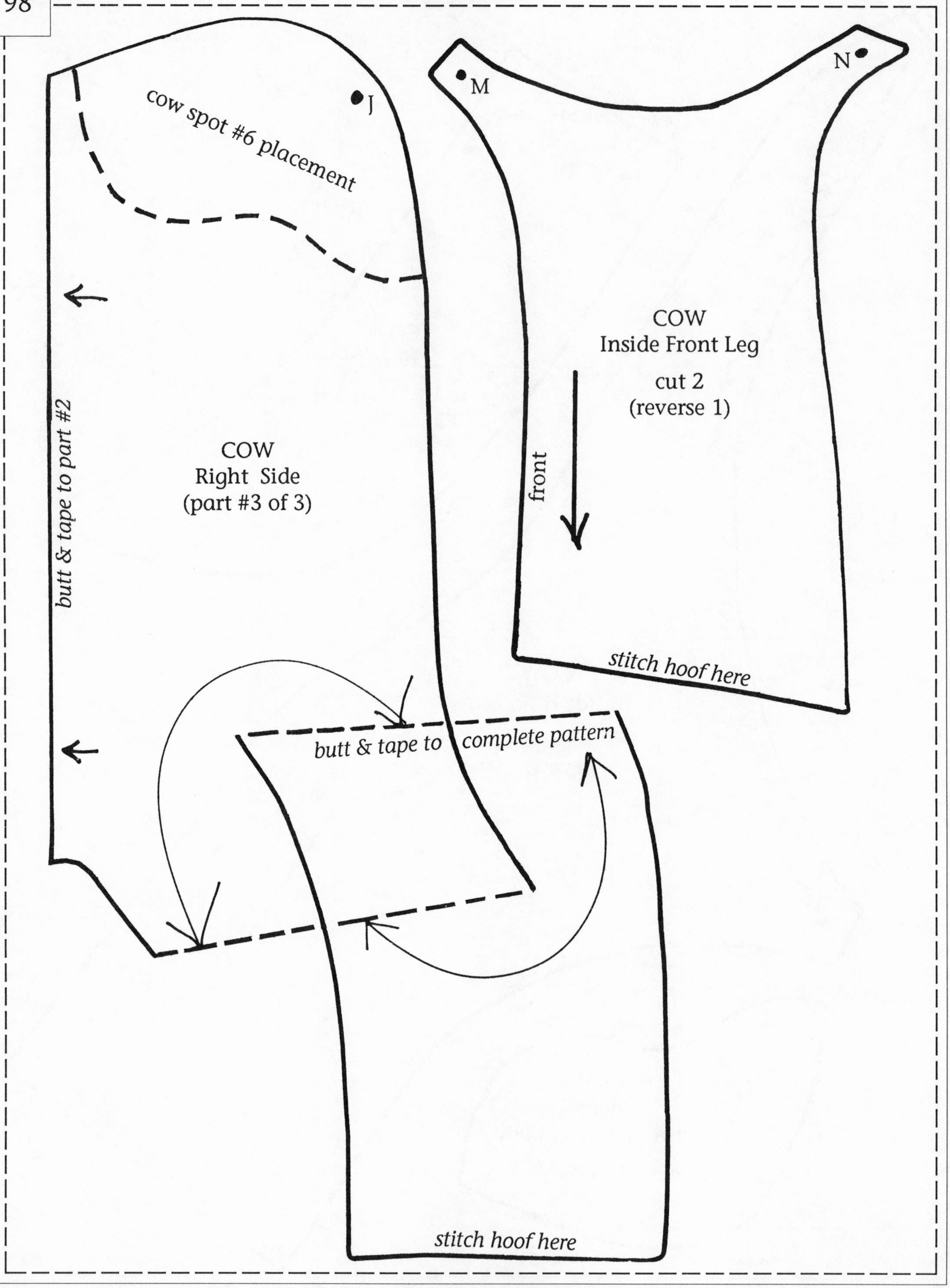

cow spot #6 placement

• J

• M   N •

COW
Inside Front Leg

cut 2
(reverse 1)

front

butt & tape to part #2

COW
Right Side
(part #3 of 3)

stitch hoof here

butt & tape to   complete pattern

stitch hoof here

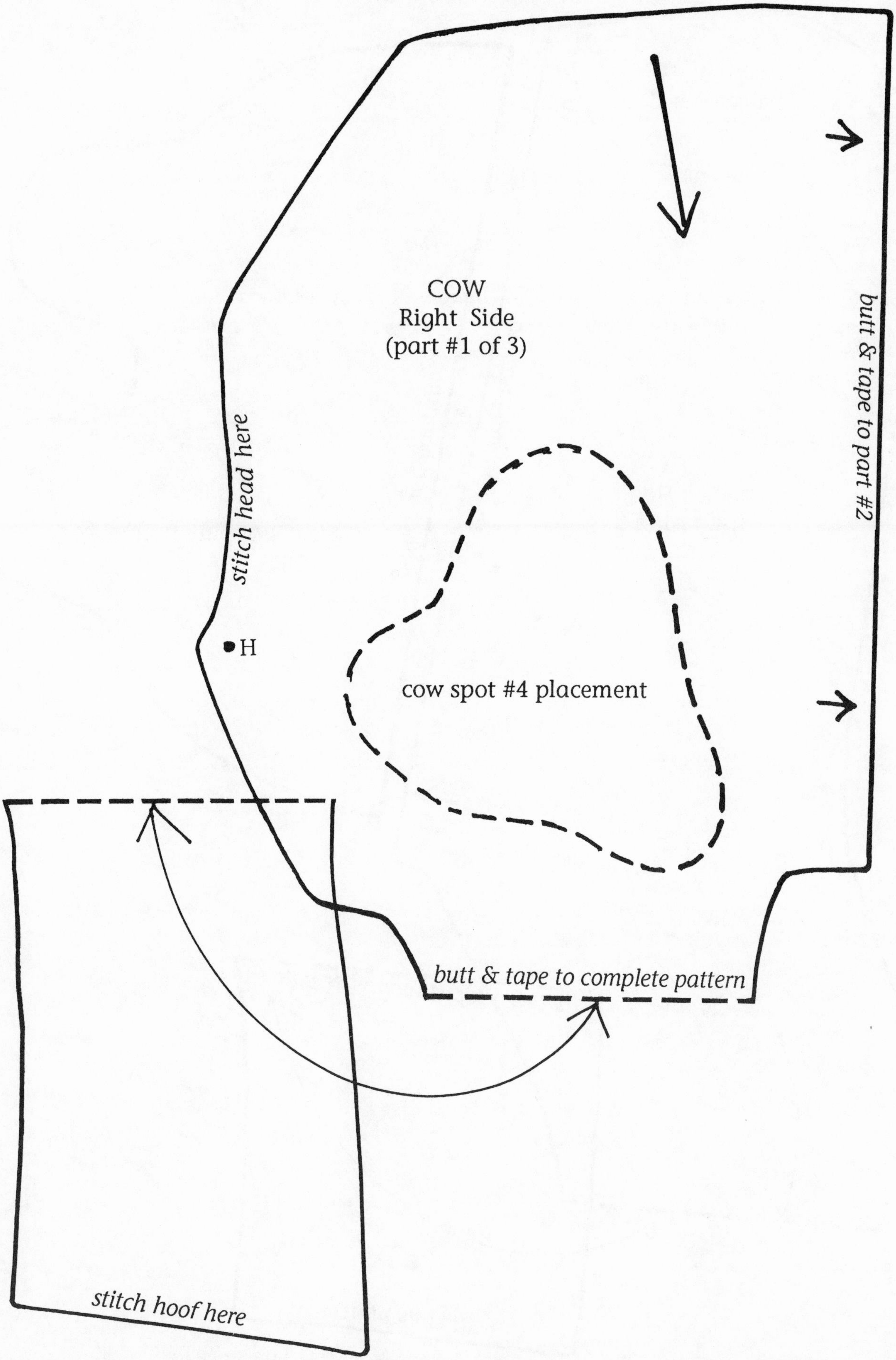

COW
Right Side
(part #1 of 3)

butt & tape to part #2

stitch head here

• H

cow spot #4 placement

butt & tape to complete pattern

stitch hoof here

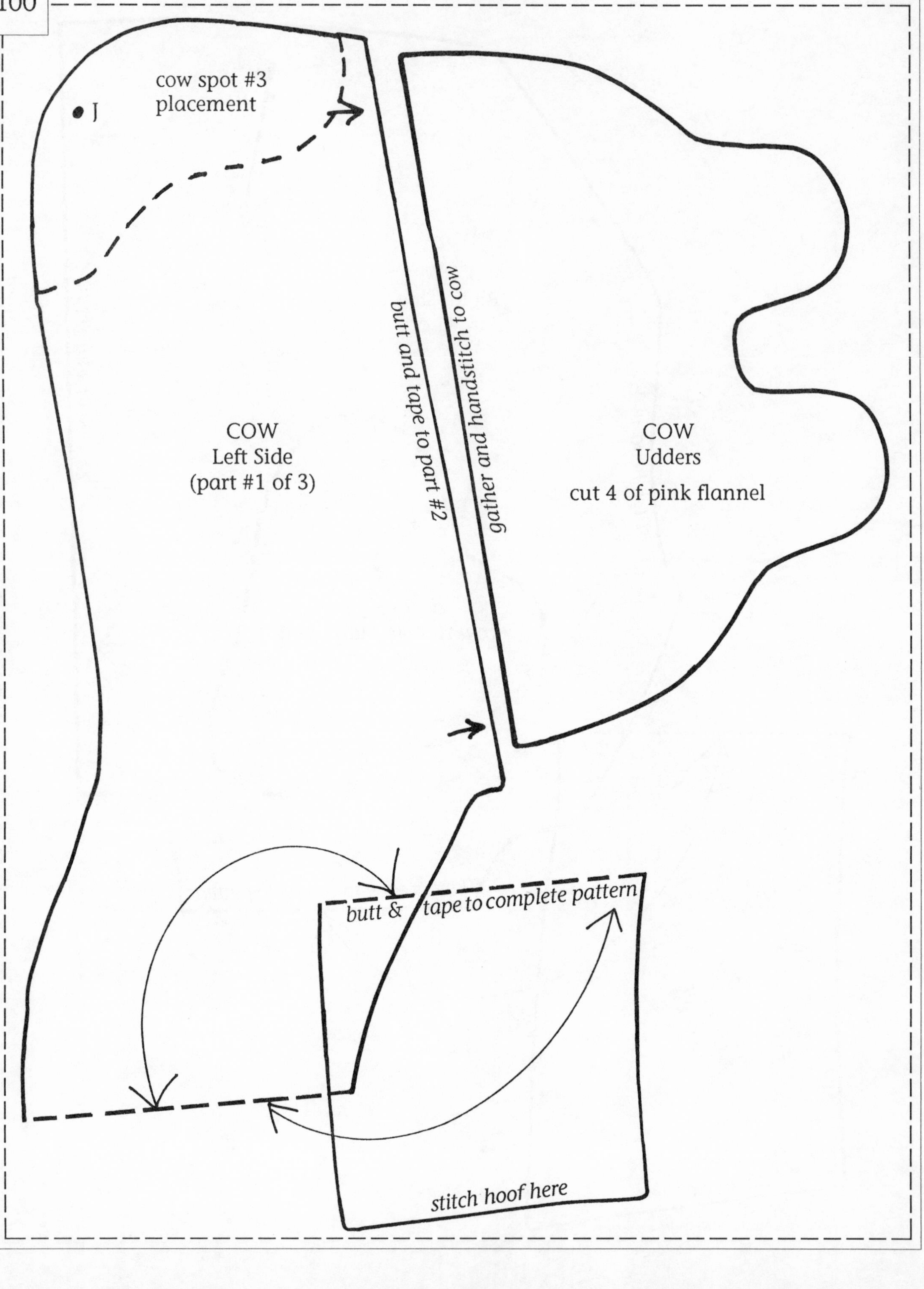

cow spot #3
placement

• J

COW
Left Side
(part #1 of 3)

butt and tape to part #2

gather and handstitch to cow

COW
Udders

cut 4 of pink flannel

butt & tape to complete pattern

stitch hoof here

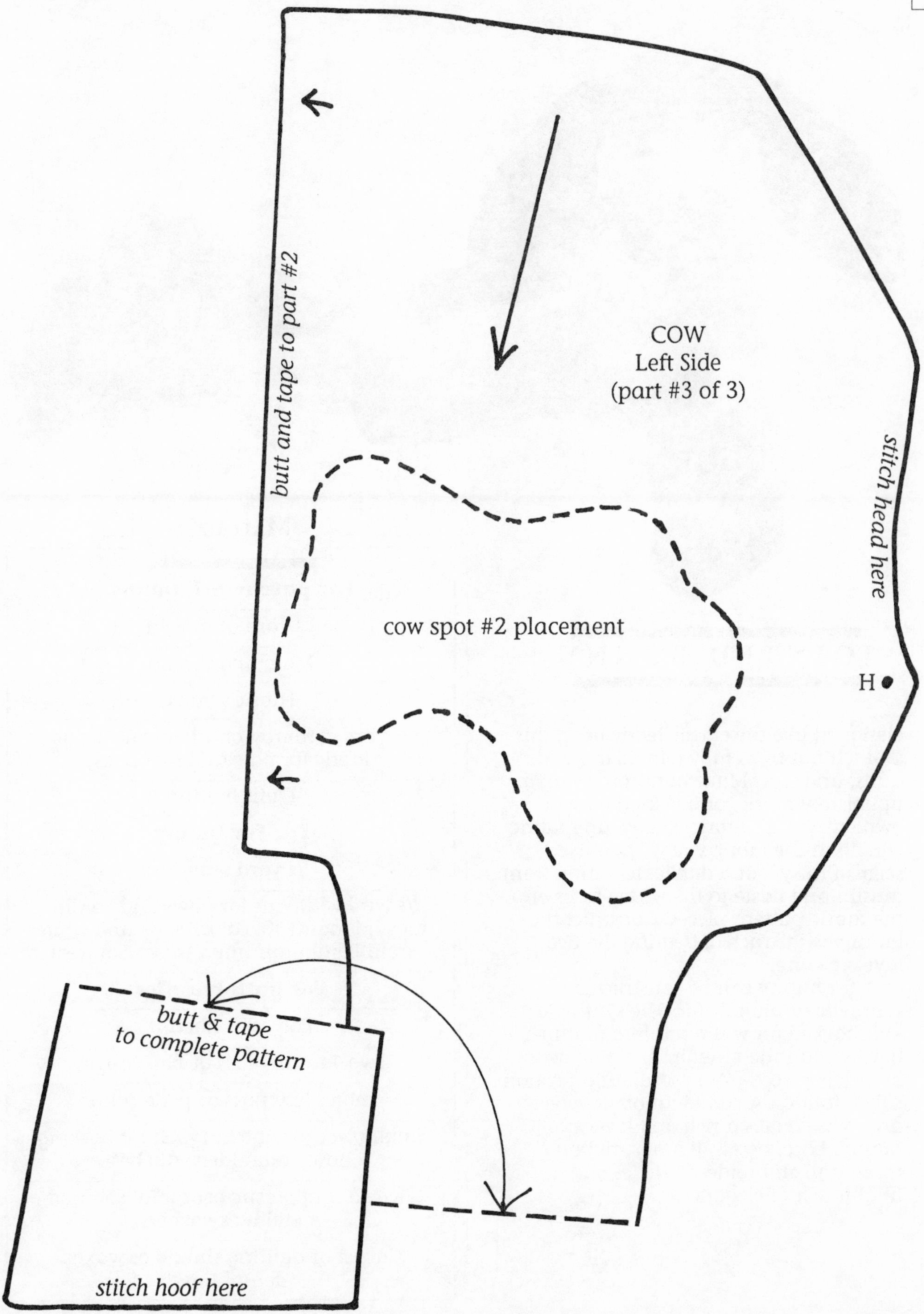

butt and tape to part #2

COW
Left Side
(part #3 of 3)

stitch head here

H •

cow spot #2 placement

butt & tape
to complete pattern

stitch hoof here

JOINTED BUNNY

Designed like the classic teddy bear, this 17-inch bunny is fully jointed at head, arms, and legs. Make him from mohair, upholstery fabric, or quick-patch your own crazy quilt fabric. Really, any fabric will do. If the fabric you wish to use seems flimsy, cut a duplicate bunny from muslin and baste to the wrong sides of the fabric pattern pieces. Construct the bunny as instructed, treating the two layers as one.

A fur bunny can be constructed of synthetic or mohair fur. The synthetic, knit-backed fur will result in a plumper bunny than the mohair. The patchwork bunny is pieced from coordinating cotton calico fabrics. A combination of velvets and silks creates a rich and lovely bunny. Lace, beads, buttons, ribbon roses, and embroidery stitches add a final touch of elegance.

MATERIALS

For patchwork bunny

½ yard of muslin

Matching thread

Fabric scraps

⅙ yard corduroy or other contrasting fabric for paw and foot pads

Quilt batting

For fur bunny

½ yard gray fur

⅙ yard white fur for paws and ear linings (Mohair F50, colors 5053 and white from Edinburgh Imports, see Sources)

For both bunnies

Polyester fiberfill

Two 14 mm glass or plastic eyes

Embroidery floss or perle cotton

Small piece of matching felt for backing nose embroidery stitches

Five 55 mm plastic bear joint sets and metal lockwashers

Carpet or quilting thread or waxed dental floss

INSTRUCTIONS

Note: *All seam allowances are ¼" unless otherwise instructed.*

Prepare, cut and mark the pattern pieces as instructed on page 10.

For the fur bunny: If using glass eyes, transfer eye markings to fur side of fabric by taking a stitch of colored thread on the right side of the fur at the markings. Leave the tails long so you can see the markings.

For the patchwork bunny: lay the pattern pieces (all but the paw and foot pads) on the muslin leaving a few inches between them. Cut the pattern pieces from the muslin adding an extra inch or so around each piece. Cut the paw and foot pads from the contrasting fabric.

Using the muslin pieces as a guide, cut batting to fit each piece, excluding paw and foot pads. Lay the batting on top of the muslin. Piece calico (or silk or velvet) over the muslin pieces as illustrated, sandwiching the batting between the muslin and the calico.

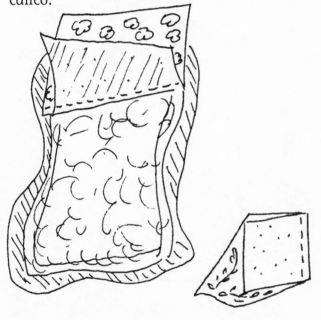

Lay the pattern pieces on top of the patchwork. Pin. Cut out the patterns through all layers. Baste ¼" from the raw edges, through all layers. Transfer markings for the joints, ears, and eyes to the muslin. For glass eyes, transfer the eye markings to the calico side of the head sides.

For patchwork and fur bunnies:

1. Pin the two body front pieces together along the center front seam, matching the single notches. Stitch.

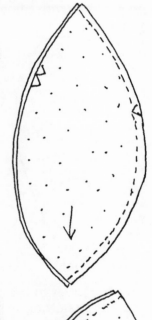

2. Pin the two body back pieces together along the center back seam. Stitch the seam from the top to the first dot, backstitching at both ends to secure. Stitch the seam from the second dot to the bottom, backstitching at both ends to secure. The gap left in the stitching between the dots will provide access to the body cavity for jointing and stuffing the bunny.

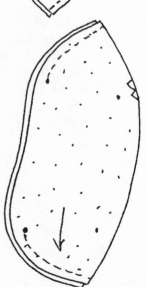

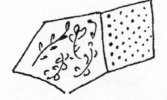

3. Pin the front and back pieces together at the sides, matching double notches and matching the seams at the top and bottom of the body backs to those at the body fronts. Stitch between the dots at the top of the body, backstitching at both ends. This small gap will allow room for insertion of a post for the neck joint.

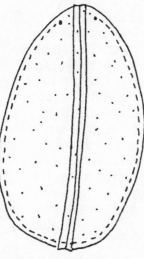

Make holes for arms and legs at markings. Turn the body right side out.

4. Pin the paw pads to the inner arms, right sides facing. Stitch. Open out the paw pads and pin the seam allowances open so they will lie flat.

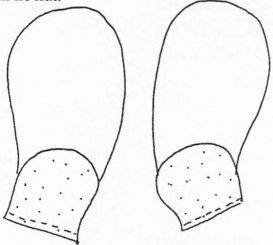

5. Pin the inner to the outer arm pieces, right sides together, with the paw pads open. Stitch all the way around the paws, leaving an opening between the dots at the top of the arms. Turn the arms right side out.

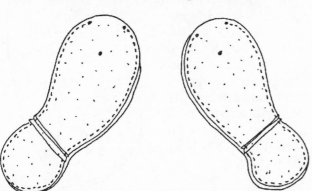

6. With right sides facing, pin two leg pieces together. Stitch from the dots down to the bottom of the leg at front and back as illustrated. Repeat for the second leg.

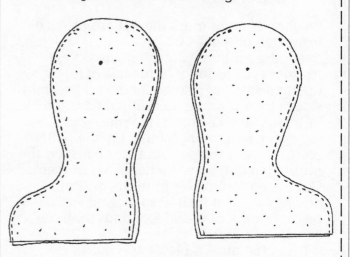

7. Pin the foot pads to the bottom of the legs, right sides facing, matching the large dot on the foot pad to the front leg seam and the small dot to the seam at the back of the leg. Stitch. Turn legs right side out.

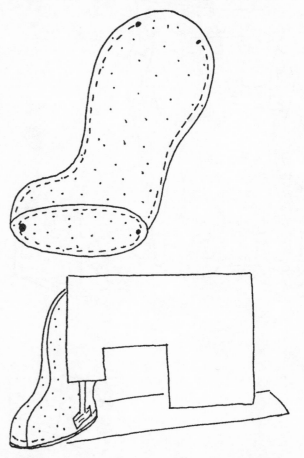

8. Right sides facing, pin and stitch each ear piece to a contrasting (inner) ear piece, leaving the bottoms open. Turn right side out.

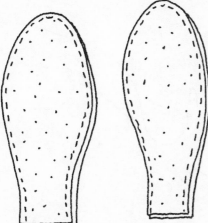

Fold the ears in half vertically and pin to the head sides as shown, the inner ear facing forward. Baste in place.

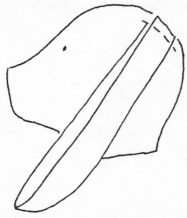

9. Pin the two head sides together, right sides facing, from the nose to the base of the neck. Stitch.

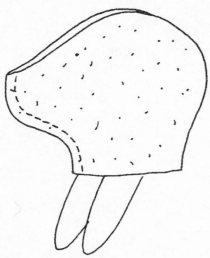

10. Pin dot A on the head gusset to the seam at the nose where the two head pieces meet, right sides facing. Pin one side of the gusset to one head side from the tip of the nose to the base of the neck at the back of the head, easing the gusset to fit as you pin. Stitch, including the ends of the ear in the seam but being careful not to catch any of the remainder of the ear in the seam. Repeat for the other side of the gusset. Turn head right side out.

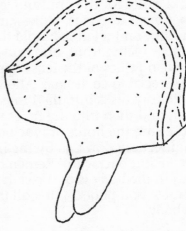

11. If you are using safety eyes, install them as instructed on page 15.

12. Starting with walnut-size pieces of fiberfill, stuff the bunny's nose. Using the handle of a wooden spoon or a dowel, push the stuffing into the nose hard. Continue stuffing the head, using golf-ball size pieces of fiberfill and packing it in with the spoon or dowel, until the stuffing reaches to within 1/2" of the raw edges at the neck opening. Using heavy thread and long (1/2") stitches, hand baste around the raw edge of the opening. Place the flat side of the stationary disk into the opening, against the fiberfill, with the post pointing out of the bottom of the neck. Pull up on the basting stitches. Stitch around once or twice more until the fabric is tight around the post. Tie the thread in a knot.

13. Following the instructions on page 15, install glass eyes, unless you have already installed the plastic eyes.

14. Insert the post protruding from the bottom of the head into the small gap in the stitching at the top of the body. From inside the body install the plastic washer, plastic lockwasher, and metal lockwasher as instructed on page 13.

15. Make holes for the arm and leg joints on the inner arms and legs. Make sure you have a right and a left leg: hold them together, toes facing front, and make the holes on the facing sides of the legs. Apply a drop of Fray Check® to each hole. Allow to dry. Put stationary disks into the limbs. Push the posts out and then into the holes in the body. (Be sure the limbs are facing in the correct direction; don't go by the head - it may be facing backward! Remember, the opening in the body is at the center back.) As instructed on page 14, install the limbs on the body.

16. Starting with small bits of fiberfill in the paws and feet and progressing to golf ball-size chunks, stuff the arms and legs of the bunny. Pack the limbs tightly. Sew the openings at the tops of the limbs and center back closed by following the easy ladder-stitch described on page 13.

17. To make the bunny's nose and mouth: Thread an long needle and knot the thread. Push the needle into the base of the neck, hiding the knot. Emerge at point A in the

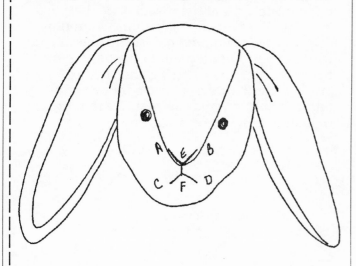

illustration. Go back in at point B. Come out at point C. Go in at point D. Come out at point E, above the loop formed between dots A and B.

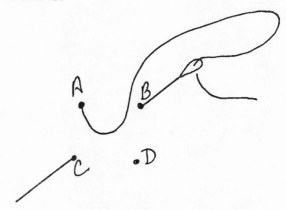

Pull the thread up. Go back in at point F, below the loop between dots C and D. Come out at the base of the neck. Adjust the loops and thread tension. Knot the thread, hiding it in the neck.

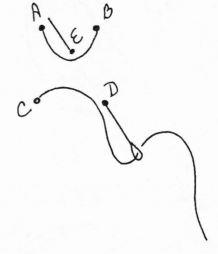

18. If making a fur bunny, free the fur caught in the seams by pulling it out with a seam ripper or a special brush available from CR's Crafts and Edinburgh Imports (see Sources).

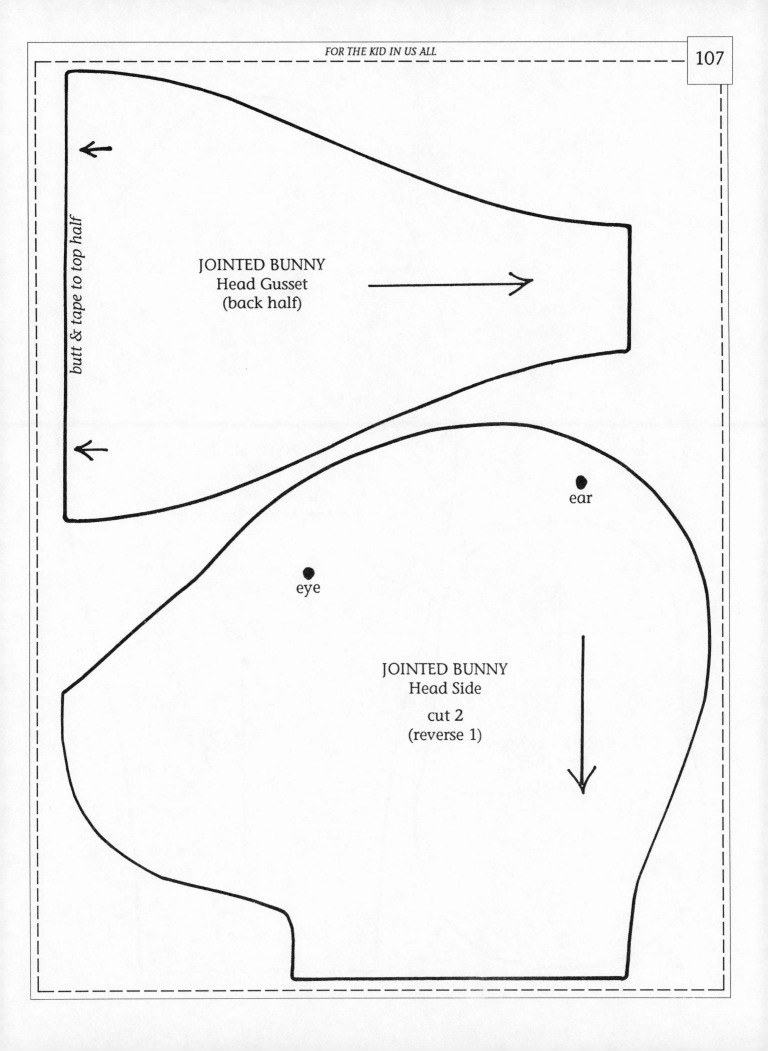

butt & tape to top half

JOINTED BUNNY
Head Gusset
(back half)

ear

eye

JOINTED BUNNY
Head Side

cut 2
(reverse 1)

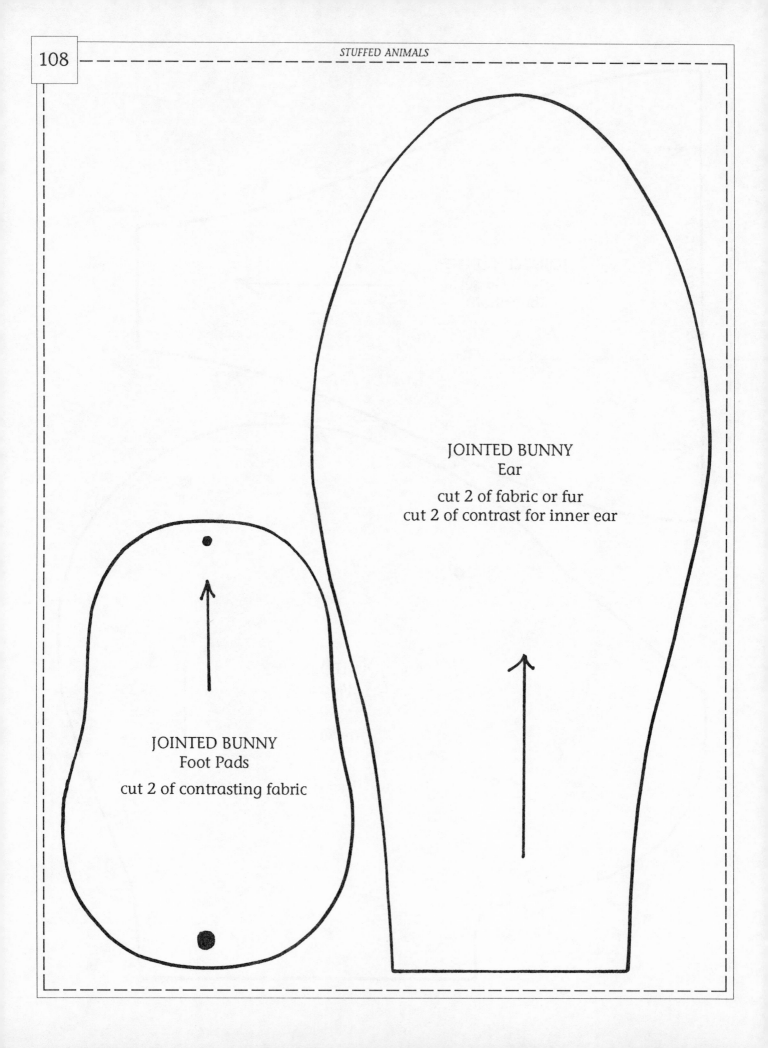

JOINTED BUNNY
Ear

cut 2 of fabric or fur
cut 2 of contrast for inner ear

JOINTED BUNNY
Foot Pads

cut 2 of contrasting fabric

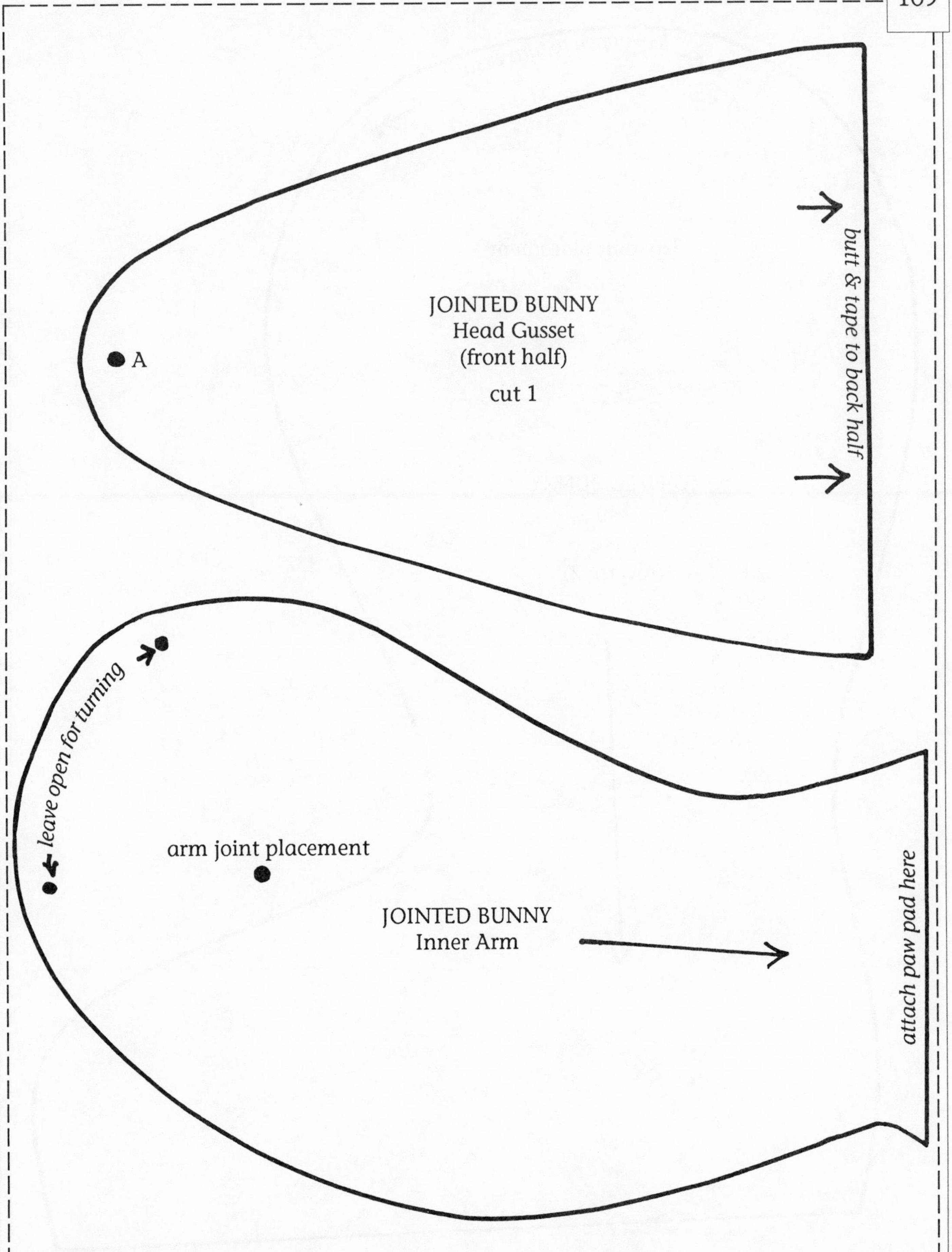

● A

JOINTED BUNNY
Head Gusset
(front half)

cut 1

butt & tape to back half

leave open for turning

arm joint placement ●

JOINTED BUNNY
Inner Arm

attach paw pad here

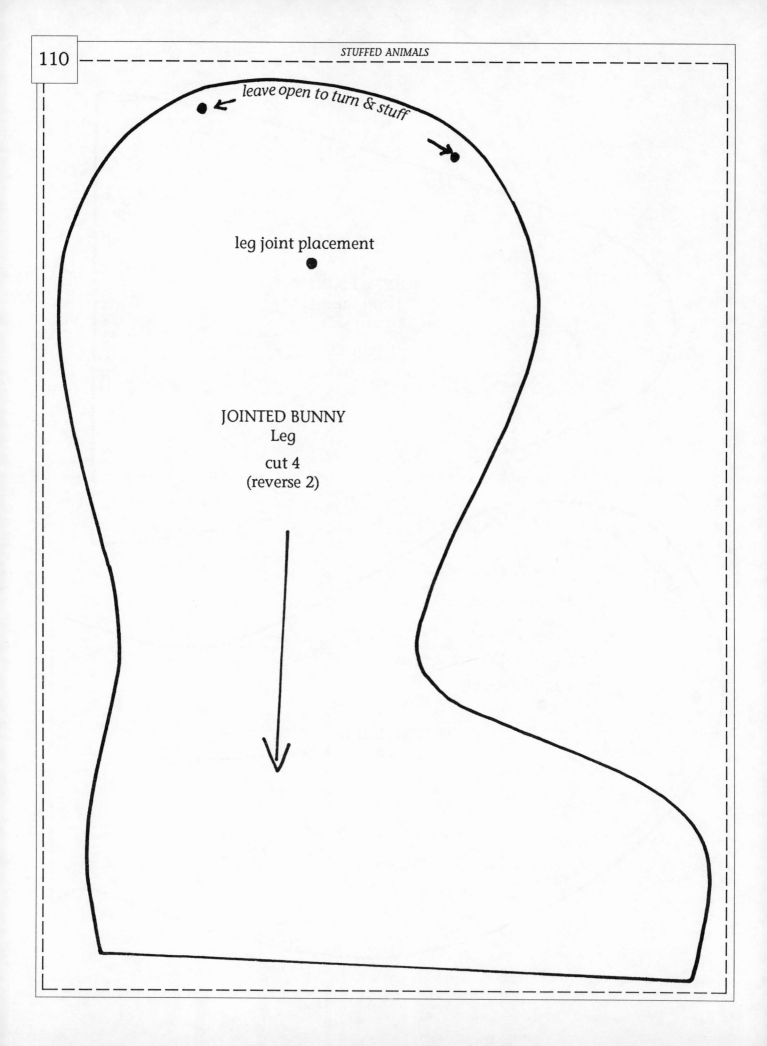

leave open to turn & stuff

leg joint placement

JOINTED BUNNY
Leg

cut 4
(reverse 2)

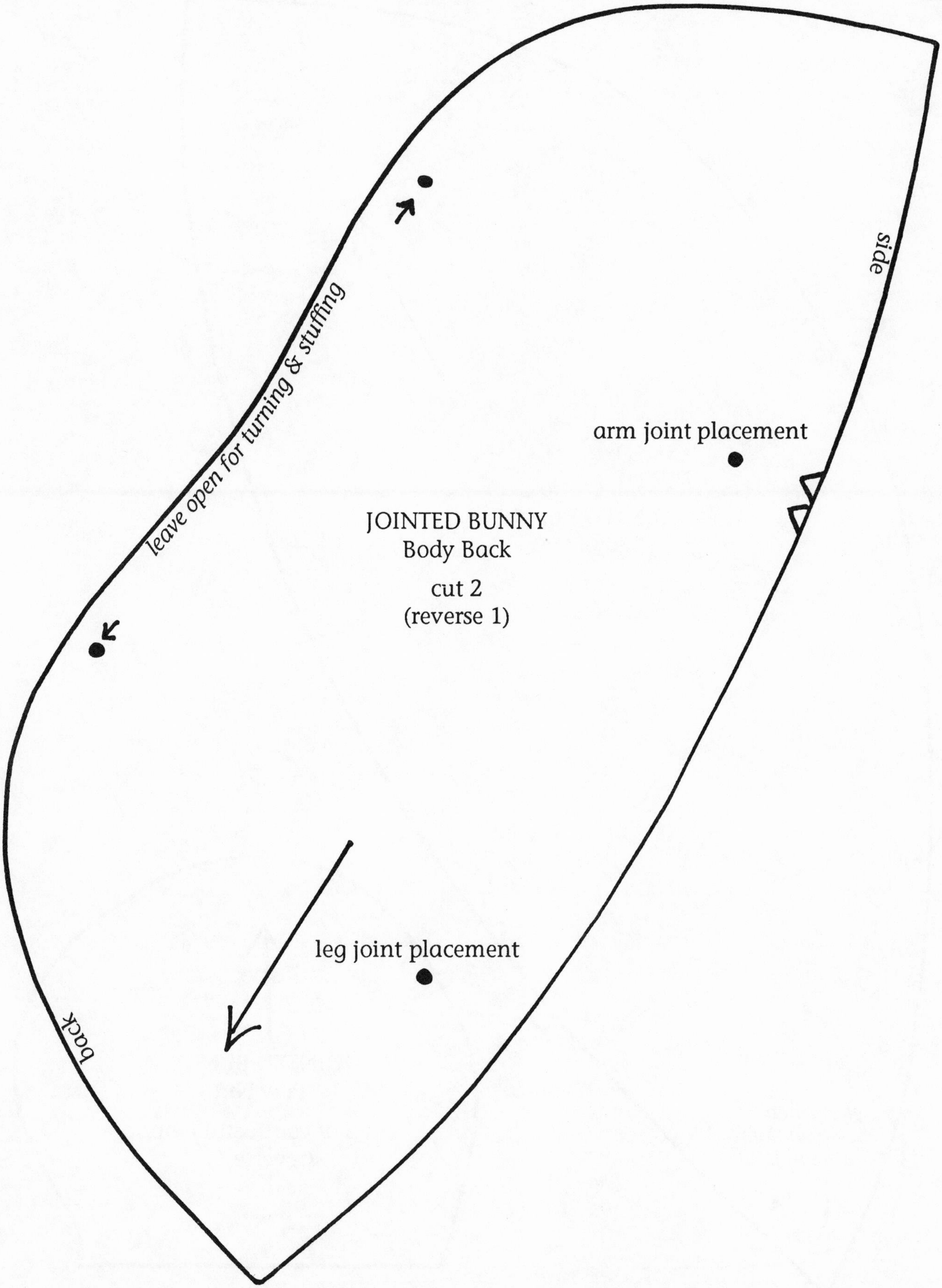

side

leave open for turning & stuffing

arm joint placement

JOINTED BUNNY
Body Back

cut 2
(reverse 1)

leg joint placement

back

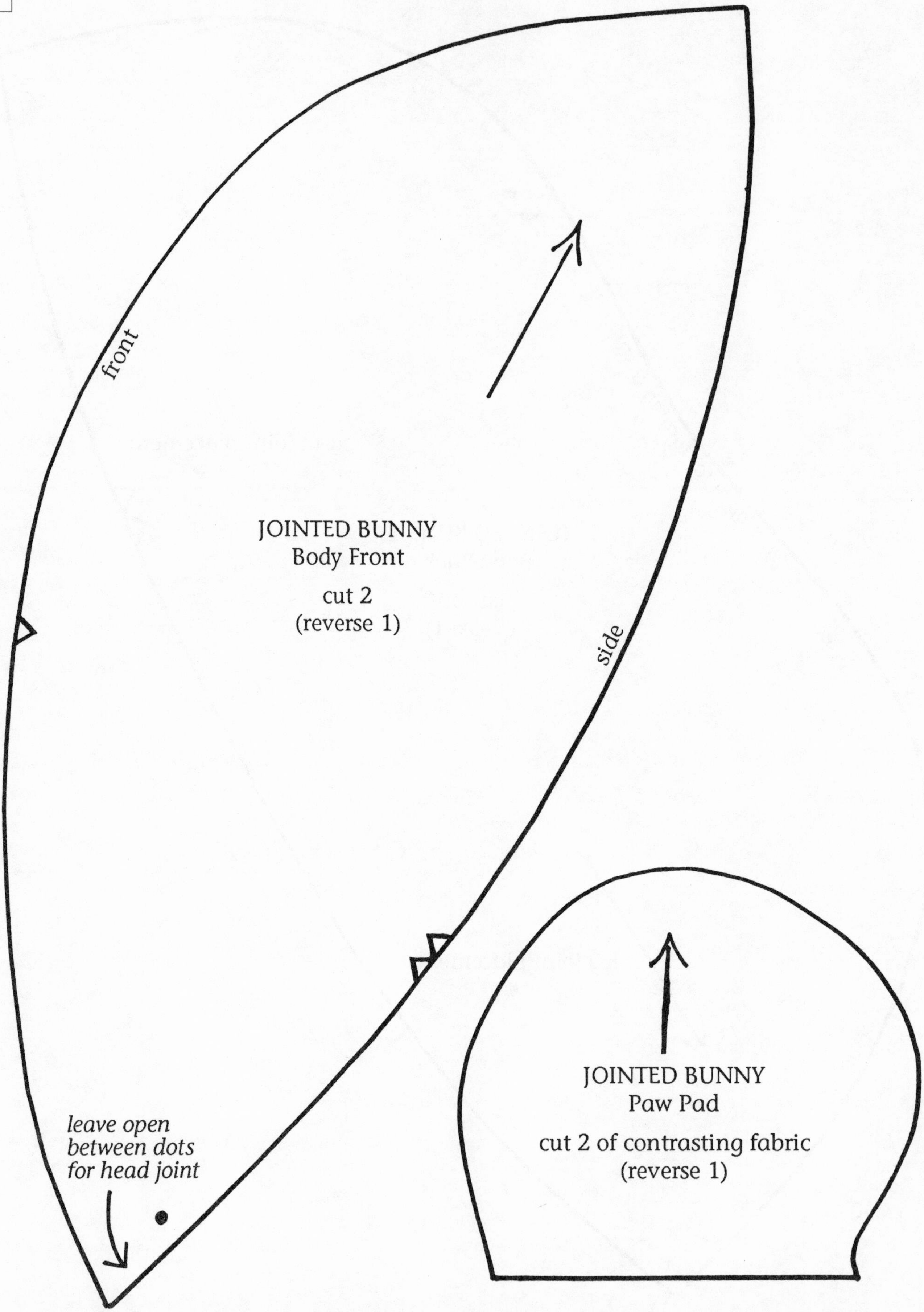

front

JOINTED BUNNY
Body Front

cut 2
(reverse 1)

side

*leave open
between dots
for head joint*

JOINTED BUNNY
Paw Pad

cut 2 of contrasting fabric
(reverse 1)

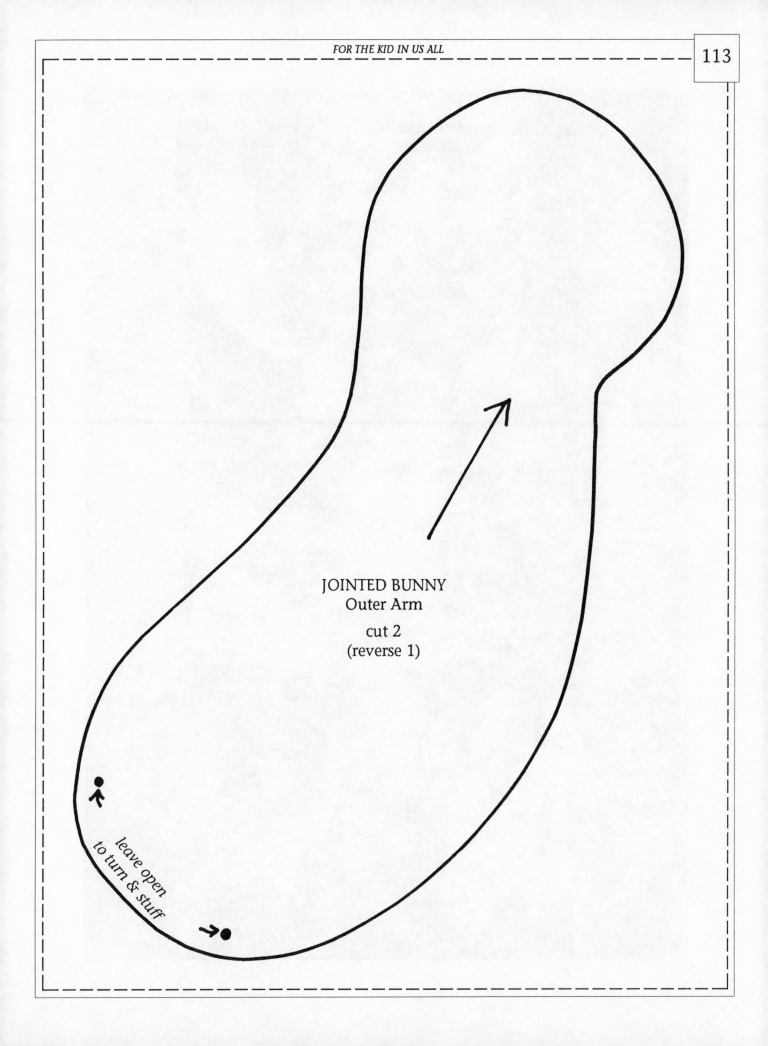

JOINTED BUNNY
Outer Arm

cut 2
(reverse 1)

leave open
to turn & stuff

♥ ♥ ♥ ♥

Standing Animal Dolls & Reclining Animals

The following 13 animals are designed with "double personalities" for twice the fun. These critters can be created as animal dolls or as reclining animals depending on which set of body instructions you choose to follow. And I've made clothing for the dolls to give them even more character.

All the head patterns (kitty, lamb, fox, dog, teddy bear, bunny, mouse, lion, piggy, cow, fawn, horse, and elephant) work with both the animal doll and reclining animal bodies. And since there are three kinds of kitties – calico, plain and Siamese – and variations on the lamb, fawn, and some of the others, the possibilities are exponential.

The animal dolls measure approximately 17 inches tall and the reclining animals, 14 inches long.

You may choose either plastic, safety, or glass eyes. To help decide, turn to page 15.

♥ ♥ ♥ ♥

K I T T Y

MATERIALS

Seal fur fabric (from by Diane or CR's Crafts, see Sources):

For solid color kitty

⅓ yard white or black seal for animal doll

½ yard white or black seal for reclining kitty

For Siamese kitty

⅓ yard tan fur for animal doll (CR's Crafts 907E)

½ yard tan fur for reclining kitty (CR's Crafts 907E)

12" x 15" piece of black seal for dark points

For calico kitty

⅓ yard white seal, scrap of black seal, and scrap of orange fur (CR's Crafts 907C) for animal doll

½ yard white seal, ¼ yard black seal, and ¼ yard orange for reclining kitty

Additional materials all types of kitties

Matching sewing thread

55 mm plastic joints: One for reclining kitty, three for animal doll

Two 12 mm plastic safety or glass cat eyes

Polyester fiberfill

Pink and black embroidery floss or perle cotton

Whiskers (see CR's Crafts in Sources)

INSTRUCTIONS

Note: All seam allowances are ¼" unless otherwise instructed. Head pattern follows. Body patterns begin on page 175 for animal dolls and page 181 for reclining animals.

As instructed on page 10, make patterns, cut and mark fur.

Transfer dots for eye placement as marked to the backing of the fur. If using glass eyes, transfer this marking to the fur side of the head. Make a stitch from the right side of the fur with colored thread, tying the ends on the right side and leaving half inch-long strings as a mark. Transfer all markings for animal doll or reclining animal as marked on pattern.

1. For calico kitty:

Right sides facing and matching dots W and X, pin black left head side top to white left head side bottom, easing to fit. Stitch.

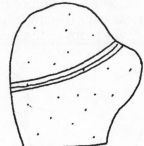

Pin orange right head side top to white right head side bottom, right sides together, matching dots Y and Z. Ease top to fit. Stitch.

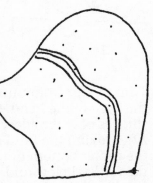

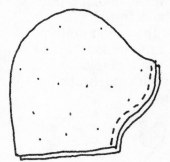

For all kitties:

Pin the head sides together, right sides facing, from dot A at nose, down to bottom of neck. Stitch.

2. For Siamese kitty:

Pin Siamese nose gusset to Siamese head gusset, matching dots C. Stitch.

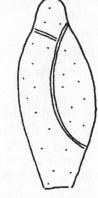

For Calico kitty:

Pin white calico kitty head gusset III to orange head gusset I, right sides facing, matching dots P and Q. Stitch from raw edge to raw edge. Pin black calico kitty head gusset II to head gussets I and III, matching dots R and S. Stitch from raw edge to raw edge.

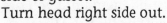

For all kitties:

Pin dot A at nose on gusset to dot A at nose on head sides. Working on one side of the head, match and pin dots B on back end of gusset to those on head side. Pin between these two points, easing any excess. Stitch. Repeat for other side of gusset. Turn head right side out.

3. For safety eyes, install as instructed on page 15. If using glass eyes, omit this step.

4. If you haven't already, turn the head right side out. Starting at the nose, stuff the head firmly. When you have stuffed to about a half inch from the raw edges at the base of the neck, insert the flat end of the stationary disk into the bottom of the neck, with the ridged post pointing out of the bottom of the head. Using doubled heavy thread or waxed dental floss, run a row of long basting stitches around the opening, one quarter inch from the raw edge. Pull up on the thread tightly. Continue around one more time, pulling the thread as you go. Secure the thread with a knot. This will pull the fabric around the joint as shown.

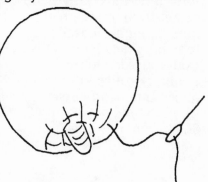

5. If using glass eyes, turn to page 15 for instructions on installing them.

6. Following the instructions on page 11, trim the fur from two solid color kitty ear pieces. For the Siamese trim the fur of two black ear pieces. For the calico kitty trim the fur of two white ear pieces. These will be the inside of the ears.

Pin and stitch a trimmed and untrimmed ear piece together, right sides facing. Trim the seam allowances at the tips of the ears. Turn right sides out.

Repeat for remaining ear.

Turn 1/4" on bottom edges of ears to inside. Whipstitch closed. Fold the ears in half lengthwise, with the trimmed side to the inside. Run a long needle through them as shown. This will make the ear concave, curved toward the front.

Pin ears to head, trimmed sides of ears facing forward, adjusting them until you are satisfied with their placement. (For calico kitty; orange ear on right, black on left, matching head color.) Studying the photograph of the kitty will help. Sew in place with doubled heavy thread as instructed on page 17. Remove the long needles holding the ears in a curve.

7. Fold tail in half lengthwise along foldline. Pin. Stitch, leaving top edge open, and pushing extra fur inside the tail so it won't get caught in or outside of the seam.

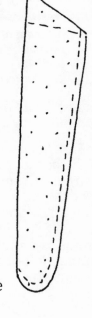

Turn tail right side out.

8. Turn to page 175 and follow the steps below to make the animal doll or to page 181 to make the reclining animal body.

9. Cut nose from felt. Place on the head, matching top, straight edge of nose with gusset seam and centering the nose over the straight up and down seam of the head sides, as illustrated.

Trim the fur from under the nose. Glue the nose to the head. Cover with vertical stitches of embroidery floss (see page 15). After taking the final stitch emerge from the center bottom of the nose. Go back into the fur 1/2" below and to the left. Emerge 1/2" directly under the nose, hooking the thread as shown. Go back into the fur 1/2" to the right and below the center bottom of the nose as shown. Emerge somewhere on the neck and knot the embroidery thread close to the fur backing. Brush the fur to hide the knot.

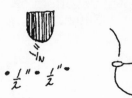

10. Cut 5 or 6 whiskers, each about 6" long. Thread the very end of each whisker in turn onto a long, large-eyed needle. Run them from one side of the muzzle to the other as shown. Clip off the end bent from going through the needle.

11. Embroider claws on paws as illustrated. Refer to page 15 for instructions on starting and ending the embroidery.

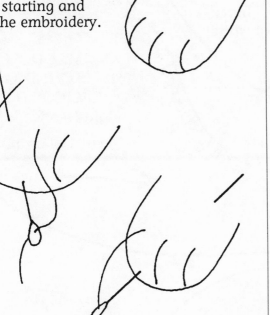

ANIMAL DOLL &
RECLINING SIAMESE KITTY
Head Gusset

cut 1 of tan

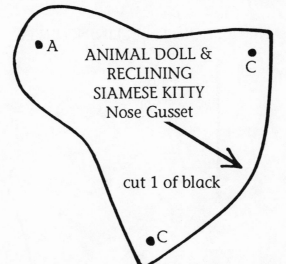

ANIMAL DOLL &
RECLINING
SIAMESE KITTY
Nose Gusset

cut 1 of black

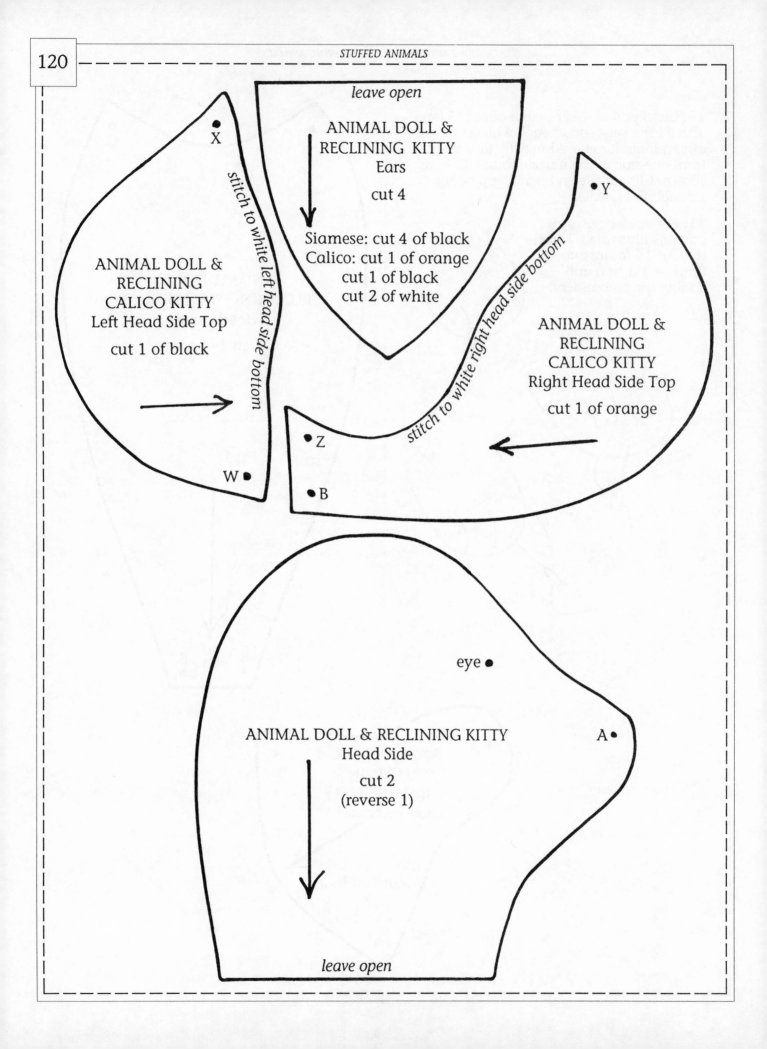

X

leave open

ANIMAL DOLL &
RECLINING KITTY
Ears

cut 4

Siamese: cut 4 of black
Calico: cut 1 of orange
cut 1 of black
cut 2 of white

• Y

ANIMAL DOLL &
RECLINING
CALICO KITTY
Left Head Side Top

cut 1 of black

stitch to white left head side bottom

stitch to white right head side bottom

ANIMAL DOLL &
RECLINING
CALICO KITTY
Right Head Side Top

cut 1 of orange

Z

W

B

eye •

A •

ANIMAL DOLL & RECLINING KITTY
Head Side

cut 2
(reverse 1)

leave open

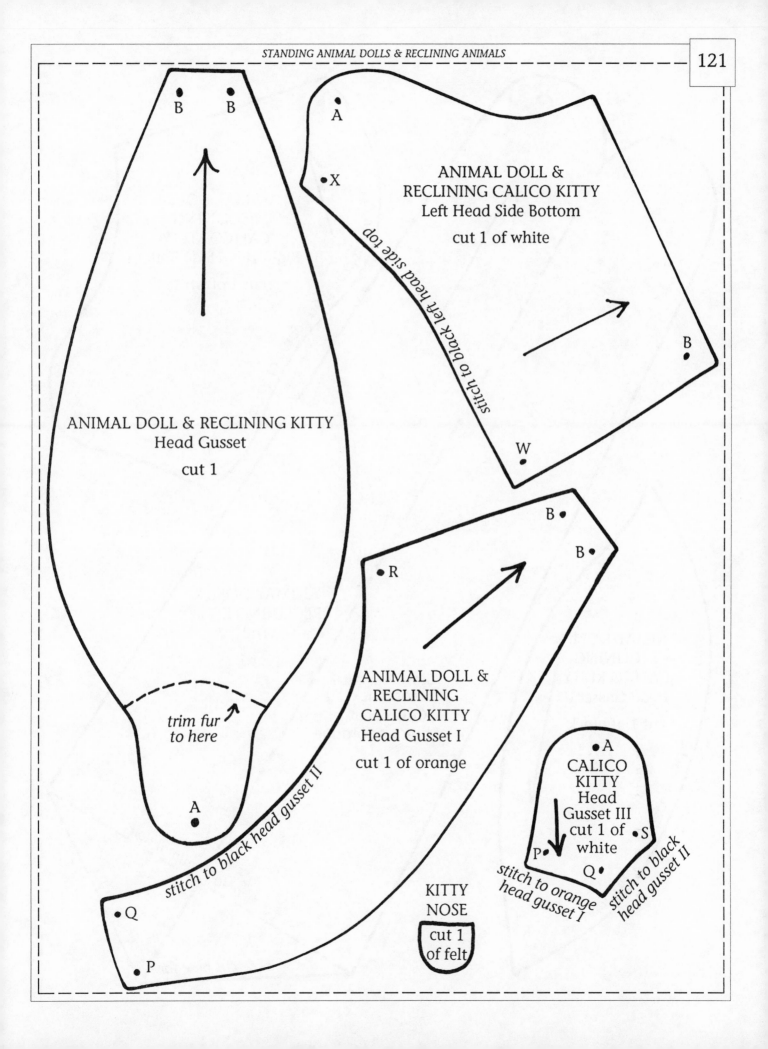

B B

A

X

**ANIMAL DOLL &
RECLINING CALICO KITTY**
Left Head Side Bottom

cut 1 of white

stitch to black left head side top

B

W

ANIMAL DOLL & RECLINING KITTY
Head Gusset

cut 1

B

B

R

**ANIMAL DOLL &
RECLINING
CALICO KITTY**
Head Gusset I

cut 1 of orange

*trim fur
to here*

A

stitch to black head gusset II

A

**CALICO
KITTY**
Head
Gusset III
cut 1 of
white

P

S

Q

*stitch to orange
head gusset I*

*stitch to black
head gusset II*

Q

**KITTY
NOSE**

cut 1
of felt

P

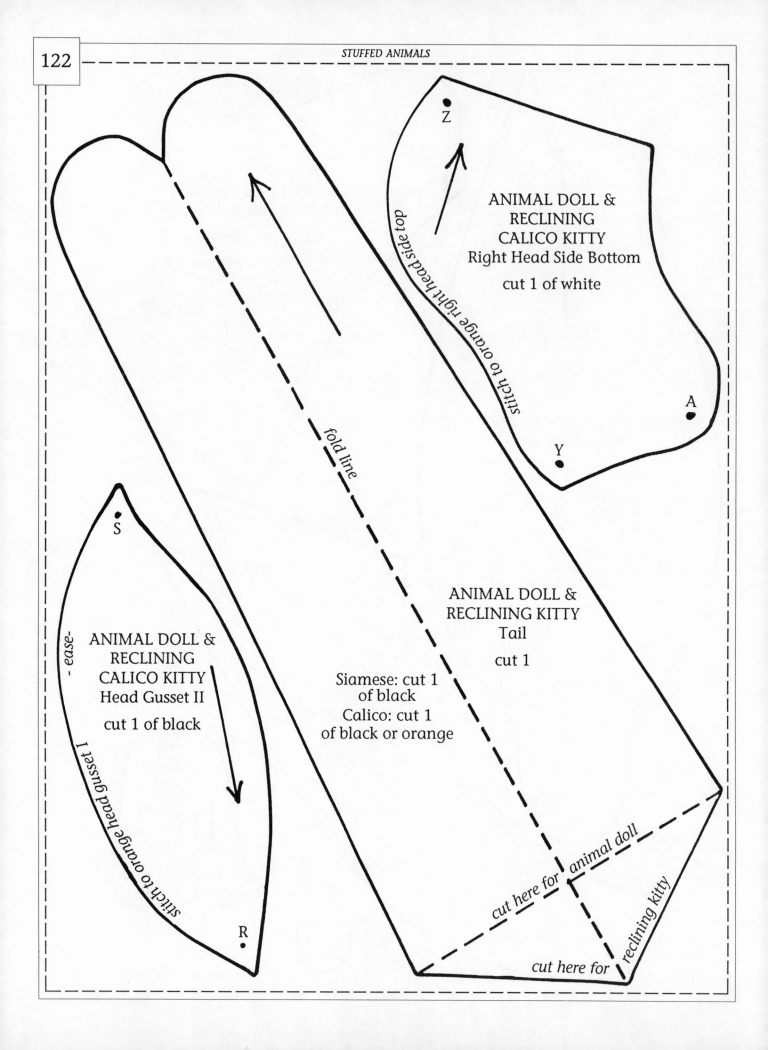

ANIMAL DOLL &
RECLINING
CALICO KITTY
Right Head Side Bottom

cut 1 of white

stitch to orange right head side top

Z

Y

A

ANIMAL DOLL &
RECLINING
CALICO KITTY
Head Gusset II

cut 1 of black

- ease -

stitch to orange head gusset I

S

R

fold line

ANIMAL DOLL &
RECLINING KITTY
Tail

cut 1

Siamese: cut 1
of black
Calico: cut 1
of black or orange

cut here for animal doll

cut here for

reclining kitty

LAMB

MATERIALS

Off-white shearling fabric
(available at most fabric stores or from CR's
Crafts, see Sources):

¹/₃ yard for animal doll
¹/₂ yard for reclining lamb

¹/₈ yard black shearling for
black and white lamb

Matching sewing thread

Heavy thread, carpet thread, or waxed
dental floss

55 mm plastic joints for head and arms:
One for reclining animal,
three for animal doll

Two 12 mm black plastic safety or glass eyes

Pink embroidery floss or perle cotton

Polyester fiberfill

¹/₂ yard ¹/₂" wide ribbon

Sheep's bell
(available from CR's Crafts, see Sources)

INSTRUCTIONS

Note: All seam allowances are ¹/₄" unless otherwise instructed. Head pattern follows. Body patterns begin on page 175 for animal dolls and page 181 for reclining animals.

For black and white lamb doll or reclining lamb, cut ears and tail from black fabric, and use two special head side patterns: muzzle (cut from black) and black and white lamb head side (cut from white). For reclining lamb, also cut feet from black fabric.

As instructed on page 10, make patterns and cut fur.

Transfer dots for eye and ear placement as marked to the backing of the fur. Using colored thread, stitch along ear placement markings through to the right side of the fur. If using glass eyes make a stitch from the right side of the fur with colored thread, tying the ends on the right side and leaving half inch long strings as a placement marking. Transfer all markings for animal doll or reclining animal to body pieces as marked on patterns and instructed on page 11.

1. Pin and stitch two ear pieces together, right sides facing, leaving short, straight edges open.

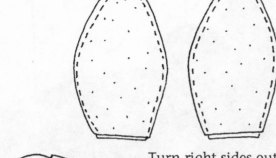

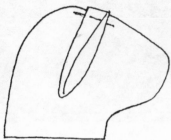

Turn right sides out. Repeat for remaining two ear pieces. Fold ears in half lengthwise. Baste. Baste to one head side between dots, folded edge facing the back of the head.

2. For black and white lamb: Pin black muzzle to white head side, matching dots M and N, easing muzzle to fit. Stitch. Treat as head side in the following instructions.

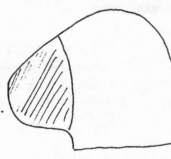

3. For both types of lamb: Pin the head sides together, right sides facing, from dot A at nose down to bottom of front of neck. Stitch.

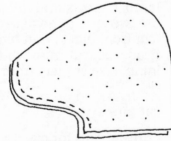

4. Gather edge of lamb back head gusset between dots B and C as marked on pattern. Right sides facing, pin back head gusset to front head gusset, matching dots B and C. Pull up on gathers to fit. Pin. Stitch.

5. Pin dot A at nose on front head gusset to dot A at seam of head sides. Pin dot D on back head gusset to dot D on one head side. Pin head gusset to head side between these dots. Stitch. Repeat for other head side.

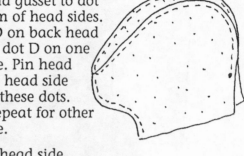

6. Stitch head side together from dot D down to the back base of the neck, leaving the bottom, straight edges of the neck open.

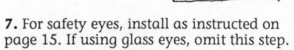

7. For safety eyes, install as instructed on page 15. If using glass eyes, omit this step.

8. If you haven't already done so, turn head right side out. Starting at the nose, stuff the head firmly. When you have stuffed to about a half inch from the raw edges at the base of the neck, insert the flat end of the stationary disk into the bottom of the neck, with the ridged post pointing out of the bottom of the head. Using heavy thread, run a row of long basting stitches around the opening by hand, one quarter inch from the raw edge. Pull up on the thread tightly. Continue around one more time, pulling the thread as you go. Secure the thread with a knot. This will pull the fabric around the joint as shown.

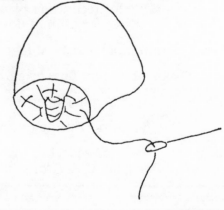

9. For glass eyes turn to page 15 for instructions on installing them.

10. Fold tail in half lengthwise, matching raw edges. Sew, leaving top, straight edge open.

Turn right side out.

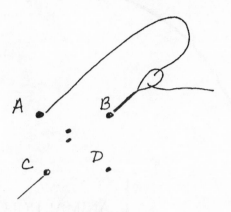

11.. Follow the directions for either the animal doll body on page 175 or reclining animal body starting on page 181.

12. To embroider the nose: Start the embroidery floss as instructed on page 15. Come up in the fabric at point A as illustrated. Go back in at point B and out at point C, leaving the thread loose. Push the needle back into the fur at point D and out at E, leaving the thread loop loose. Go under the first loop between A and B and back into the fur on the bottom side of loop C and D. Pull up on the thread, taking up slack in the two loops until they are even. Finish off the thread as instructed on page 17.

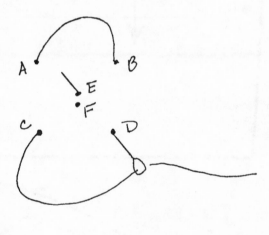

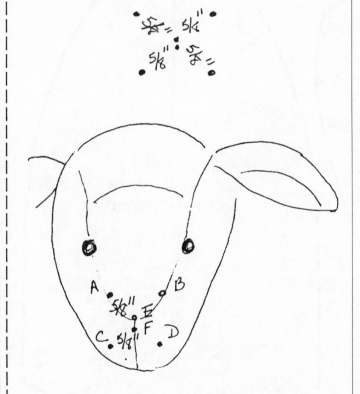

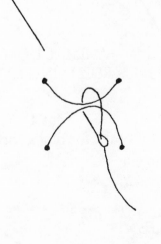

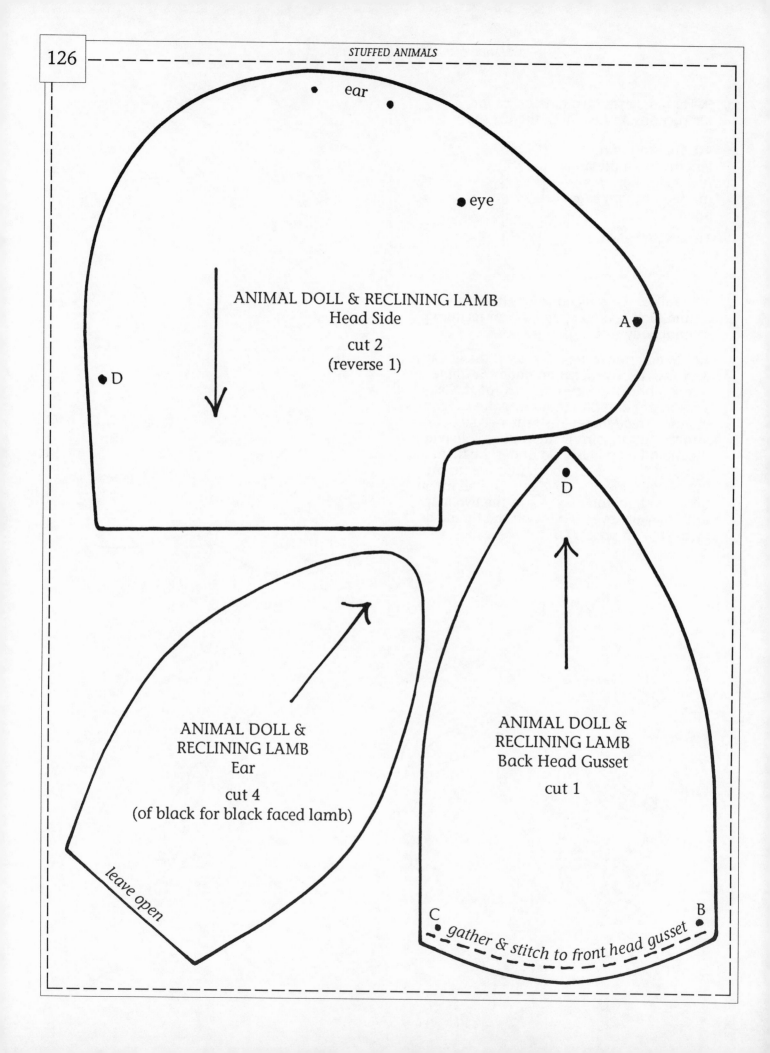

• ear •

• eye

ANIMAL DOLL & RECLINING LAMB
Head Side

cut 2
(reverse 1)

A •

• D

• D

ANIMAL DOLL &
RECLINING LAMB
Ear

cut 4
(of black for black faced lamb)

leave open

ANIMAL DOLL &
RECLINING LAMB
Back Head Gusset

cut 1

C •

• B

gather & stitch to front head gusset

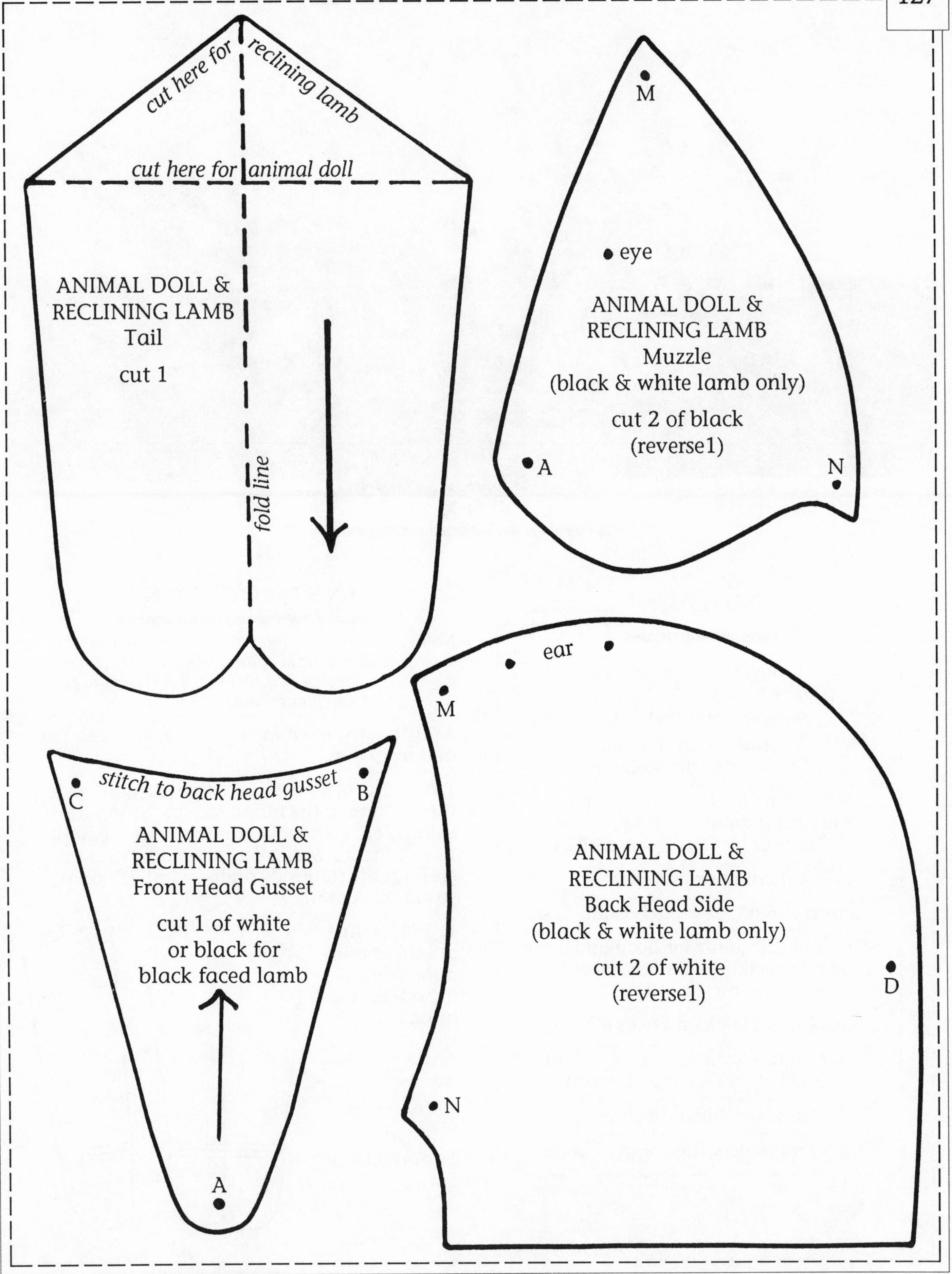

cut here for reclining lamb

cut here for animal doll

ANIMAL DOLL &
RECLINING LAMB
Tail

cut 1

fold line

ANIMAL DOLL &
RECLINING LAMB
Muzzle
(black & white lamb only)

cut 2 of black
(reverse1)

• M

• eye

• A

• N

stitch to back head gusset

• C
• B

ANIMAL DOLL &
RECLINING LAMB
Front Head Gusset

cut 1 of white
or black for
black faced lamb

• A

• ear •
• M

ANIMAL DOLL &
RECLINING LAMB
Back Head Side
(black & white lamb only)

cut 2 of white
(reverse1)

• D

• N

F O X

MATERIALS

Red fox fur fabric
(from CR's Crafts or by Diane,
see Sources):

¹/₃ yard for animal doll
¹/₂ yard for reclining animal

¹/₈ yard white fur fabric for animal doll
or reclining animal (white seal from
CR's Crafts or by Diane was used here)

Matching sewing thread

Carpet thread, or waxed dental floss

55 mm plastic joints for head and arms:
One for reclining animal, three for
animal doll

Two 12 mm plastic safety or glass eyes

One 21 mm plastic bear nose (see CR's
Crafts or by Diane in Sources)

Polyester fiberfill stuffing

Black embroidery floss or perle cotton

INSTRUCTIONS

*Note: All seam allowances are ¹/₄" unless otherwise
instructed. Head pattern follows. Body patterns
begin on page 175 for animal dolls and page
181 for reclining animals.*

As instructed in chapter 1, make patterns, cut
and mark fur.

Transfer dots for eye placement as marked to
the backing of the fur on the fox head side. If
using glass eyes make a stitch from the right
side of the fur with colored thread, tying the
ends on the right side and leaving ¹/₂" long
strings as a mark.

1. Stitch white
tail tip to tail,
right sides
facing. Fold tail
in half length-
wise, matching
raw edges. Sew,
leaving top,
straight edge
open.

Turn right side
out.

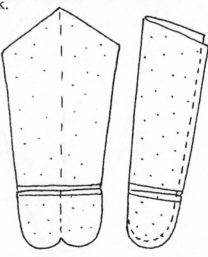

2. Pin white muzzles to head sides, matching dots A and B. Stitch.

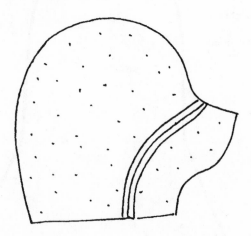

3. Pin the head sides together, right sides facing, matching dots C at nose, down to bottom of neck. Stitch.

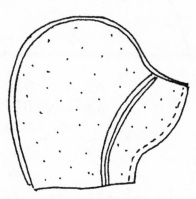

4. Pin dot C at nose tip of gusset to dot C at seam of head sides. Match and pin dot D at bottom back edge of one side of gusset to respective dot D at bottom back of one head side. Pin between these two points, easing any excess. Stitch from dot E to through dot D to bottom back neck edge. Repeat for other side of gusset. The gap left in the stitching is for the later insertion of the nose.

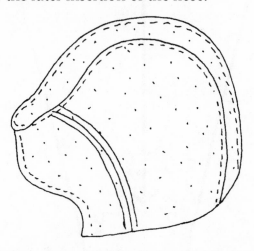

5. If using safety eye follow the instructions on page 15. If using glass eyes omit this step.

6. Install the plastic nose in the small opening in the stitching as instructed on page 15.

7. If you haven't already, turn head right side out. Starting at the nose, stuff the head firmly. When you have stuffed to about a half inch from the raw edges at the base of the neck, insert the flat end of the stationary disk into the bottom of the neck, with the ridged post pointing out of the bottom of the head. Using heavy thread, run a row of long basting stitches around the opening by hand, one quarter inch from the raw edge. Pull up on the thread tightly. Continue around one more time, pulling the thread as you go. Secure the thread with a knot. This will pull the fabric around the joint as shown.

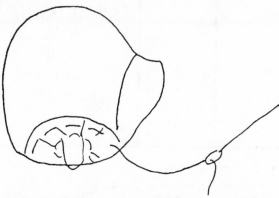

8. If using glass eyes, install them as instructed on page 15.

9. Pin and stitch a white and a fox colored ear piece together along the two curved edges, right sides facing. Turn right sides out. Repeat for remaining ear. Trim the white fur of both ear pieces. This will be the inside ear. Turn 1/4" on bottom edges of ears to inside. Whipstitch closed. Fold the ears in half lengthwise. Run a long needle through them as shown. This will make a pucker.

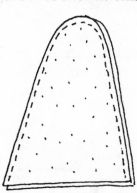
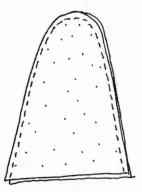

10. Follow the directions for either the animal doll body on page 175 or reclining animal body on page 181.

11. Pin ears to head, adjusting them until you are satisfied with their placement. Sew in place as instructed on page 17.

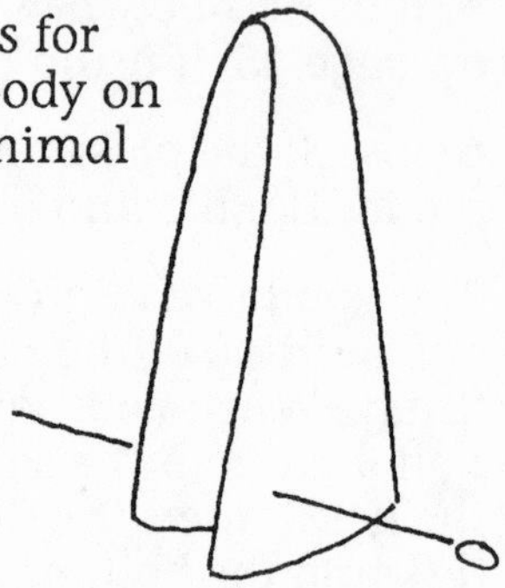

12. Turn to page 15 for instructions for embroidering the mouth.

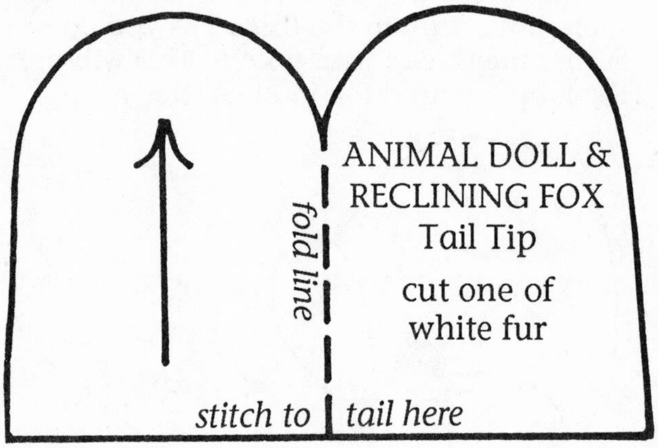

ANIMAL DOLL &
RECLINING FOX
Tail Tip

cut one of
white fur

fold line

stitch to tail here

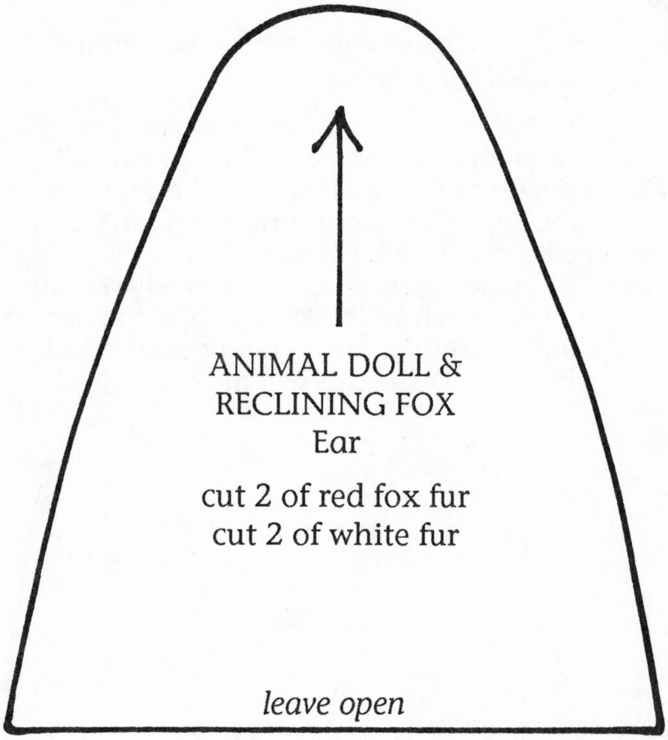

ANIMAL DOLL &
RECLINING FOX
Ear

cut 2 of red fox fur
cut 2 of white fur

leave open

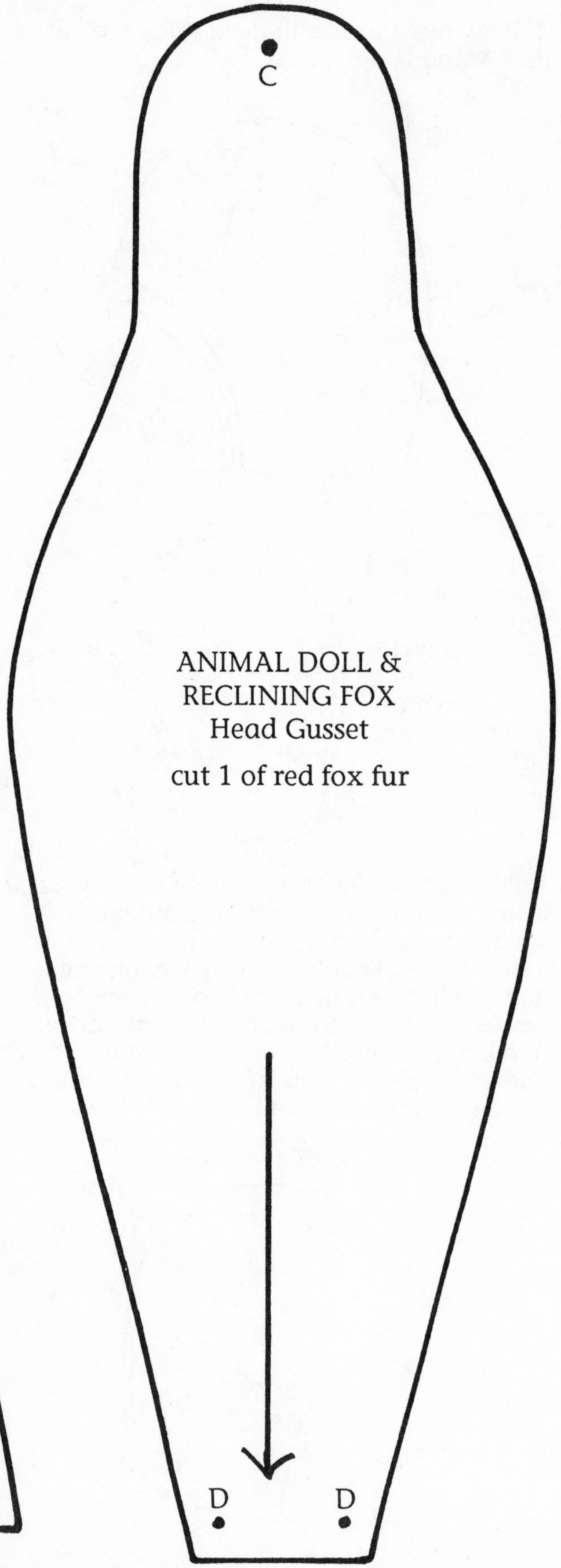

C

ANIMAL DOLL &
RECLINING FOX
Head Gusset

cut 1 of red fox fur

D   D

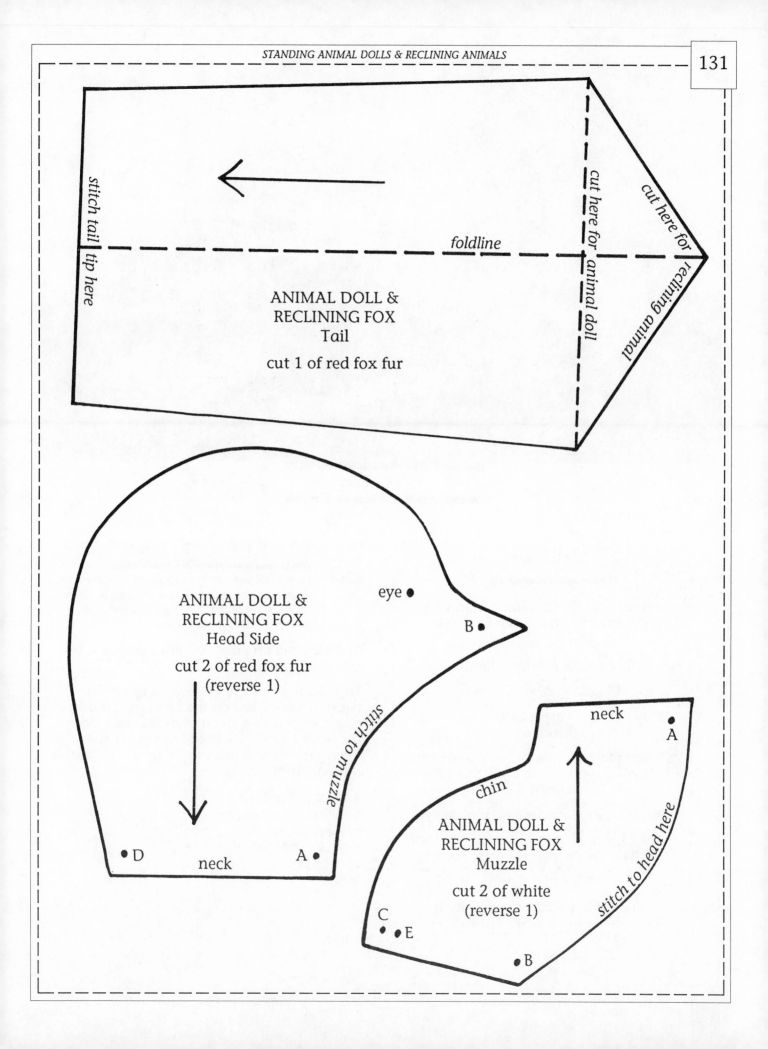

stitch tail tip here

foldline

cut here for animal doll

cut here for reclining animal

ANIMAL DOLL &
RECLINING FOX
Tail

cut 1 of red fox fur

ANIMAL DOLL &
RECLINING FOX
Head Side

cut 2 of red fox fur
(reverse 1)

eye •

B •

stitch to muzzle

• D   neck   A •

neck

• A

chin

ANIMAL DOLL &
RECLINING FOX
Muzzle

cut 2 of white
(reverse 1)

stitch to head here

C •
• E

• B

D O G

MATERIALS

Camel seal fur (available from CR's Crafts or by Diane, see Sources):

¹/₃ yard for animal doll

¹/₂ yard for reclining animal

Matching sewing thread

Heavy thread, carpet thread, or waxed dental floss

55 mm plastic joints for head and arms: One for reclining animal, three for animal doll

Two 15 mm plastic safety or glass eyes

One 21 mm plastic bear nose (see CR's Crafts or by Diane in Sources section)

Polyester fiberfill

Embroidery floss or perle cotton

INSTRUCTIONS

Note: All seam allowances are ¹/₄" unless otherwise instructed. Head and tail patterns follow. Body patterns begin on page 175 for animal dolls and page 181 for reclining animals.

As instructed on page 10, make patterns, cut and mark fur.

Transfer dots for eye placement to the fur backing as marked on the head side. If using glass eyes make a stitch from the right side of the fur with colored thread, tying the ends on the right side and leaving ¹/₂" long strings as a placement marking.

1. Fold tail in half lengthwise, matching raw edges. Sew, leaving top, straight edge open. Turn right side out.

2. Make darts in two ear pieces. These will be inside ears. Pin two ear pieces together, one darted and one not. Stitch, leaving short, straight edges open. Repeat for second set.

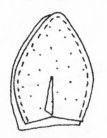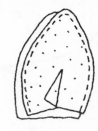

Turn right side out.

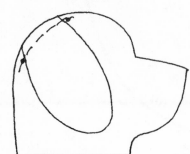

Pin to head sides as shown, between dots, darted sides of ears facing head sides. Baste in place.

3. Pin the head sides together, right sides facing, matching dots A at nose, down to bottom of neck. Stitch.

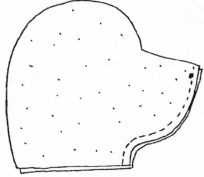

4. Pin dot A at nose on gusset to dot A at seam of head sides. Match and pin dot B at bottom back edge of one side of gusset to respective dot B at bottom back of one head side. Pin between these two points, easing any excess. Stitch from dot C to through dot B to bottom back neck edge, including the ear in the seam. Repeat for other side of gusset. The opening created between the dots C will allow installation of the nose.

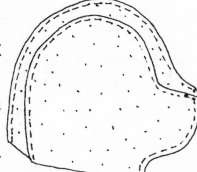

5. If using safety eyes, turn to page 15 for installing instructions. If using glass eyes, omit this step.

6. Turn head right side out. Install the plastic nose in the small opening in the stitching between dots C as instructed on page 15.

7. Starting at the nose, stuff the head firmly. When you have stuffed to about a half inch from the raw edges at the base of the neck, insert the flat end of the stationary disk into the bottom of the neck, with the ridged post pointing out of the bottom of the head. Using heavy thread run a row of long basting stitches around the opening by hand, one quarter inch from the raw edge. Pull up on the thread tightly. Continue around one more time, pulling the thread as you go. Secure the thread with a knot. This will pull the fabric around the joint as shown.

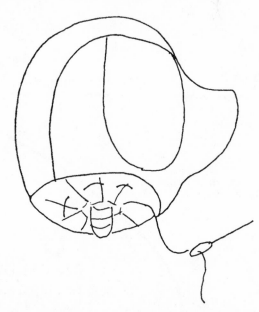

8. If using glass eyes, follow the instructions for their installation on page 15. If you've already installed safety eyes, omit this step.

9. Turn to page 15 and follow the mouth embroidery instructions.

10. Next, follow the instructions to make either the animal doll body on page 175 or reclining animal body on page 181.

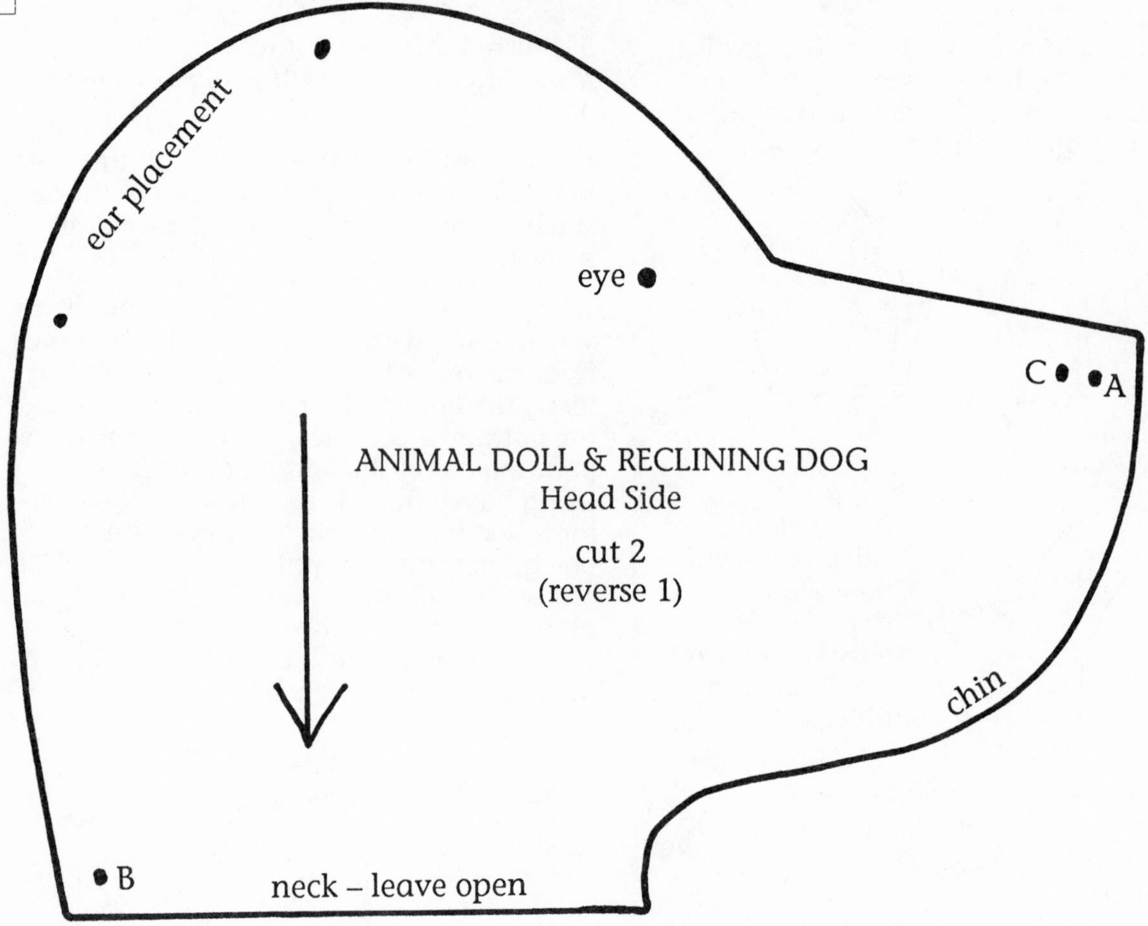

ear placement

eye •

C • •A

ANIMAL DOLL & RECLINING DOG
Head Side

cut 2
(reverse 1)

chin

• B

neck – leave open

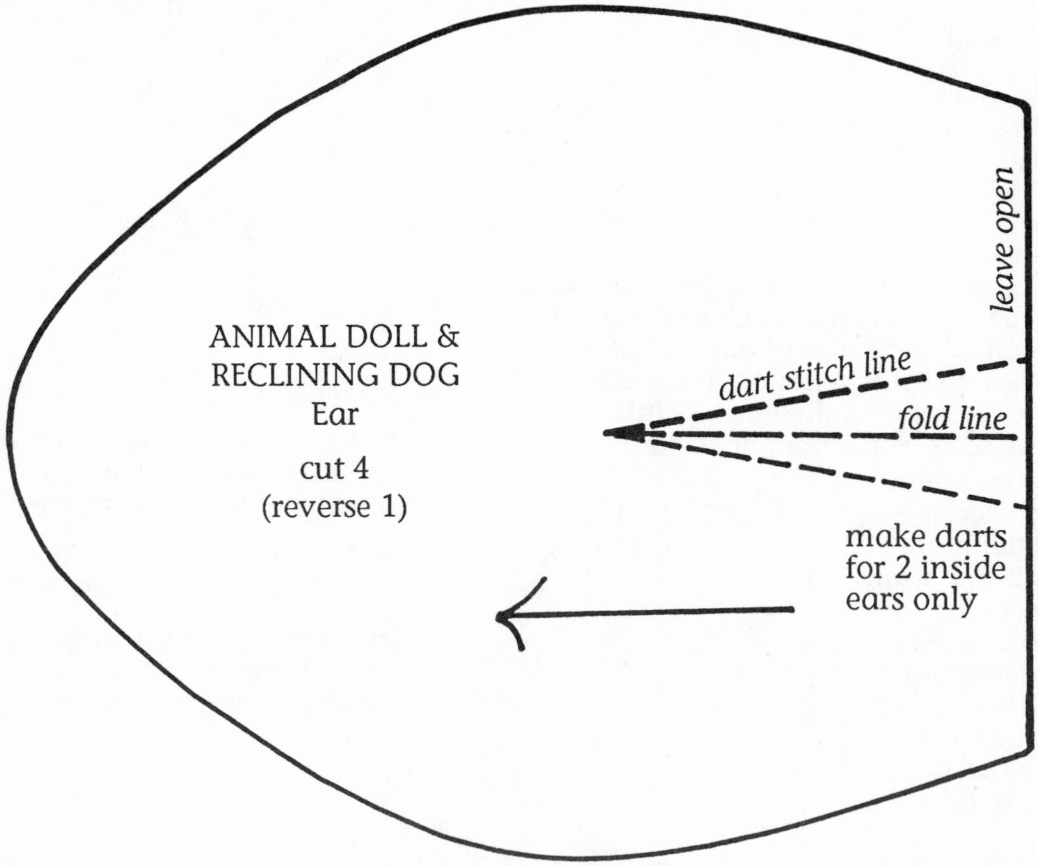

ANIMAL DOLL &
RECLINING DOG
Ear

cut 4
(reverse 1)

leave open

dart stitch line

fold line

make darts
for 2 inside
ears only

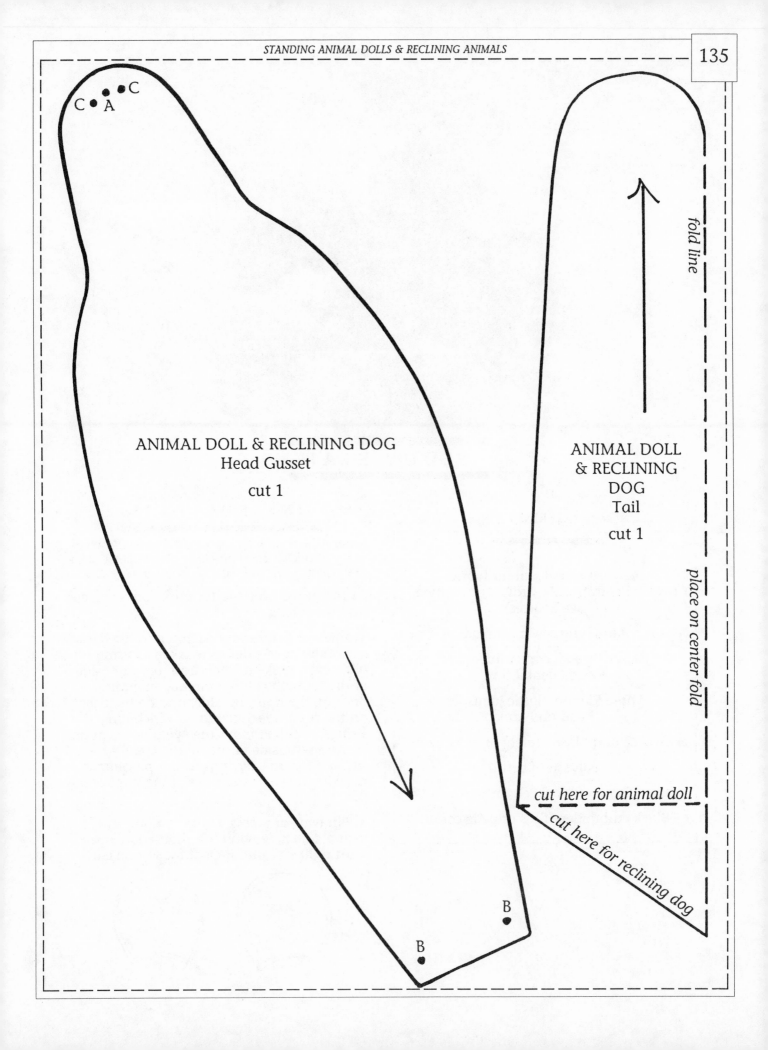

C• •C
C• •A

ANIMAL DOLL & RECLINING DOG
Head Gusset

cut 1

B
B
B

ANIMAL DOLL
& RECLINING
DOG
Tail

cut 1

fold line

place on center fold

cut here for animal doll

cut here for reclining dog

TEDDY BEAR

MATERIALS

⅓ yard camel seal fur fabric
(available from CR's Crafts or by Diane,
see Sources)

Matching sewing thread

Heavy thread, carpet thread, or
waxed dental floss

Three 55 mm plastic joints for
head and arms

Two 12 mm plastic safety or glass eyes

Polyester fiberfill

Scrap of black felt for nose

Black embroidery floss or perle cotton

INSTRUCTIONS

*Note: All seam allowances are ¼" unless otherwise
instructed. Head and tail patterns follow. Body
patterns for animal dolls begin on page 175.*

As instructed on page 10, make patterns, cut
and mark fur.

Transfer dots for eye placement to the backing of the head sides as marked. If using
glass eyes, make a stitch from the right side
of the fur with colored thread, emerging
back on the right, fur side, and tie the ends
on the right side, leaving half inch long
strings. This will mark the eye placement on
the front, fur side of the fabric. Use the same
method for transferring the ear placement
marking on the head sides to the front of the
fur.

1. Pin two ear pieces together, right sides
facing. Stitch, leaving the short edges open.
Turn right side out. Repeat for second ear.

2. Pin the head sides together, right sides facing, matching dot A at nose, down to bottom of neck. Stitch from raw edge to raw edge.

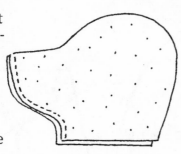

3. Pin dot A at nose on gusset to dot A at nose at seam of head sides. Pin dot B at bottom back edge of one side of gusset to dot B at bottom back of one head side. Pin between these two points, easing any excess. Stitch. Repeat for other side of gusset.

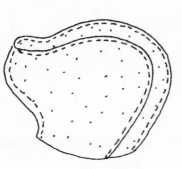

4. For safety eyes, follow the installation instructions on page 15. If using glass eyes omit this step.

5. Turn head right side out. Starting at the nose, stuff the head firmly. When you have stuffed to about a half inch from the raw edges at the base of the neck, insert the flat end of the stationary disk into the bottom of the neck, with the ridged post pointing out of the bottom of the head. Using heavy thread, run a row of long basting stitches around the opening by hand, one quarter inch from the raw edge. Pull up on the thread tightly. Continue around one more time, pulling the thread as you go. Secure the thread with a knot. This will pull the fabric around the joint as shown.

6. For glass eyes follow the instructions on page 15 for installation.

7. Follow the instructions starting on page 175 to make the animal doll body.

8. Turn under ¼" on bottom edges of ears to inside. Whipstitch closed. As instructed on page 17, handstitch to head at markings, centering the ears over the head side/gusset seam. Remove thread markings

10. Glue the felt nose to the fur, just below the horizontal head side/gusset seam, centered over the under chin seam, as shown. Let dry. As instructed on page 15, embroider over the felt. After your last stitch over the felt, emerge from the center bottom of the nose, just below the felt. To form the mouth, follow the illustration. Finish off the embroidery thread as instructed on page 17.

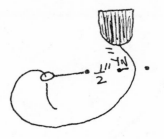

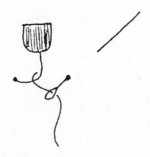

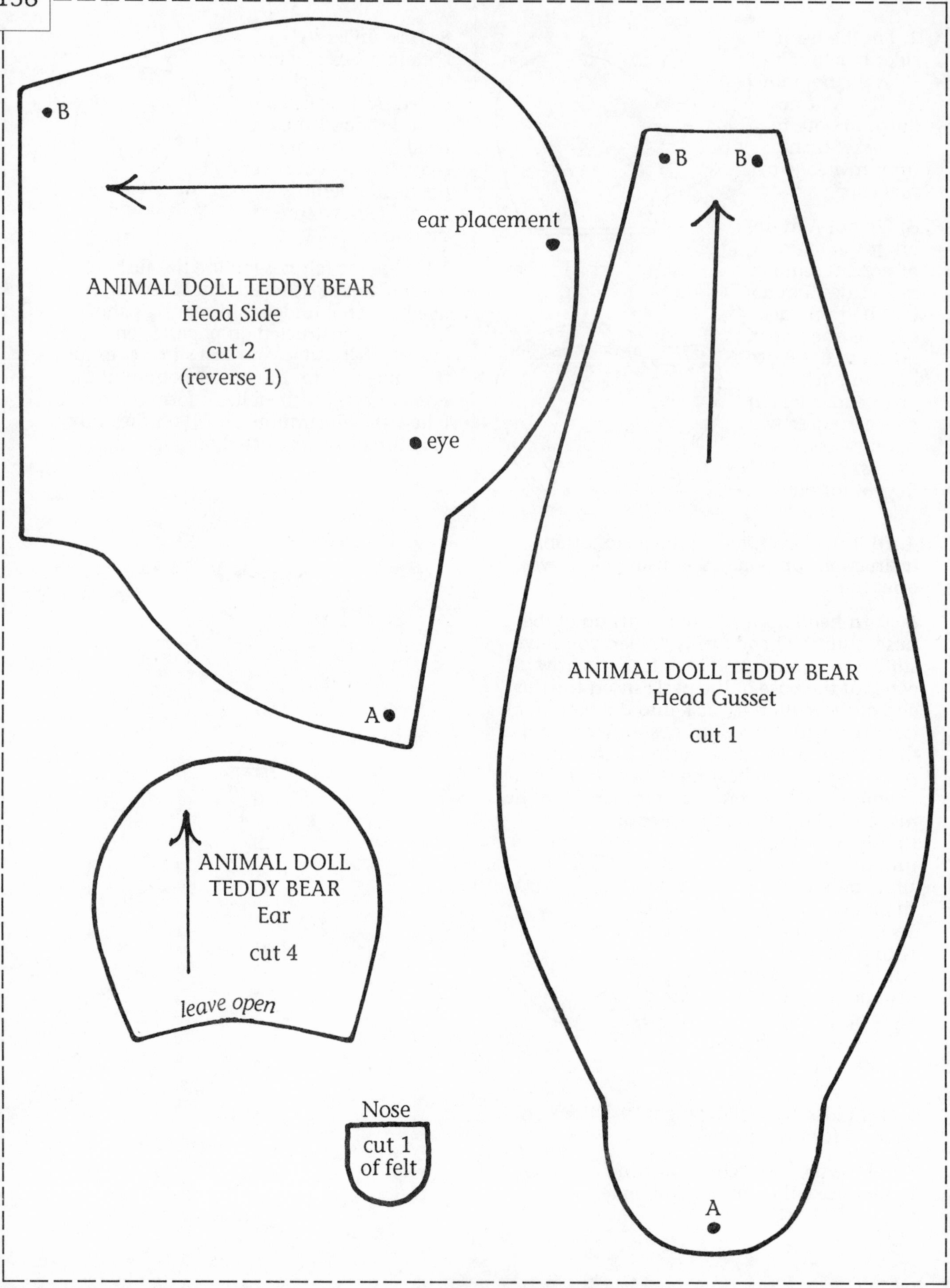

• B

ANIMAL DOLL TEDDY BEAR
Head Side

cut 2
(reverse 1)

ear placement •

• eye

A •

• B   B •

ANIMAL DOLL TEDDY BEAR
Head Gusset

cut 1

ANIMAL DOLL
TEDDY BEAR
Ear

cut 4

leave open

Nose

cut 1
of felt

A •

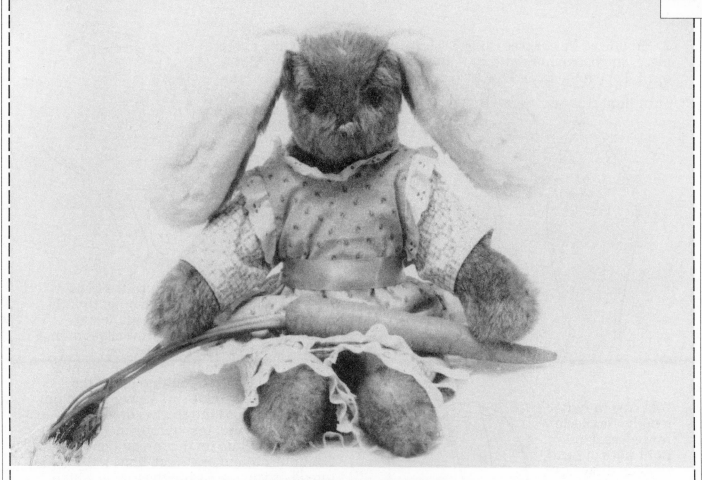

BUNNY

MATERIALS

¹/₃ yard gray-brown fur fabric for animal doll (907G Ginger short from CR's Crafts or Tan muted shade from by Diane, see Sources)

Matching sewing thread

10" x 10" scrap of white fur

Heavy thread, or waxed dental floss

One 55 mm plastic joint for head

Two 12 mm plastic safety or glass eyes

Polyester fiberfill stuffing

Scrap of pink felt

Pink embroidery floss or perle cotton

INSTRUCTIONS

Note: All seam allowances are ¹/₄" unless otherwise instructed. Head and tail patterns follow. Body patterns for animal dolls begin on page 175.

As instructed on page 10, make patterns, cut and mark fur.

Transfer dots for eye placement to the backing of the fur as marked on the head side. If using glass eyes make a stitch from the right side of the fur with colored thread, tying the ends on the right side and leaving ¹/₂" long strings as a mark.

1. Fold tail in half along foldline, matching raw edges. Sew, leaving short, straight edge open.

Turn right side out.

2. Pin one white ear piece to one colored ear piece. Stitch, leaving short, straight edges open. Repeat for second ear.

Turn right side out.

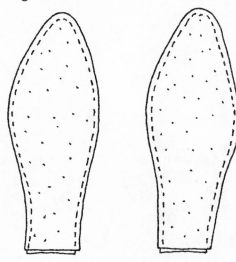

Fold ears in half lengthwise. Baste raw edges. Pin to right sides of head sides as shown, between dots, white side of ears facing forward. Baste in place.

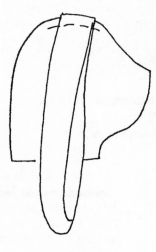

3. Pin the head sides together, right sides facing, matching dots A at nose, down to bottom of front of neck. Stitch.

4. Pin dot A at nose on gusset to dot A at seam of head sides. Match and pin dot B at bottom back edge of one side of gusset to respective dot B at bottom back of one head side. Pin between these two points,

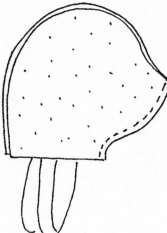

easing any excess. Stitch from dot A through dot B to bottom back neck edge, including the ear in the seam. Repeat for other side of gusset.

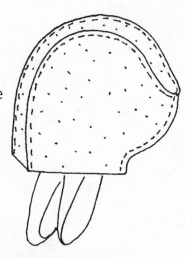

5. If using safety eyes turn to page 15 for installation instructions. If using glass eyes, omit this step.

6. If you haven't already, turn the head right side out. Starting at the nose, stuff the head firmly. When you have stuffed to about a half inch from the raw edges at the base of the neck, insert the flat end of the stationary disk into the bottom of the neck, with the ridged post pointing out of the bottom of the head. Using heavy thread run a row of long basting stitches around the opening by hand, one quarter inch from the raw edge. Pull up on the thread tightly. Continue around one more time, pulling the thread as you go. Secure the thread with a knot. This will pull the fabric around the joint as shown.

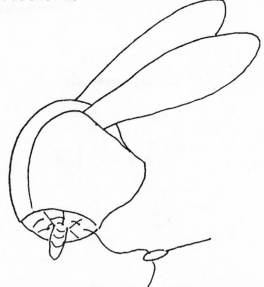

7. If using glass eyes turn to the instructions on page 15. If using safety eyes, omit this step.

8. To make the bunny's body, follow the general instructions for the animal doll on page 175.

9. Trim the fur where the nose is to attach. Glue the felt nose in place. Set aside to dry. Embroider the nose as instructed on page 15.

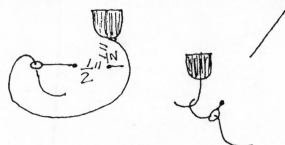

After the last stitch, come up at the bottom center of the nose, just below the felt.

Go back into the fur $1/2$" below and to the left of the bottom of the nose. Emerge $1/2$" directly under the nose, hooking the thread as shown. Go back into the fur $1/2$" to the right and below the center bottom of the nose as shown. Emerge somewhere on the neck and finish off as instructed on page 17.

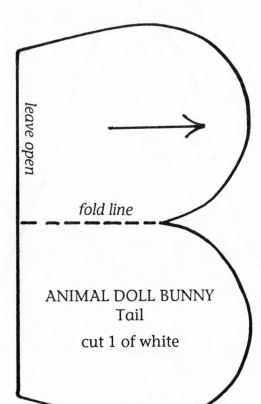

leave open

fold line

ANIMAL DOLL BUNNY
Tail

cut 1 of white

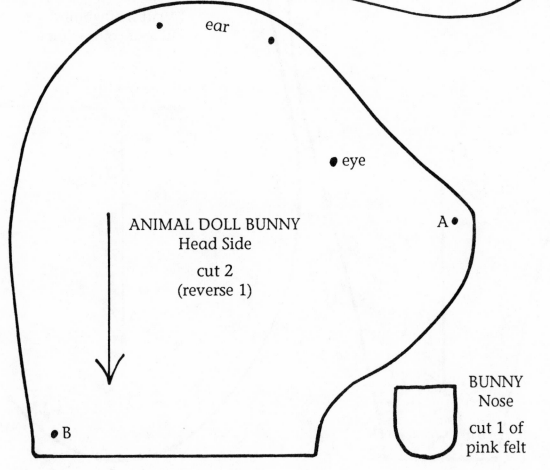

ear

eye

A

ANIMAL DOLL BUNNY
Head Side

cut 2
(reverse 1)

B

BUNNY
Nose

cut 1 of
pink felt

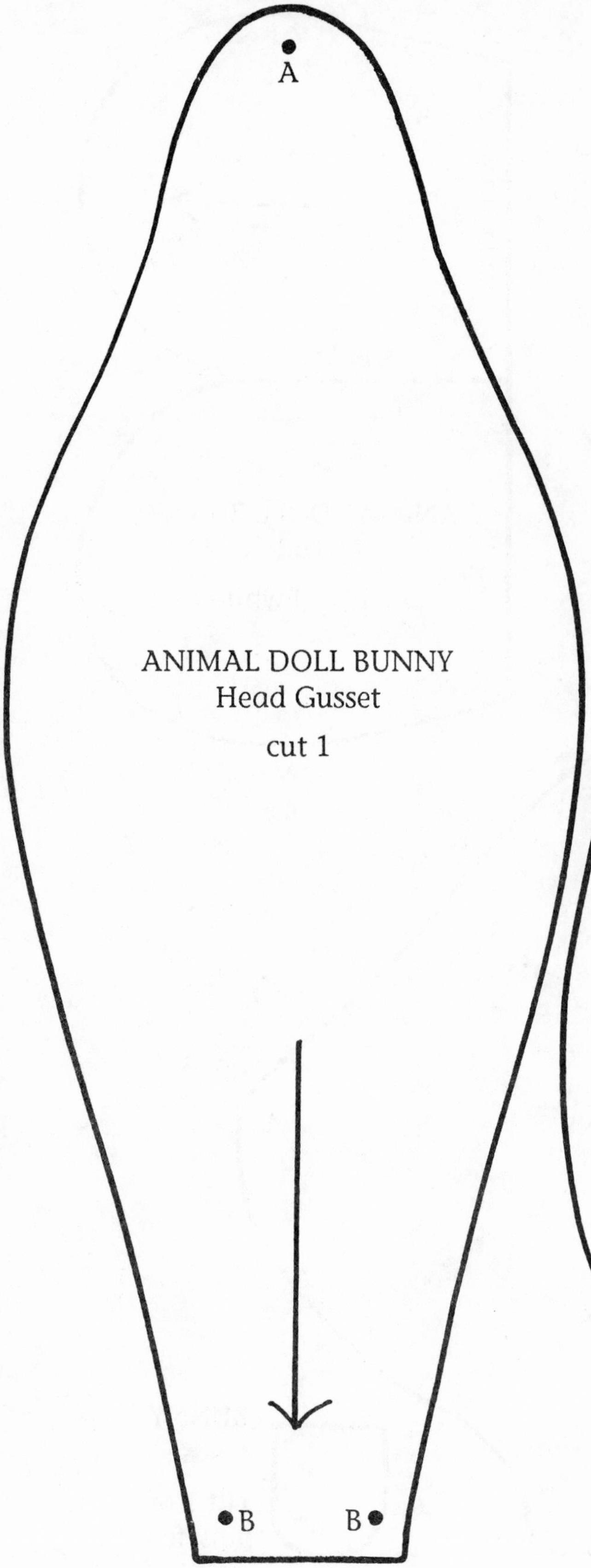

A

ANIMAL DOLL BUNNY
Head Gusset

cut 1

•B   B•

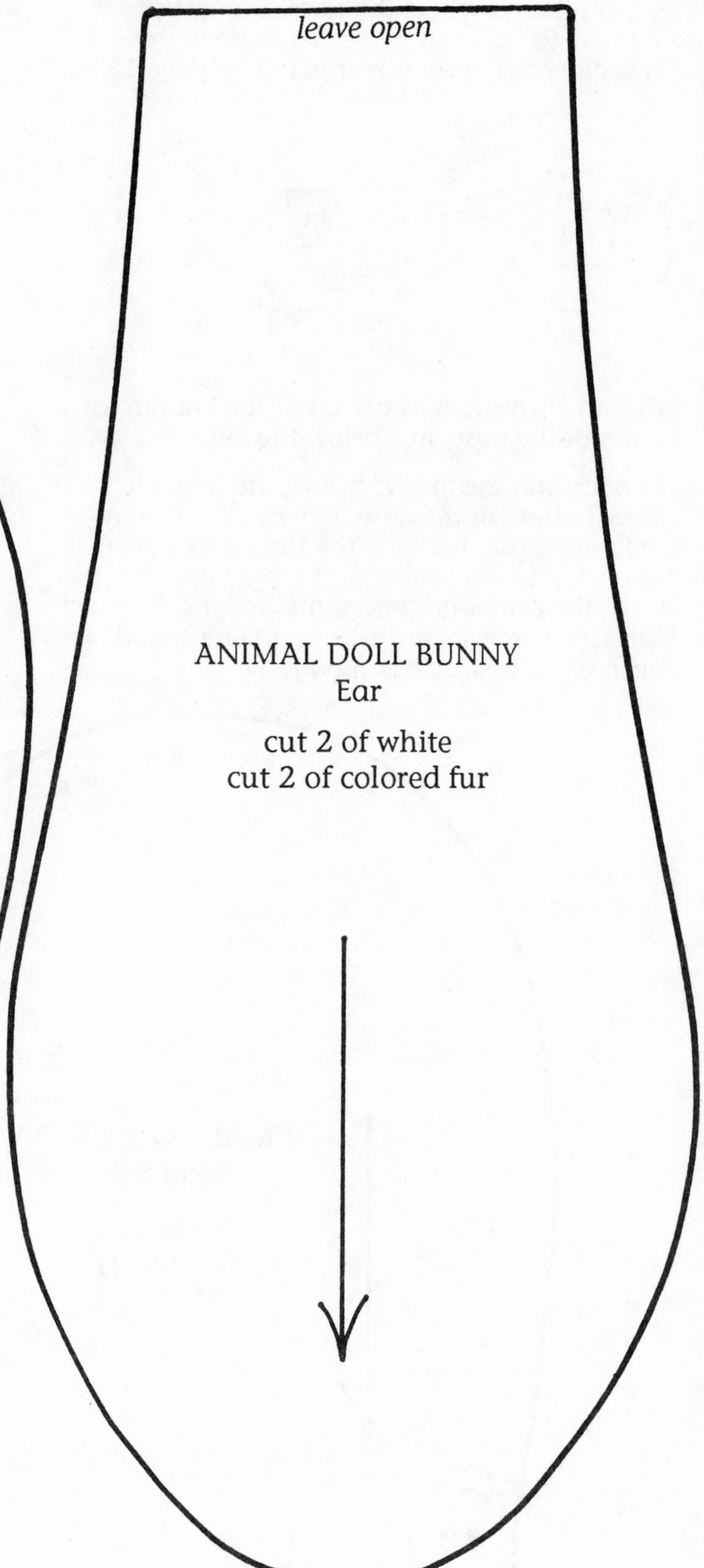

leave open

ANIMAL DOLL BUNNY
Ear

cut 2 of white
cut 2 of colored fur

MOUSE

MATERIALS

¹/₃ yard gray-brown fur fabric for animal doll (907G Ginger short from CR's Crafts or Tan muted shade from by Diane, see Sources)

Matching sewing thread

Scrap of white fur for ears

Carpet thread or waxed dental floss

One 55 mm plastic joints for head

Two 12 mm plastic safety or glass eyes

Polyester fiberfill

12 mm teddy bear nose

Embroidery floss or perle cotton

INSTRUCTIONS

Note: All seam allowances are ¹/₄" unless otherwise instructed. Head and tail patterns follow. Body patterns for animal dolls begin on page 175.

As instructed on page 10, make patterns, cut and mark fur.

Transfer dots for eye placement to the backing of the fur as marked on the head side. If using glass eyes make a stitch from the right side of the fur with colored thread, tying the ends on the right side and leaving ¹/₂" long strings as a mark.

1. Fold tail in half along foldline, matching raw edges. Sew, leaving one short, straight edge open.

Turn right side out.

2. Pin one white ear piece to one colored ear piece. Stitch, leaving short, straight edges open. Repeat for second ear.

Turn right side out.

3. Stitch the darts in the head sides.

4. Pin the head sides together, right sides facing, matching dots A under nose, and B at back bottom of neck. Stitch, leaving an opening between the markings for the nose as noted on pattern.

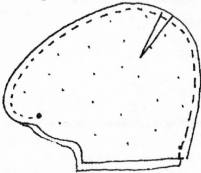

5. Pin dot A on gusset to dot A at seam under chin of head sides. Match and pin dot C at bottom edge of one side of gusset to respective dot C at bottom front of one head side. Pin between these two points. Stitch from dot A through dot C to bottom neck edge. Repeat for other side of gusset.

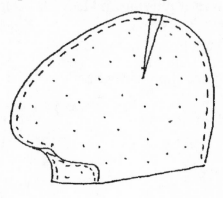

6. If using safety eyes, follow the installation instructions on page 15. If using glass eyes, omit this step.

7. Turn head right side out. Install the plastic nose in the small opening in the stitching as instructed on page 15.

8. Starting at the nose, stuff the head firmly. When you have stuffed to about a half inch from the raw edges at the base of the neck, insert the flat end of the stationary disk into the bottom of the neck, with the ridged post pointing out of the bottom of the head. Using heavy thread run a row of long basting stitches around the opening by hand, one quarter inch from the raw edge. Pull up on the thread tightly. Continue around one more time, pulling the thread as you go. Secure the thread with a knot. This will pull the fabric around the joint as shown.

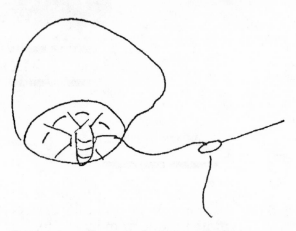

9. If using glass eyes, follow the instructions on page 15. Omit this step if you've installed safety eyes.

10. To make the mouse's body, follow the animal doll instructions on page 175.

11. Turn the bottom, raw edges of the ears to the inside, 1/4". Whipstitch. As instructed in chapter 1, stitch the ears to the head, easing them (almost gathering them) to fit over the darts, so that the inside edges of the ears are 1 1/2" apart.

12. Turn to page 15 and follow the mouth embroidery instructions.

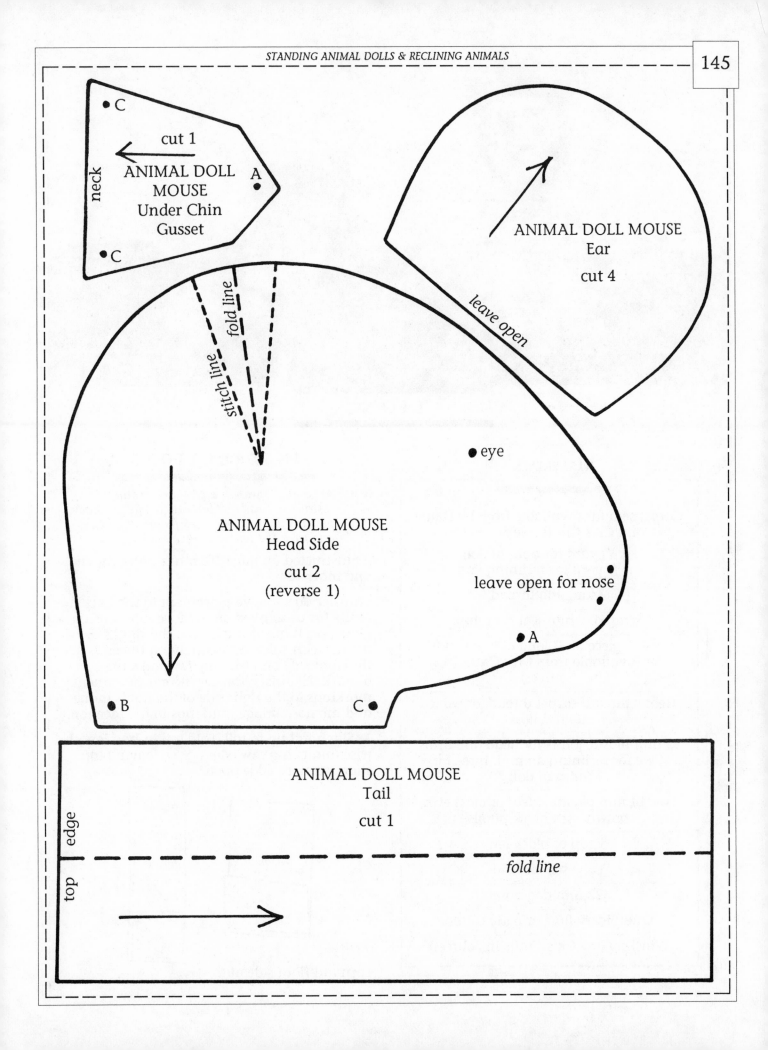

ANIMAL DOLL MOUSE
Under Chin Gusset

cut 1

neck

• C

• C

A •

ANIMAL DOLL MOUSE
Ear

cut 4

leave open

stitch line

fold line

ANIMAL DOLL MOUSE
Head Side

cut 2
(reverse 1)

• eye

leave open for nose

• A

• B

C •

ANIMAL DOLL MOUSE
Tail

cut 1

edge

top

fold line

LION

MATERIALS

Camel seal fur (available from by Diane and CR's Crafts, see Sources):

¹/₃ yard for animal doll
¹/₂ yard for reclining lion

Matching thread

Scrap of white seal fur fabric

9" x 12" piece of 3" long pile brown fun fur (available from CR's Crafts, see Sources)

Heavy thread, carpet thread, or waxed dental floss

55 mm plastic joints for head and arms: One for reclining animal, three for animal doll

Two 14 mm plastic safety or glass eyes, brown with black pupils

Scrap of black felt

Polyester fiberfill

22 mm dog nose

Embroidery floss or perle cotton

Whiskers (see CR's Crafts in Sources)

INSTRUCTIONS

Note: All seam allowances are ¹/₄" unless otherwise instructed. Head and tail patterns follow. Body patterns begin on page 175 for animal dolls and page 181 for reclining animals.

As instructed on page 10, make patterns, cut and mark fur.

Transfer dots for eye placement to the backing of the fur as marked on the face top. If using glass eyes make a stitch from the right side of the fur with colored thread, tying the ends on the right side and leaving ¹/₂" long strings as a mark. Likewise, transfer the ear placement markings to the right side of the lion's mane and the nose bridge markings to the face top.

1. Stitch tail tip to tail. Fold tail in half lengthwise, matching raw edges. Sew, leaving top short, straight edge open.

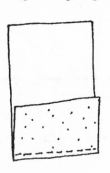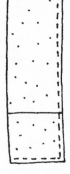

Turn tail right side out.

2. Pin two ear pieces together. Stitch, leaving short, bottom edges open. Repeat for second ear.

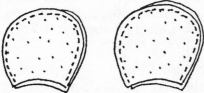

Turn right side out.

3. Pin the two mane pieces together, right sides facing, as shown.

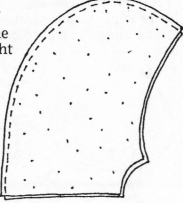

4. Right sides facing, pin one side of chin to one cheek, matching dots A and B. Stitch.

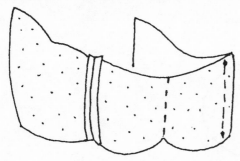

Repeat for other side of chin and other cheek.

5. Right sides facing, pin chin/cheek to face top, matching dots C and D.

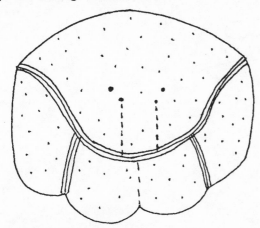

6. Right sides facing, pin face top/chin/cheek to mane, matching dots F and E. Stitch.

7. Pin chin/cheek/mane together from dot G down to bottom edge of neck. Stitch from H down to bottom of neck. The space left between G and H will allow installation of the nose in step 9.

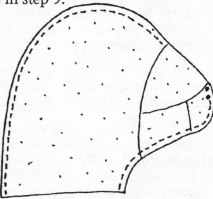

8. If using safety eyes, follow the instructions on; page 15. Remember to install the eye backings (see step 11). If using glass eyes, omit this step.

9. Turn head right side out. Install the plastic nose in the small opening in the stitching between G and H as instructed on page 15.

10. Starting at the nose, stuff the head firmly. When you have stuffed to about a half inch from the raw edges at the base of the neck, insert the flat end of the stationary disk into the bottom of the neck, with the ridged post pointing out of the bottom of the head. Using heavy thread run a row of long basting stitches around the opening by hand, one quarter inch from the raw edge. Pull up on the thread tightly. Continue around one more time, pulling the thread as you go. Secure the thread with a knot. This will pull the fabric around the joint as shown.

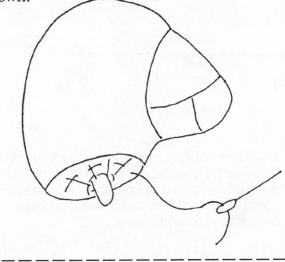

11. If using glass eyes, turn to the instructions on page 15. Remember to install the eye backing; make a hole at the dot marked in the center of the eye backing. When the needle emerges from the eye hole thread the black felt eye backing before threading the needle through the eye wire loop. If you've already installed safety eyes, omit this step.

12. To construct the lion's body, follow the instructions for either the animal doll or reclining animal on page 175 or page 181.

13. To form the bridge of the lion's nose, thread and knot a long needle with carpet thread or dental floss. Push the needle into the fur somewhere at the side of the head, come up at the top point of one side (closest to the eye) of the nose bridge markings. Pull on the thread, hiding the knot in the fur. Go back in a few threads over from where you just emerged. Come out at the top point of the other side of the nose bridge. Go back and forth across the nose, taking just a few threads each time you emerge on each side of the nose, until you get to the bottom. After your last stitch, emerge somewhere in the side of the head. Make a knot at the fur and clip the thread. Remove colore thread markings.

15. Cut five or six whiskers, each about 6" long. Thread the very end of each whisker in turn onto a long, large-eyed needle. Run them from one side of the muzzle to the other as shown. Clip off the end bent from going through the needle.

16. Turn to page 15 and follow the instructions to embroider the lion's mouth.

17. Embroider claws on paws as illustrated. Refer to page 15 for instructions on starting and ending the embroidery.

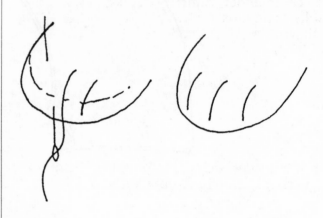

14. Turn bottom raw edges of ears to inside. Whipstitch openings closed. Using the easy method described on page 13, attach the ears to the mane at markings. Remove colored marking threads.

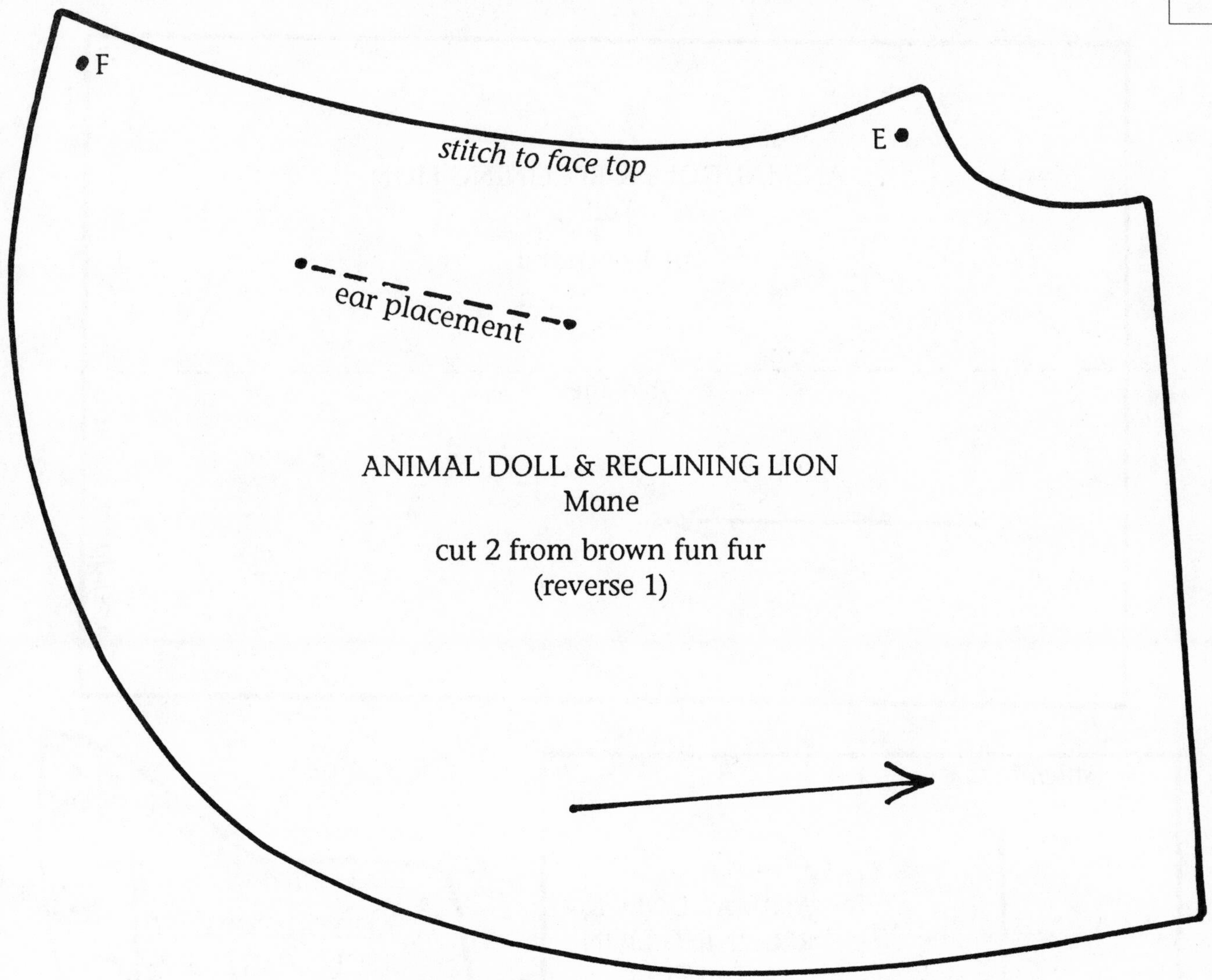

• F

stitch to face top

E •

•- - - - - - - - - -
ear placement - - - •

ANIMAL DOLL & RECLINING LION
Mane

cut 2 from brown fun fur
(reverse 1)

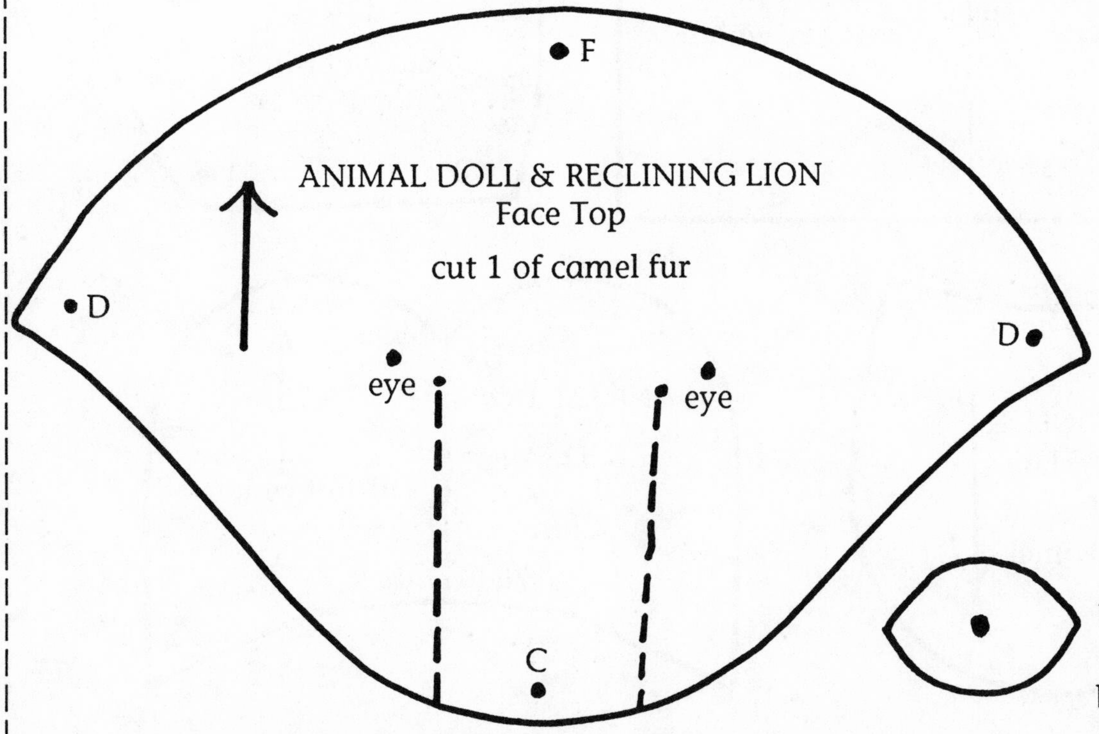

⟶

• F

ANIMAL DOLL & RECLINING LION
Face Top

cut 1 of camel fur

↑

• D

D •

eye •

• eye

C •

LION
Eye Back

cut 2 of
black felt

ANIMAL DOLL & RECLINING LION
Tail

cut 1 of camel

fold line

stitch tail tip here

stitch to tail

fold line

ANIMAL DOLL &
RECLINING LION
Tail Tip

cut 1 of white

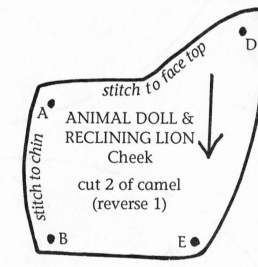

A•

stitch to chin

stitch to face top

•D

ANIMAL DOLL &
RECLINING LION
Cheek

cut 2 of camel
(reverse 1)

B•   E•

leave open

ANIMAL DOLL &
RECLINING LION
Ear

cut 4 of camel

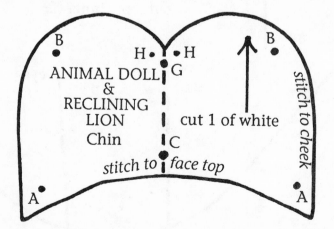

B•   H• •H   •B

G

ANIMAL DOLL
&
RECLINING
LION
Chin

cut 1 of white

stitch to cheek

•C

stitch to face top

A•   •A

COW

White seal fur fabric (available from CR's Crafts or by Diane, see Sources):

¹/₂ yard for reclining cow
¹/₃ yard for animal doll

Matching sewing thread

¹/₄ yard black seal fur fabric

Scrap of black wool or felt for hooves

Heavy thread, carpet thread, or waxed dental floss

55 mm plastic joints for head and arms:
One for reclining cow,
three for animal doll

Two 12 mm plastic safety or glass eyes

One square of bone-colored felt

Scrap of black or brown yarn or Pretty Hair® for tail tip

Polyester fiberfill

Embroidery floss or perle cotton

INSTRUCTIONS

Note: All seam allowances are ¹/₄" unless otherwise instructed. Head and tail patterns follow. Body patterns begin on page 175 for animal dolls and page 181 for reclining animals.

As instructed on page 10, make patterns, cut and mark fur.

Transfer dots for eye placement as marked to the backing of the head sides. If using glass eyes, make a stitch from the right side of the fur with colored thread, emerging back on the right, fur side, and tie the ends on the right side, leaving ¹/₂" long strings. This will mark the eye placement on the front, fur side of the fabric.

1. Trim fur of white pieces for ears to within ¹/₄" of backing. Make darts. These are the inside of the ears. Pin a white ear piece to a black ear piece, right sides facing. Stitch, leaving the short, straight edges open. Turn right side out. Repeat for second ear.

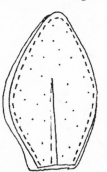
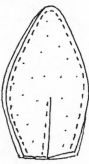

Fold ears as illustrated, white sides to inside, and baste. Pin ears to head sides between dots A and C as marked, having white sides of ears facing fur of head sides. Baste in place.

2. Match and pin dots C on back head gusset to dots C on head front gusset/muzzle. Stitch.

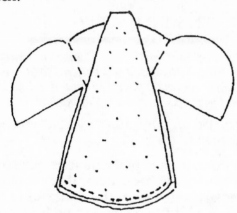

3. Working on one side of the head, match and pin dot D on head side to dot D on head front gusset/muzzle. Match and pin dots F on head side to back head gusset. Pin gussets to head side between dots. Stitch from dot B to dot D. Stitch from dot C down to dot F, including the ear in the seam. Leave a gap in the stitching between the dots for the horn.

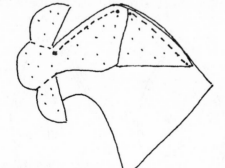

Right sides together, pin front gusset/muzzle to head side matching dots D and dots G. Stitch between the dots.

Repeat for second head side.

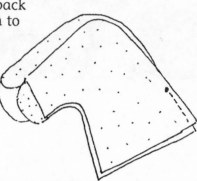

4. Pin head sides together at head back from dot F down to bottom of neck. Stitch.

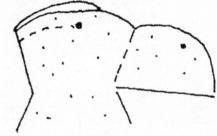

5. Fold one side of front gusset/muzzle along foldline, right sides facing, matching dots J. Pin. Stitch from folded edge to center dot J.

Repeat for other side.

6. Pin chin/neck matching dots G. Stitch from dot J, through dot G, down to bottom raw edge of neck.

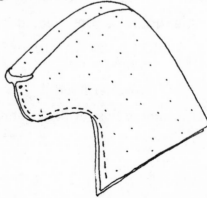

7. If using safety eyes, install them according to the instructions on page 15.

8. Pin the two horn pieces together. Stitch, leaving an opening for turning as marked.

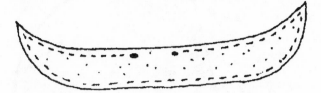

Trim seam allowances across tips. Turn right side out. Stuff, carefully filling in the points. Handstitch the opening closed. Turn the head right side out. Insert one end of the horns into the opening in the head in front of the ears. Push and pull the horns through until they are even in the head. Handstitch the fur fabric to the horns, turning the raw edges ¼" to the inside.

9. Starting at the nose, stuff the head firmly. When you have stuffed to about a half inch from the raw edges at the base of the neck, insert the flat end of the stationary disk into the bottom of the neck, with the ridged post pointing out of the bottom of the head. Using heavy thread, run a row of long basting stitches around the opening by hand, one quarter inch from the raw edge. Pull up on the thread tightly. Continue around one more time, pulling the thread as you go. Secure the thread with a knot. This will pull the fabric around the joint as shown.

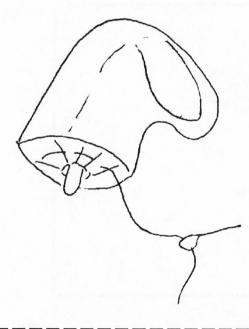

10. If you are using glass eyes, turn to page 15 for instructions. If you've already installed safety eyes, continue.

11. For reclining cow: Pin black tail piece to white tail piece with black nap pointing toward white, and white nap pointing away from black, as illustrated.

For both: Measure 7" of Pretty Hair®. To cut, rub the wool against the blade of a scissors. This will form a jagged, or uneven cut in the wool. Fold the wool in half and place on bottom end of right side of the tail as shown. Baste.

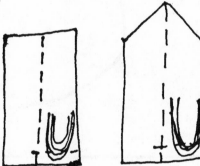

Fold tail along foldline. Pin. For reclining cow: Stitch along long side, and across short white edge, leaving short angled, black edge open. For animal doll: Stitch across bottom short edge and long edge, leaving one short edge open, as marked. Turn right side out.

12. Follow instructions to make either a reclining cow (page 181) or animal doll body (page 175).

13. Turn to page 15 for nose and mouth embroidery instructions.

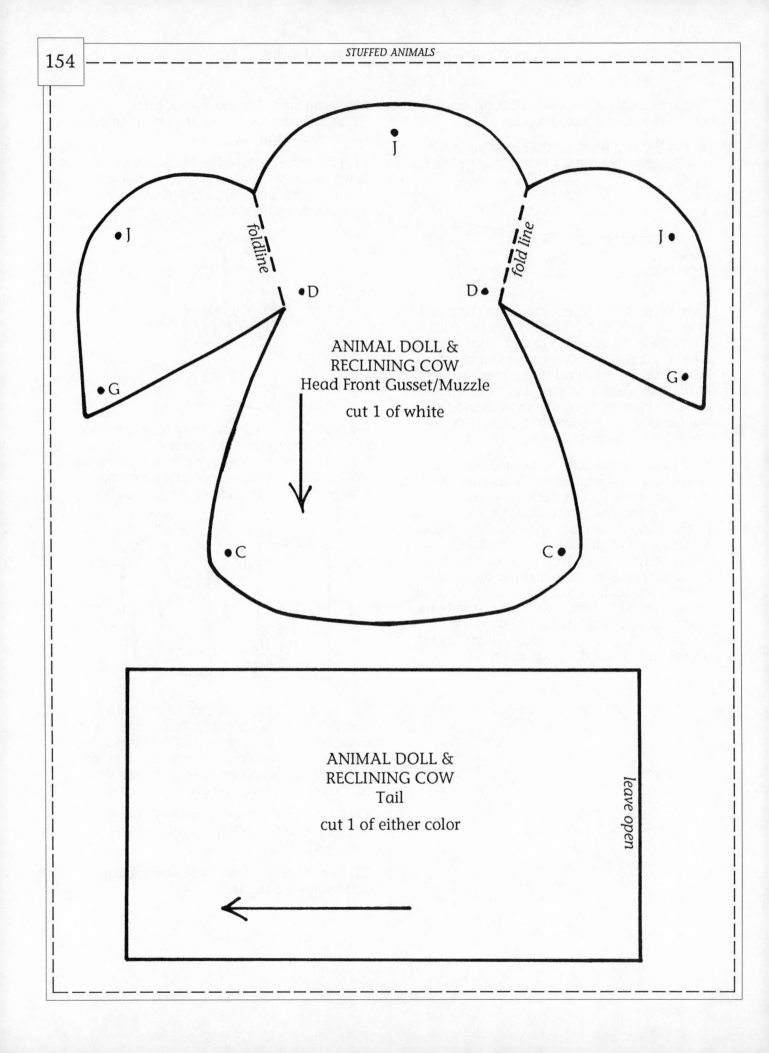

J

J

foldline

•D

fold line

D•

J

ANIMAL DOLL &
RECLINING COW
Head Front Gusset/Muzzle

cut 1 of white

•G

G•

•C

C•

ANIMAL DOLL &
RECLINING COW
Tail

cut 1 of either color

leave open

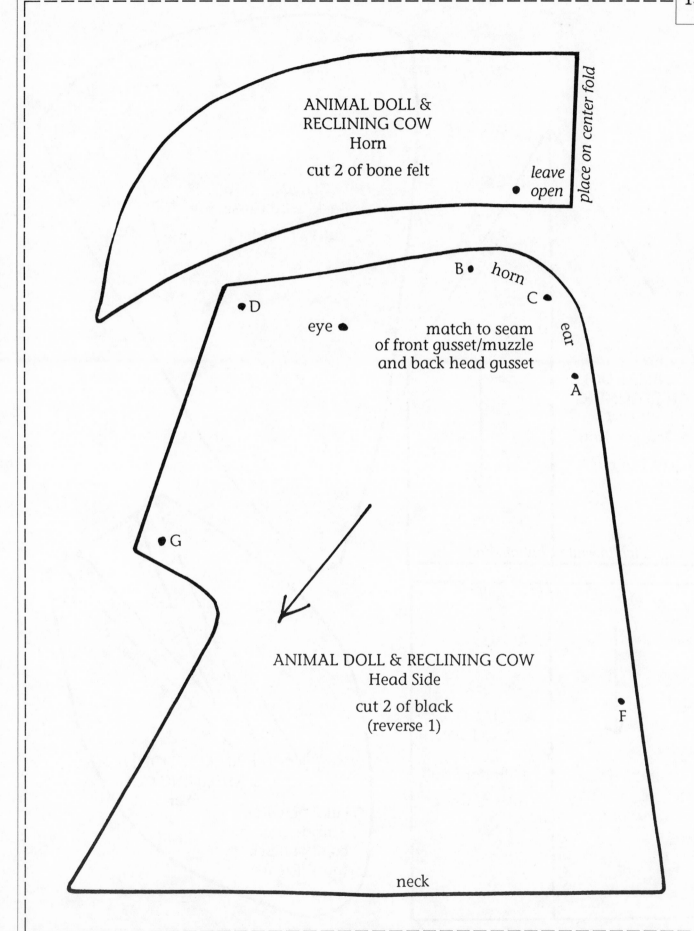

**ANIMAL DOLL &
RECLINING COW
Horn**

cut 2 of bone felt

leave
open

place on center fold

B•

horn

C•

D•

eye •

ear

•A

**match to seam
of front gusset/muzzle
and back head gusset**

•G

**ANIMAL DOLL & RECLINING COW
Head Side**

**cut 2 of black
(reverse 1)**

•F

neck

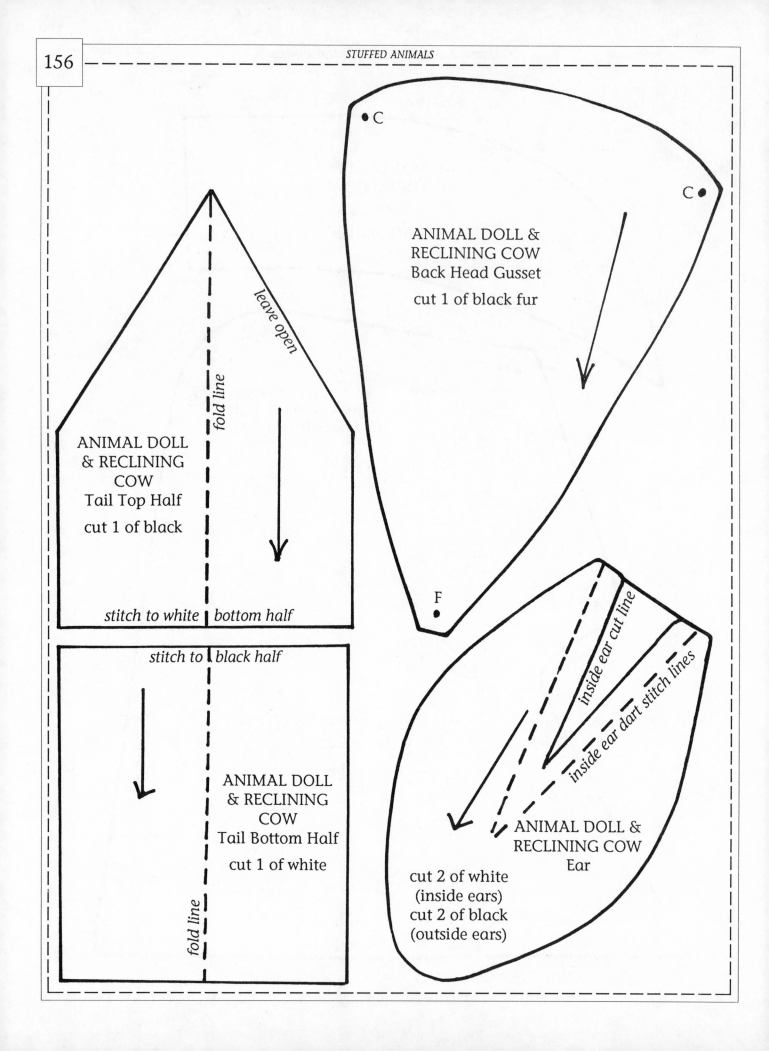

• C

C •

ANIMAL DOLL &
RECLINING COW
Back Head Gusset

cut 1 of black fur

leave open

fold line

ANIMAL DOLL
& RECLINING
COW
Tail Top Half

cut 1 of black

stitch to white | *bottom half*

F

stitch to | *black half*

ANIMAL DOLL
& RECLINING
COW
Tail Bottom Half

cut 1 of white

fold line

inside ear cut line

inside ear dart stitch lines

ANIMAL DOLL &
RECLINING COW
Ear

cut 2 of white
(inside ears)
cut 2 of black
(outside ears)

FAWN OR RUDOLPH

MATERIALS

Mustang short pile fur fabric (from CR's Crafts or by Diane, see Sources):

¹/₂ yard for reclining animal
¹/₃ yard for animal doll

Matching sewing thread

Scrap of white fur

White thread

Large scrap of black wool fabric or felt

Carpet thread, or waxed dental floss

---

55 mm plastic joints for head and arms: One for reclining animal, three for animal doll

---

Two 12 mm plastic safety or glass eyes

One blinking musical Rudolph nose (see CR's Crafts in Sources) or one plastic 21 mm bear nose

---

For Rudolph: ¹/₄ yard brown suede-like or cotton fabric for antlers

---

Polyester fiberfill

Embroidery floss or perle cotton

INSTRUCTIONS

Note: All seam allowances are ¹/₄" unless otherwise instructed. Head and tail patterns follow. Body patterns begin on page 175 for animal dolls and page 181 for reclining animals.

As instructed in chapter 1, make patterns, cut and mark fur.

Transfer dots for eye and (optional) antler placement as marked, onto the fur backing. If using glass eyes make a stitch from the right side of the fur with colored thread, tying the ends on the right side and leaving half inch long strings as a mark. Using the colored thread method transfer the antler placement markings to the right side of the fur.

1. Pin the white and colored two tail pieces together, right sides facing. Sew, leaving short, straight edge open.

Trim seam allowance to ¹/₈" at tip of tail. Turn tail right side out.

2. As instructed on page 11, trim the fur of the white ears. These are the inside ears. Match and pin colored ear pieces to white ones. Stitch, leaving the straight edges open.

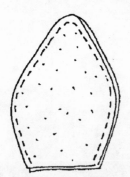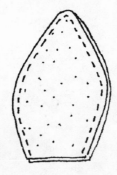

Trim seam allowances to ⅛" at tips of ear pieces. Fold ears in half lengthwise, white to the inside. Baste raw edges together ¼" from raw edge.

3. Cut slash along dashed line as marked on head side. Fold head, right sides facing, along this line. Insert unfinished end of ear between the two raw edges creating a dart as shown, white side facing down, toward neck edge of head side. Pin. Stitch dart. Repeat for other ear and side of head.

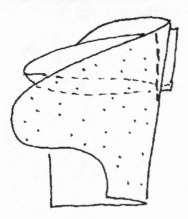

4. Pin the head sides together, right sides facing, from dot A at nose, down to bottom of neck. Stitch.

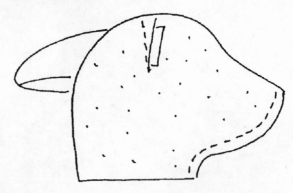

5. Pin dot A at nose on gusset to dot A at top of chin seam on head sides. Pin dot B at bottom back edge of one side of gusset to dot B on respective bottom back of one head side. Pin between these two points, easing any excess. Stitch from dot C, around top of head, through dot B to the neck edge. Repeat for other side of gusset.

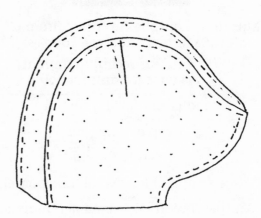

6. If using safety eyes, follow the instructions on page 15. Omit this step if using glass eyes.

7. Turn head right side out.

For fawn, install the plastic nose as instructed on page 15.

For Rudolph nose, unhook wires for nose at plastic attachment leading to music mechanism. From the right side, wire-end first, insert the half with nose through hole, seating nose flat on head. Reattach music box. Leave the wires and music mechanism hanging from the head until you have stuffed the head about 1/3 full.

For both fawn and Rudolph, starting at the nose, stuff the head firmly. For Rudolph, push the wires into the head and place the "button" of the music box flush against the fur backing inside the center back of the head. It will look like the "x-ray" illustration.

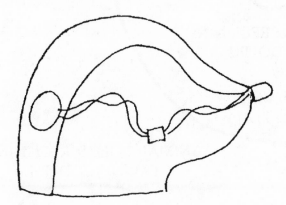

Continue stuffing. When you have stuffed to about a half inch from the raw edges at the base of the neck, insert the flat end of the stationary disk of the joint into the bottom of the neck, with the ridged post pointing out of the bottom of the head. Using heavy thread run a row of long basting stitches around the opening by hand, 1/4" from the raw edge. Pull up on the thread tightly. Continue around one more time, pulling the thread as you go. Secure the thread with a knot. This will pull the fabric around the joint as shown.

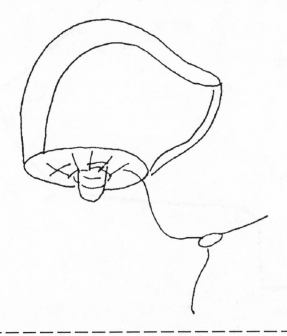

8. If you are using glass eyes, follow the instructions on page 15. If you already installed safety eyes, continue.

9. Make the body of the animal doll or reclining animal according to the instructions on page 175 or 181.

10. For Rudolph, stitch two antler pieces together, right sides facing. Repeat for other antler.

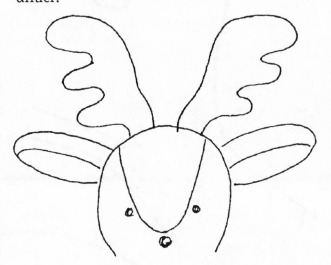

Turn right side out. Stuff carefully, making sure the stuffing is even. Stop stuffing when you have stuffed to about 1/4" from the end of the bottom of the antlers. Handstitch antlers to head at markings, fingers of antlers facing outward, pushing raw edges of bottom of antlers under antler, out of sight.

11. For mouth embroidery instructions turn to page 15.

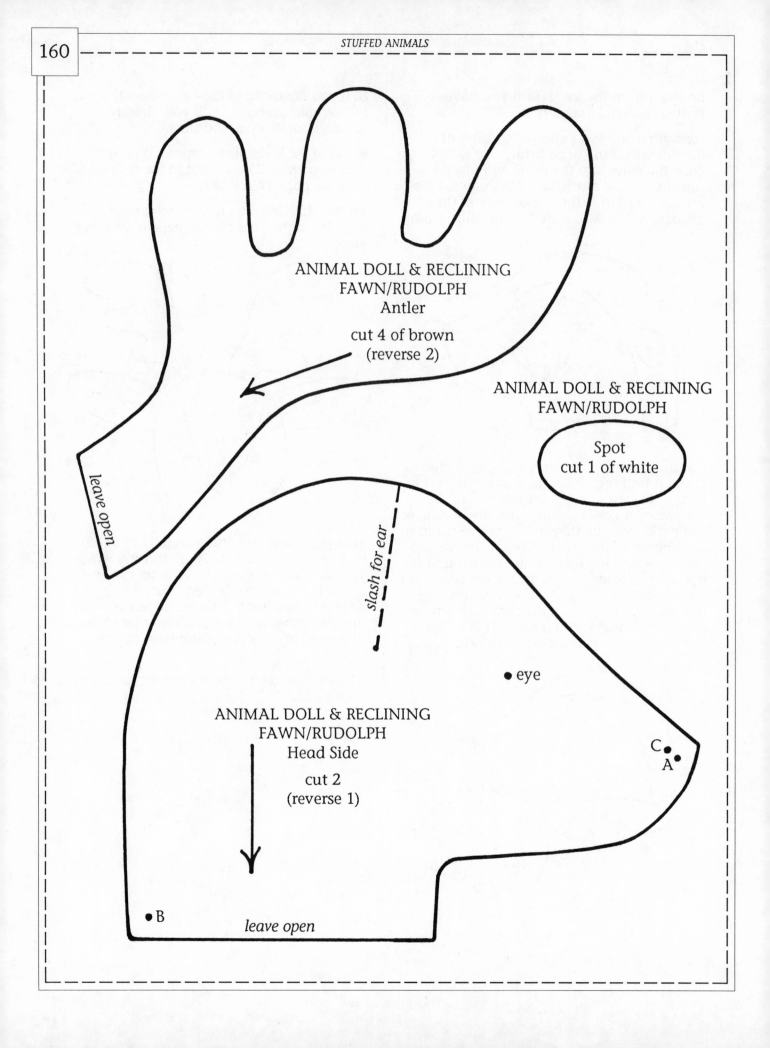

ANIMAL DOLL & RECLINING
FAWN/RUDOLPH
Antler

cut 4 of brown
(reverse 2)

ANIMAL DOLL & RECLINING
FAWN/RUDOLPH

Spot
cut 1 of white

leave open

slash for ear

• eye

ANIMAL DOLL & RECLINING
FAWN/RUDOLPH
Head Side

cut 2
(reverse 1)

C •
A •

• B

leave open

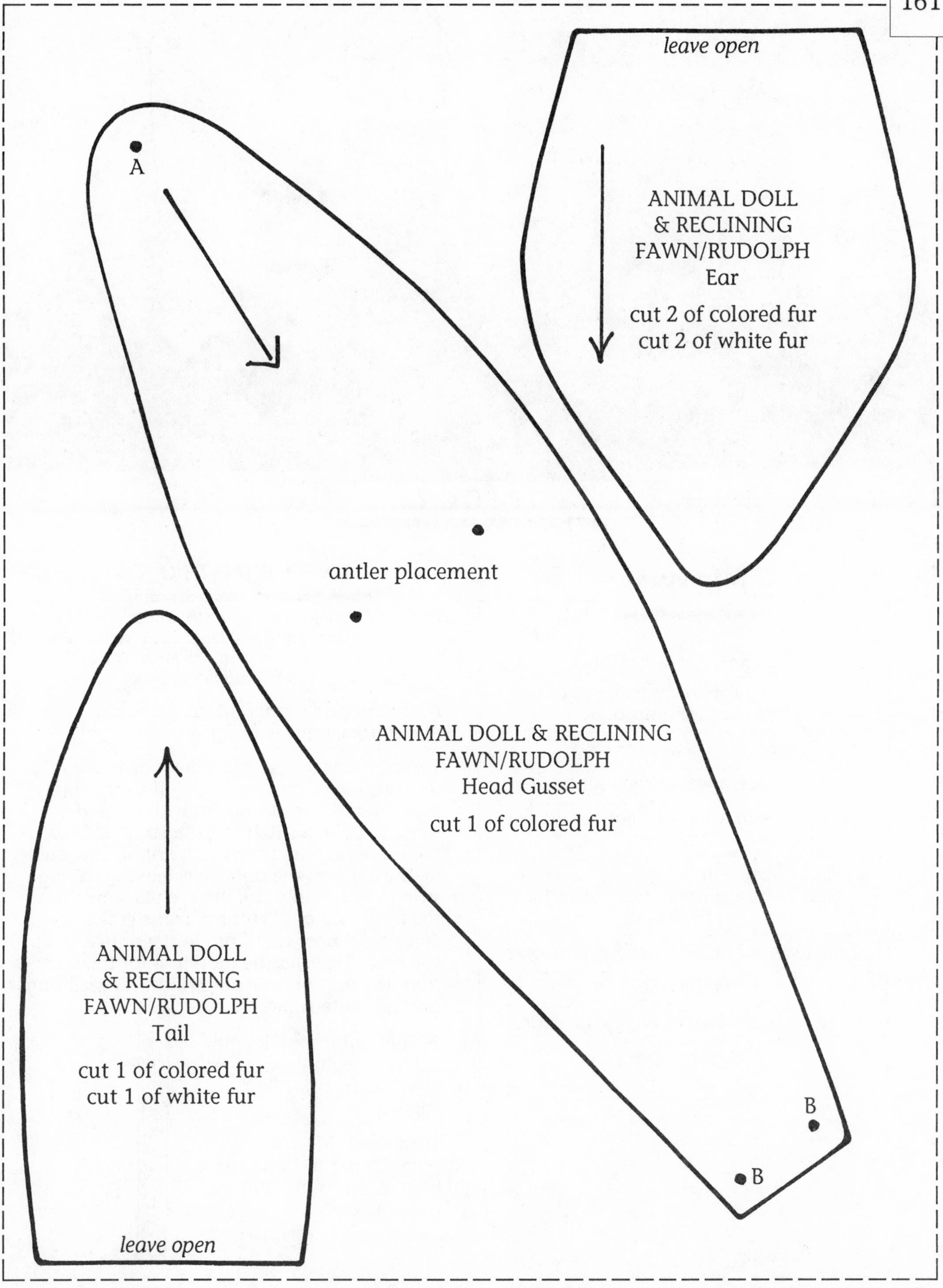

leave open

A

ANIMAL DOLL
& RECLINING
FAWN/RUDOLPH
Ear

cut 2 of colored fur
cut 2 of white fur

antler placement

ANIMAL DOLL & RECLINING
FAWN/RUDOLPH
Head Gusset

cut 1 of colored fur

ANIMAL DOLL
& RECLINING
FAWN/RUDOLPH
Tail

cut 1 of colored fur
cut 1 of white fur

B

B

leave open

P I G G Y

MATERIALS

Pink corduroy or fur fabric:
½ yard for reclining pig
⅓ yard for animal doll

Matching sewing thread

Scrap of brown wool or felt for hooves

Heavy thread, carpet thread, or waxed dental floss

55 mm plastic joints for head and arms:
One for reclining animal, three for animal doll

Two 12 mm plastic safety or glass eyes

Polyester fiberfill

Brown embroidery floss or perle cotton

One pipe cleaner

INSTRUCTIONS

Note: All seam allowances are ¼" unless otherwise instructed. Head and tail patterns follow. Body patterns begin on page 175 for animal dolls and page 181 for reclining animals.

As instructed on page 10, make patterns, cut and mark corduroy or fur.

Transfer dots for eye placement as marked to the backing of the head sides. If using glass eyes, mark their placement with colored thread: make a stitch from the right side of the fur, emerging back on the right side, and tie the ends on the right side, leaving ½" long strings. This will mark the eye placement on the front side of the fabric. Transfer the French dot nose markings to the right side of the nose. Transfer the markings for the body from the appropriate animal doll or reclining animal pattern pieces.

1. Fold tail in half lengthwise, matching raw edges. Sew, leaving one short edge open.

Turn right side out. Fold a pipe cleaner in half. Insert bent end into tail. Push it in to the end.

2. Pin two ear pieces together, right sides facing. Stitch, leaving the short, straight edges open. Turn right side out. Repeat for second ear.

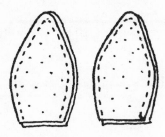

Fold ears in half lengthwise. Pin to head sides at marking as shown, fold facing the back of the head. Baste.

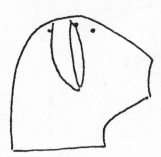

3. Pin one side of head gusset to one head side, right sides facing from dot A at nose, down to dot B at bottom of neck, easing the gusset to fit. Stitch. Repeat for other side of head gusset and other head side.

4. Pin head sides together below nose from dot C to dot D. Stitch from raw edge to raw edge.

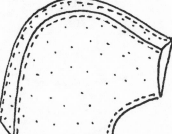

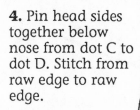

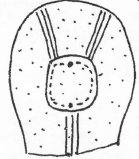

5. Pin nose to head, matching one dot on nose to under neck seam and the other dot to dot E on gusset. Stitch.

6. If you have chosen safety eyes, install them by following the instructions on page 15. If you are using glass eyes, omit this step.

7. Turn head right side out. Starting at the nose, stuff the head firmly. When you have stuffed to about a half inch from the raw edges at the base of the neck, insert the flat end of the stationary disk into the bottom of the neck, with the ridged post pointing out of the bottom of the head. Using heavy thread, run a row of long basting stitches around the opening by hand, one quarter inch from the raw edge. Pull up on the

thread tightly. Continue around one more time, pulling the thread as you go. Secure the thread with a knot. This will pull the fabric around the joint as shown.

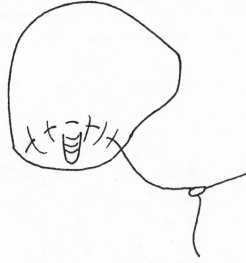

8. If you are using glass eyes, follow the instructions on page 15. If you have already installed safety eyes, continue.

9. To form nostrils, thread a long dollmaking needle with brown embroidery floss. Knot one end. Enter the head at the bottom of the neck so the knot will not show when the head is installed on the body. Emerge at the marking on the pig's nose. Make a French knot by pushing the tip of the needle back into the fabric a few threads away from where you just came out. Wind the thread around the needle five or six times. Push the needle into the fabric. Emerge at the second nostril marking. Pull on the thread to form the knot. Repeat for the second nostril. End the thread by coming out at the neck again. Knot.

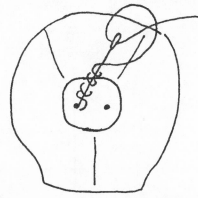

10. To make the body, follow the instructions for either the animal doll (page 175) or reclining animal (page 181).

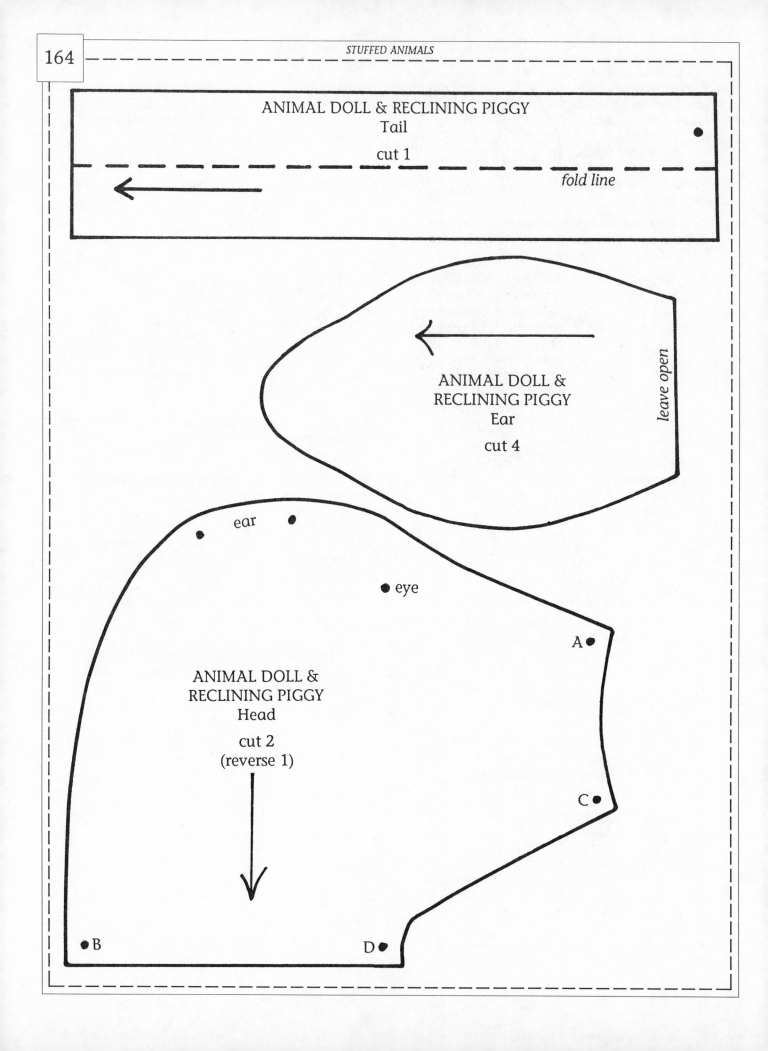

ANIMAL DOLL & RECLINING PIGGY
Tail

cut 1

fold line

ANIMAL DOLL &
RECLINING PIGGY
Ear

cut 4

leave open

ear

eye

A

ANIMAL DOLL &
RECLINING PIGGY
Head

cut 2
(reverse 1)

C

B

D

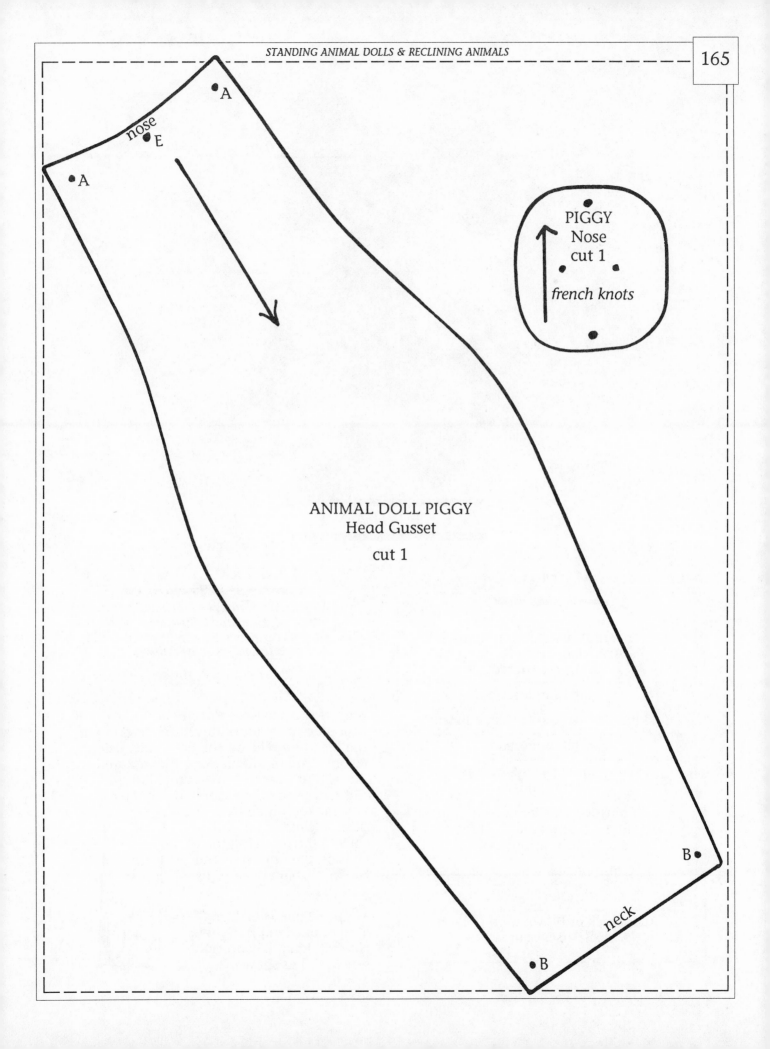

• A

nose
• E

• A

PIGGY
Nose
cut 1

french knots

ANIMAL DOLL PIGGY
Head Gusset

cut 1

B •

• B

neck

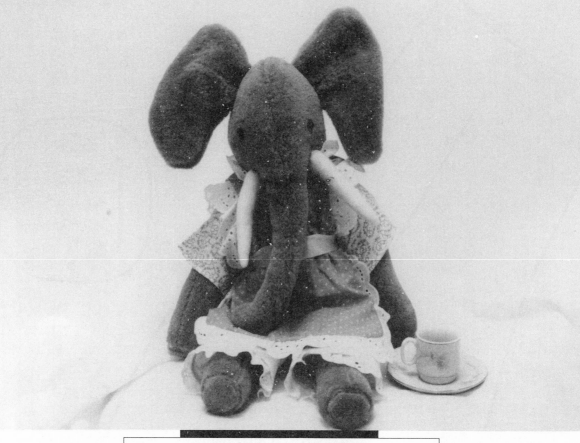

ELEPHANT

MATERIALS

³/₈ yard short pile fur for animal doll (907K Antelope, available from CR's Crafts, see Sources)

Matching thread

One piece of bone-colored felt for tusk

Matching thread

Heavy carpet thread, or waxed dental floss

55 mm plastic joints for head and arms: one for reclining animal, three for animal doll

Two 12 mm plastic safety or glass eyes

Polyester fiberfill

Gray, black or brown yarn or Pretty Hair® (see Sources)

INSTRUCTIONS

Note: All seam allowances are ¼" unless otherwise instructed. Head and tail patterns follow. Body patterns begin on page 175 for animal dolls and page 181 for reclining animals.

As instructed on page 10, make patterns, cut and mark fur.

Transfer dots for eye placement and ear and tusk placement markings to the backing of the fur as marked on the head side. Using colored thread, stitch along the tusk and ear placement lines to transfer them to the right, fur side of the fabric. If using glass eyes make a stitch from the right side of the fur with colored thread, tying the ends on the right side and leaving ½" long strings as a mark.

1. Cut 30 pieces of yarn 3" long or one length of Pretty Hair® 3" long. Lay on right side of tail as shown.

Fold tail in half lengthwise. Stitch as shown, leaving the short straight top edge (not the end where you laid the tail "hairs") open for turning.

Turn right side out.

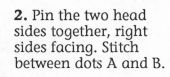

2. Pin the two head sides together, right sides facing. Stitch between dots A and B.

3. Pin head gusset to one head side, right sides facing, matching dots A and raw edges. Stitch from dot A down to bottom of neck edge. Repeat for other side of head gusset and other head side.

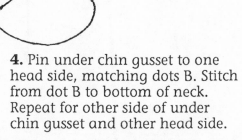

4. Pin under chin gusset to one head side, matching dots B. Stitch from dot B to bottom of neck. Repeat for other side of under chin gusset and other head side.

5. If using safety eyes, follow the instructions on page 15 to install them. If you chose glass eyes, omit this step.

6. Turn head right side out. Starting at the trunk, stuff the head. Be sure the trunk is stuffed evenly before proceeding on to the head. When you have stuffed to about a half inch from the raw edges at the base of the neck, insert the flat end of the stationary disk into the bottom of the neck, with the ridged post pointing out of the bottom of the head. Using heavy thread, run a row of long basting stitches around the opening by hand, one quarter inch from the raw edge. Pull up on the thread tightly. Continue around one more time, pulling the thread as you go. Secure the thread with a knot. This will pull the fabric around the joint as shown.

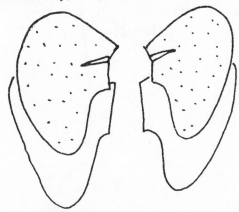

7. If using glass eyes, follow the instructions on page 15 to install them. If you have already installed safety eyes, continue.

8. To make the elephant's body, turn to the instructions for the animal doll on page 175 or the reclining animal on page 181.

9. Lay the ears out, wrong side up, as shown. Make darts in two ear pieces as marked. These will be the inside (facing elephant's body) of the ears.

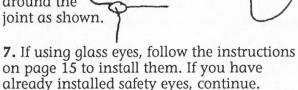

Stitch a darted to an undarted ear piece. Repeat. Turn right side out.

Turn seam allowances of open, straight edges to inside. Whipstitch closed. Pin to head at markings, darts facing the back of the elephant. Following the method described on page 17, handstitch the ears to the head at the markings.

10. Pin two tusk pieces together. Stitch, leaving short, straight edges open. Trim seam allowances to 1/8" from stitching. Repeat for other tusk pieces. Turn tusks right side out. Stuff. Turn 1/4" at bottom edge of tusks to center. To secure, stitch across as shown.

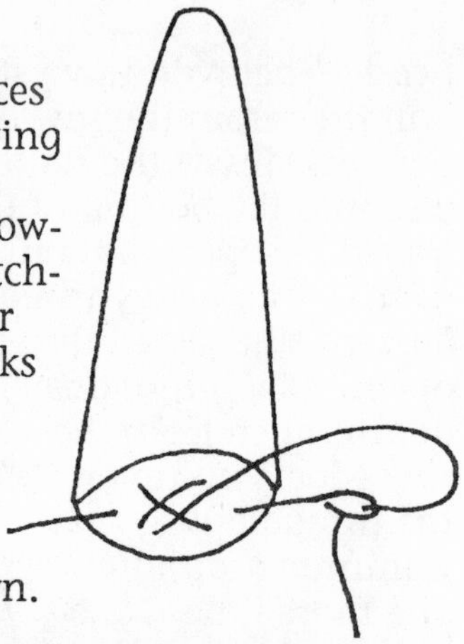

Pin tusks to head at markings. Stitch to head. Bend tusks gently to turn slightly up and in, toward the trunk.

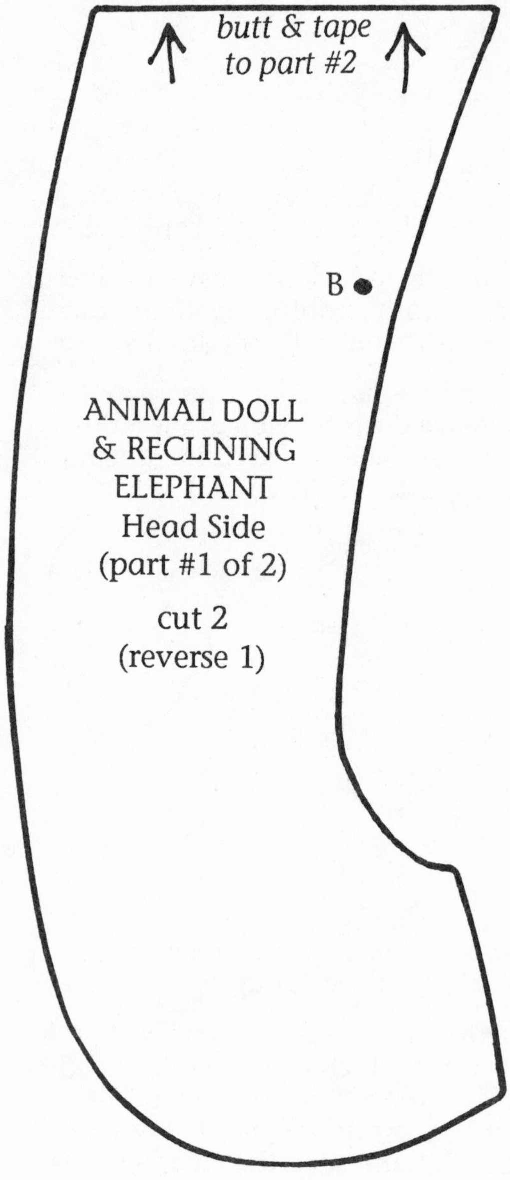

butt & tape to part #2

B

ANIMAL DOLL & RECLINING ELEPHANT Head Side (part #1 of 2) cut 2 (reverse 1)

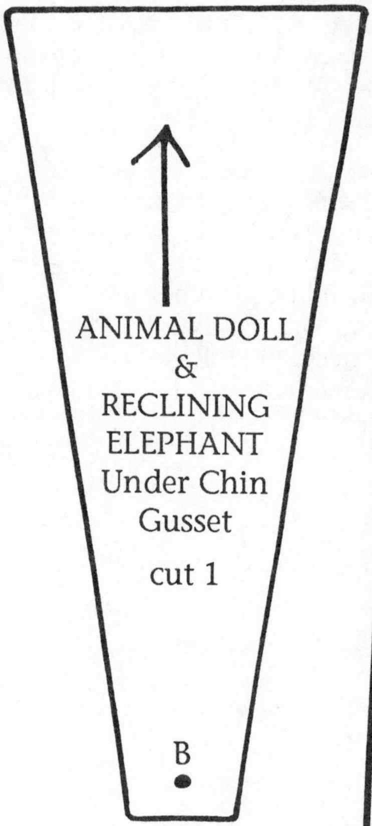

ANIMAL DOLL & RECLINING ELEPHANT Under Chin Gusset cut 1

B

A

ANIMAL DOLL & RECLINING ELEPHANT Head Gusset cut 1

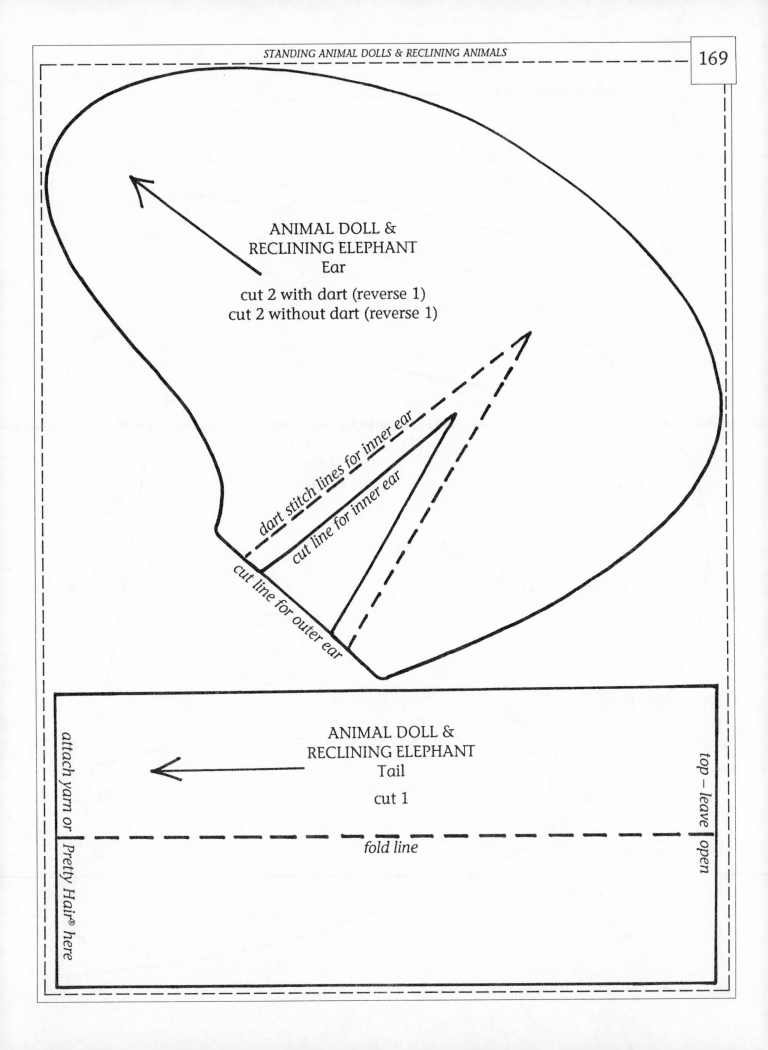

ANIMAL DOLL &
RECLINING ELEPHANT
Ear

cut 2 with dart (reverse 1)
cut 2 without dart (reverse 1)

dart stitch lines for inner ear

cut line for inner ear

cut line for outer ear

ANIMAL DOLL &
RECLINING ELEPHANT
Tail

cut 1

fold line

attach yarn or Pretty Hair® here

top – leave open

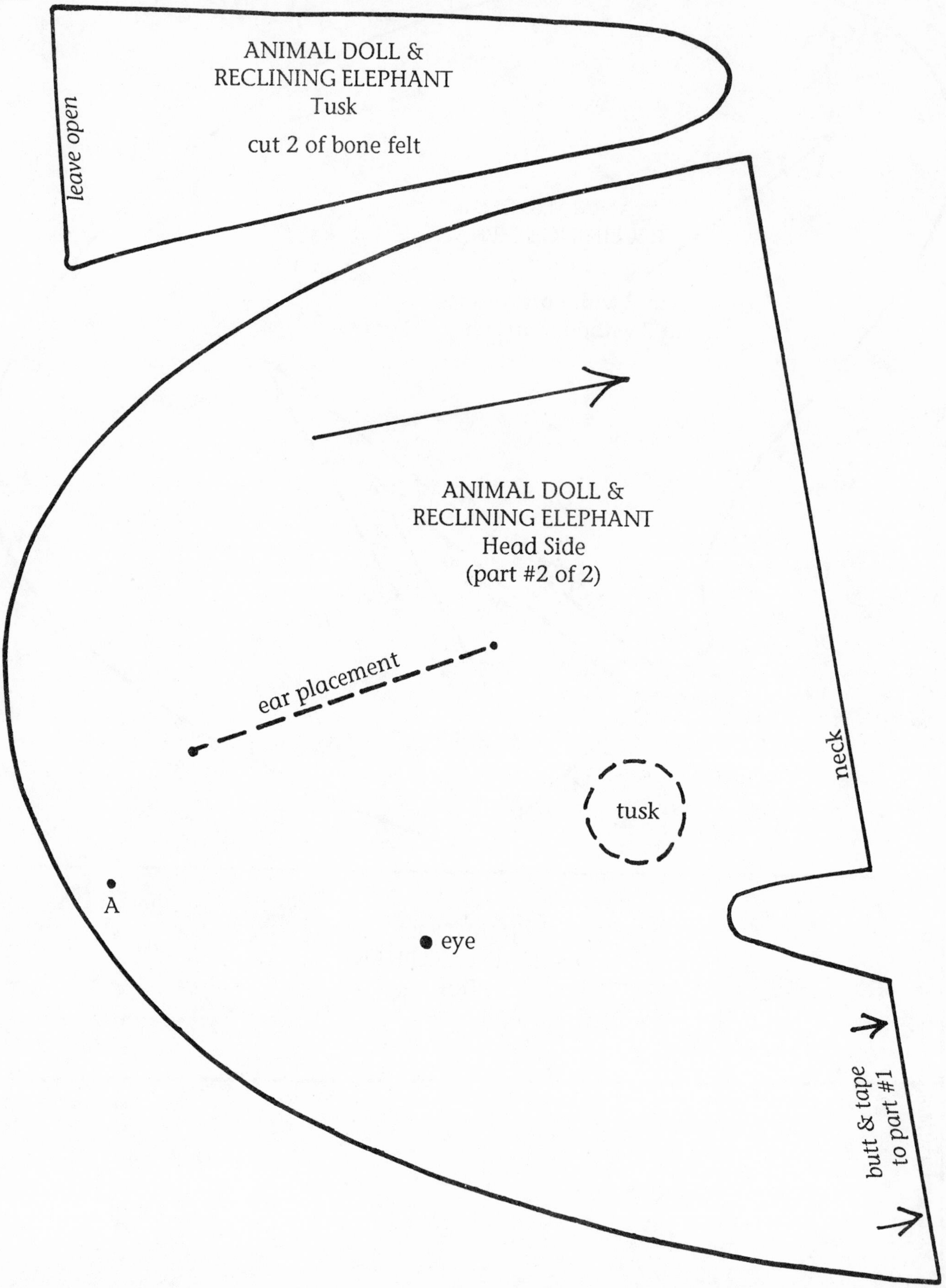

ANIMAL DOLL &
RECLINING ELEPHANT
Tusk

cut 2 of bone felt

leave open

ANIMAL DOLL &
RECLINING ELEPHANT
Head Side
(part #2 of 2)

ear placement

neck

tusk

A

eye

butt & tape
to part #1

HORSE OR UNICORN

MATERIALS

Camel, dark brown, black, or white seal fur (available from by Diane or CR's Crafts, see Sources):

> 1/2 yard for reclining animal
> 1/3 yard for animal doll

Matching thread

Scrap of white fur for star

Matching thread

Scrap of black wool or felt for hooves

Two 14 mm glass or plastic safety eyes

55 mm plastic joints for head and arms: One for reclining animal, three for animal doll

Polyester fiberfill stuffing

Heavy thread, carpet thread, or waxed dental floss

Embroidery floss or perle cotton

INSTRUCTIONS

Note: All seam allowances are 1/4" unless otherwise instructed. Head and tail patterns follow. See page 40 for unicorn's fabric specifications for body, hooves, and mane. Body patterns begin on page 175 for animal dolls and page 181 for reclining animals.

As instructed on page 10, make patterns and cut fur. Transfer markings for ear and star placement to the backing of the fur. To transfer these markings to the right side of the fur, hand or machine stitch over the markings using a bright, contrastingly colored thread, as instructed on page 7.

Transfer dots for eye placement as marked to the backing of the fur. If using glass eyes make a stitch from the right side of the fur with colored thread, tying the ends on the right side and leaving half inch long strings as a mark.

1. As instructed on page 11, trim two opposite ear pieces. (Right side up so they will point in opposite directions.) Pin them to the other two ear pieces,

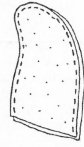

right sides facing. Stitch, leaving the bottom edges open for turning as shown.

Turn right side out.

2. From the right side of the head gusset, hold the star over the fur. Line up the star within the placement lines. Clip the fur from the gusset that will be under the star. Pin the star to the gusset. Using a small zigzag stitch, applique the edge of the star to the head gusset. Omit for unicorn.

3. Right sides facing, pin the dart in the head gusset. Stitch ¼" from the straight, raw edge along the stitching lines on the pattern.

4. Pin the head sides together, right sides facing, matching dots A and B. Stitch from dot A down to bottom of neck.

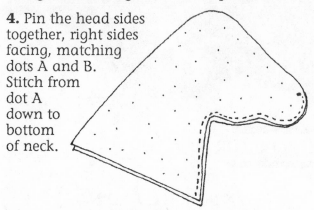

5. Pin dot A on gusset to dot A at junction of head sides, right sides together. Matching dots C, pin one side of gusset to respective head side, easing and pinning between dots A and C. Stitch. Repeat for other side. Pin and stitch head sides together from dot C through dot D.

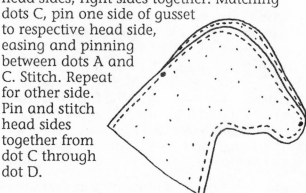

6. If using safety eyes, turn to page 15 and follow the instructions to install them. For glass eyes, omit this step.

7. Turn head right side out. Starting at the nose, stuff the head firmly.

When you have stuffed to about a half inch from the raw edges at the base of the neck, insert the flat end of the stationary disk of the joint into the bottom of the neck, with the ridged post pointing out of the bottom of the head. Using heavy thread, run a row of

long basting stitches around the opening by hand, ¼" from the raw edge. Pull up on the thread tightly. Continue around one more time, pulling the thread as you go. Secure the thread with a knot. This will pull the fabric tightly around the joint as shown.

8. If you chose glass eyes, follow the instructions on page 15 to install them. If you have already installed safety eyes, continue.

9. To make the body of the animal doll or reclining horse, turn to the instructions on page 175 or 181.

10. Turn the bottom edges of the ears ¼" to the inside. Whipstitch closed. Handstitch to head at markings, having points of ears facing center and trimmed ears facing forward.

11. Cut a length of Pretty Hair® 10" long. Find the middle of the hair and stitch it to the dart seam at the top of the horse's neck, about a half inch behind the ears. One half of the hair will fall forward for the forelock and the other half will fall to one side of the neck to begin the mane.

Cut three more lengths of Pretty Hair®, each 10" long. Fold them in half and stitch the folds down the neck, on the seam, each about an inch below the preceding one. Brush all mane hair to one side of the neck.

12. Turn to page 15 for nose and mouth embroidery instructions.

Unicorn

Make a white horse as previously instructed, substituting gold yarn for the mane and tail and gold fabric rather than black wool for the hooves.

To make the horn: Right sides facing fold the horn in half as shown. Stitch along the stitching lines. Trim seam allowances to 1/8" at top of horn. Turn horn right side out. Stuff to 1" from bottom open edge. Baste 1/2" from raw edge. Pull up on basting stitches tightly. Knot. Sew to head between and just in front of the ears.

To curl the yarn: Wrap yarn around metal skewers or knitting needles, securing the ends with tape. Soak in water. Place in 200-degree oven for 10 or 15 minutes or until completely dry. Cool. Remove from skewers. Apply the yarn as instructed for the Pretty Hair®.

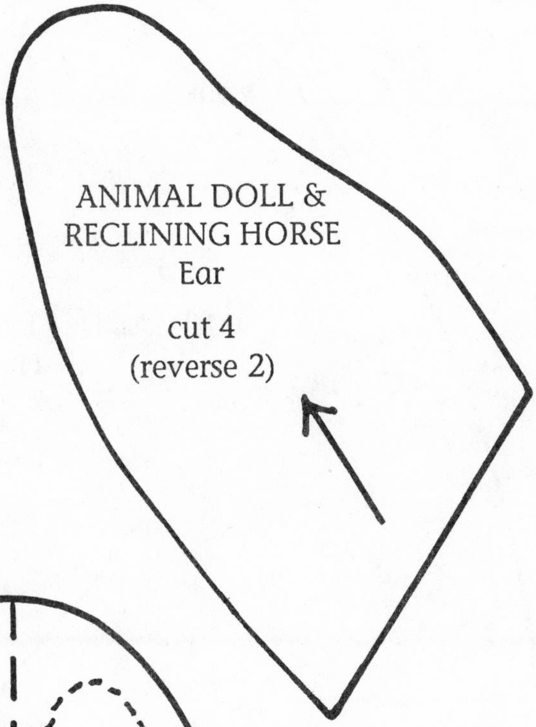

ANIMAL DOLL & RECLINING HORSE
Ear

cut 4
(reverse 2)

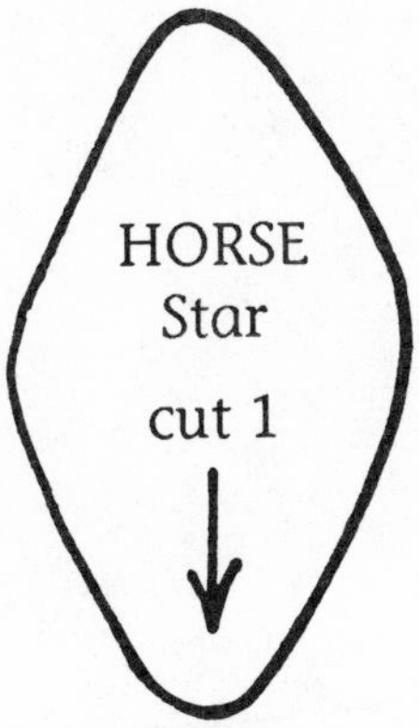

HORSE
Star

cut 1

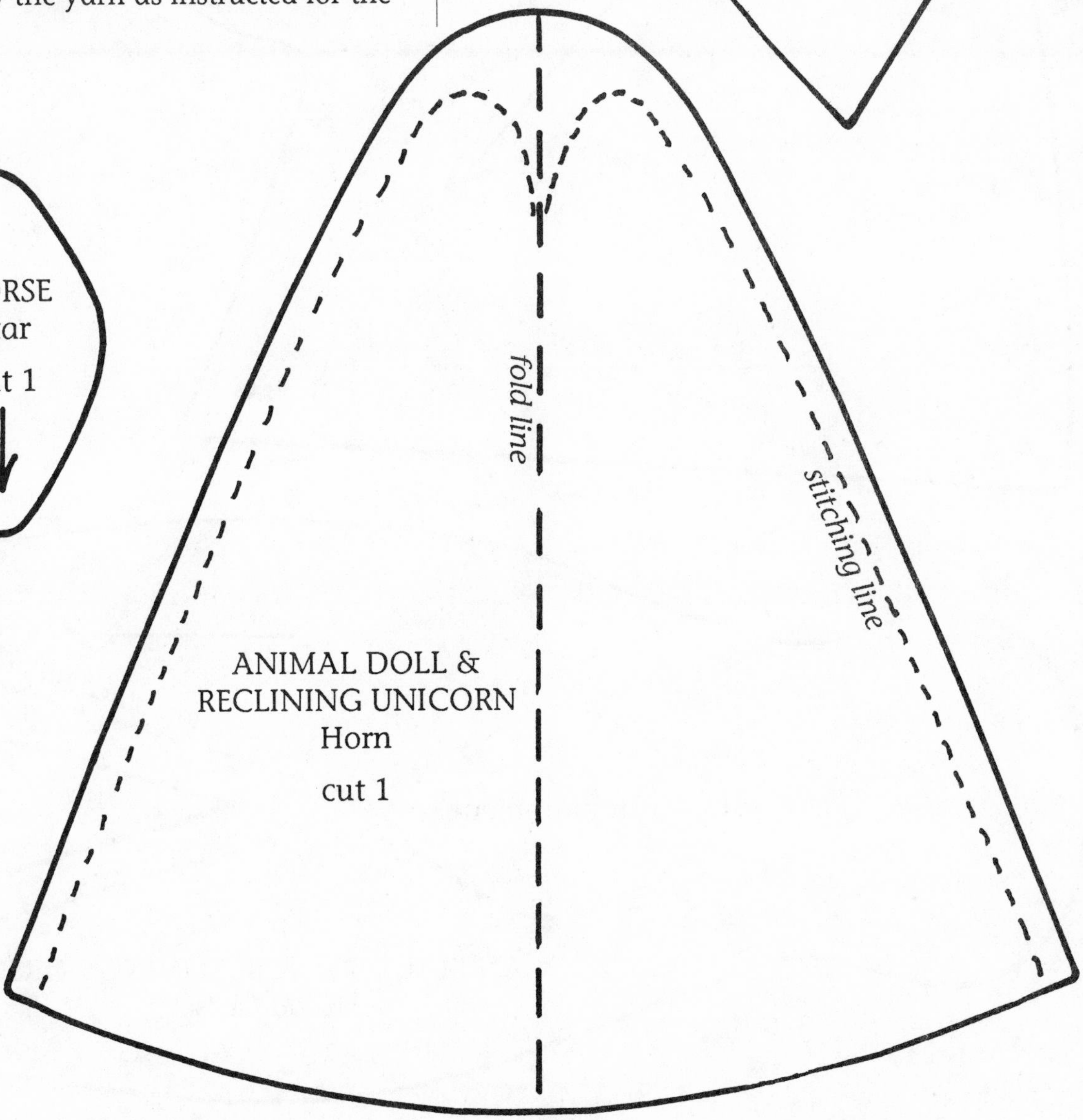

fold line

stitching line

ANIMAL DOLL & RECLINING UNICORN
Horn

cut 1

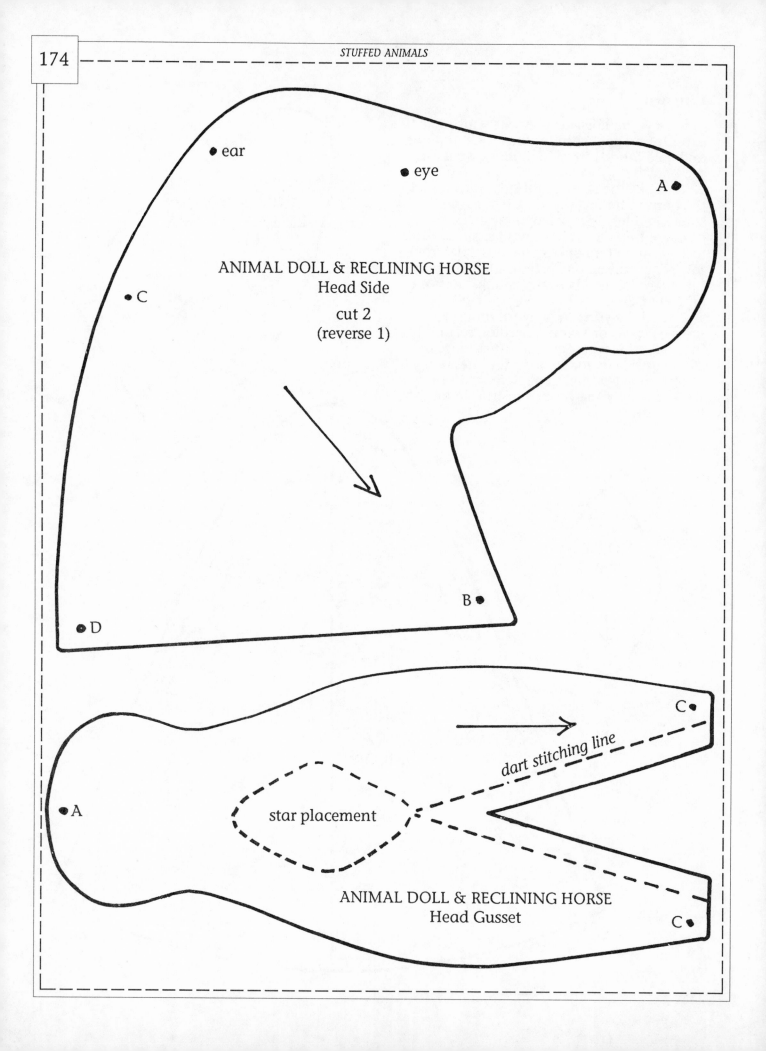

• ear

• eye

A•

ANIMAL DOLL & RECLINING HORSE
Head Side

cut 2
(reverse 1)

•C

B•

•D

•A

star placement

dart stitching line

C•

ANIMAL DOLL & RECLINING HORSE
Head Gusset

C•

GENERAL INSTRUCTIONS FOR ANIMAL DOLLS

INSTRUCTIONS

Note: All seam allowances are ¼" unless otherwise instructed.

As instructed on page 10, make patterns, cut and transfer all markings from the animal doll body pattern pieces to the fur backing or "wrong" side of the fabric.

1. Pin and sew the two body pieces together, right sides facing, leaving the bottom, straight edges open.

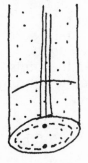

Make holes for arms and head at markings on body pieces. Turn the body right side out.

2. For piggy, cow, fawn/Rudolph, and horse: Stitch hooves to bottoms of arms and legs.

For all: Right sides facing, pin two arm pieces together. Stitch, leaving an opening between the dots for turning and stuffing.

Repeat for second arm.

Right sides facing stitch leg pieces together, leaving the top straight edges open.

For piggy, cow and fawn/Rudolph: Match seams in front and back of arms and legs as shown to form an upside down V in the bottom of the hooves. Stitch as shown. To reduce bulk, trim across the points of the seam allowances.

For horse and elephant: Pin foot soles to bottoms of arms and legs, matching dots to seams at front and back. Stitch.

For all: Turn arms and legs right side out. Stuff legs to within about an inch of the top.

3. For all except teddy bear: Find center of bottom, straight edge of body back. Pin tail to right side as shown. (Omit for teddy bear.)

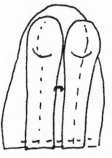

For all: Pin legs over tail as illustrated. Make sure back of each leg (center back seam) is against the fur of the back body. Stitch through legs, tail, and body back, leaving body front free.

4. Hold the arms together as shown. Make holes at the dots marked for jointing on the sides of the arms that face each other. This will make a right and a left arm. One arm at a time, insert the stationary disk into the arm, threaded post first and push the post out of the hole.

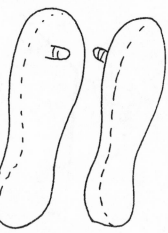

6. To install the head, insert the post of the stationary disk into the hole in top of the body. Put the large washer over the post and then push the locking disk into place, and then the metal lockwasher. As instructed on page 14, tighten with the socket or nut and hammer, until the joint is tight when the head is turned.

7. Making sure the arms are pointing to the front of the animal, push the post of the joint from the arm into the body. From inside the body, place a washer on the post. Push a lockwasher on the post. Using the hammer and socket or nut, make the joints as tight as possible. Turn back to the jointing instructions on page 14 if needed.

8. Stuff the arms. As instructed on page 13, ladderstitch the openings at the tops of the arms closed.

9. Stuff the body to a medium firmness, making sure to pack stuffing around the head and arm joints. Turn under $1/4$" at the bottom front of the body opening. Slipstitch closed.

10. To finish, return to the earlier instructions for the specific animal you are making.

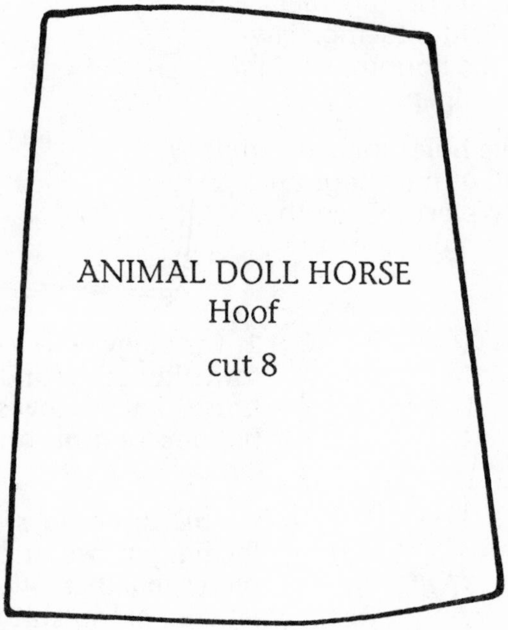

ANIMAL DOLL HORSE
Hoof
cut 8

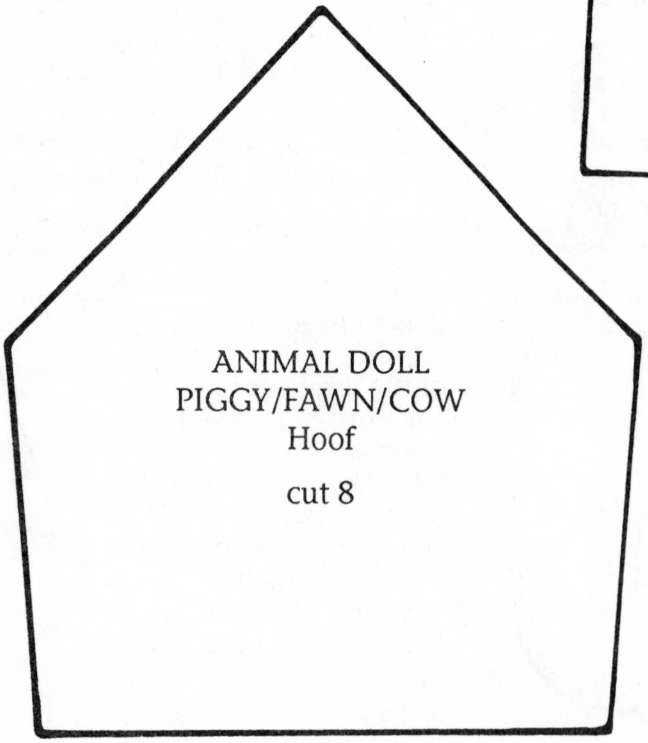

ANIMAL DOLL
PIGGY/FAWN/COW
Hoof
cut 8

ANIMAL DOLL
HORSE/ELEPHANT
Hoof Sole
cut 4

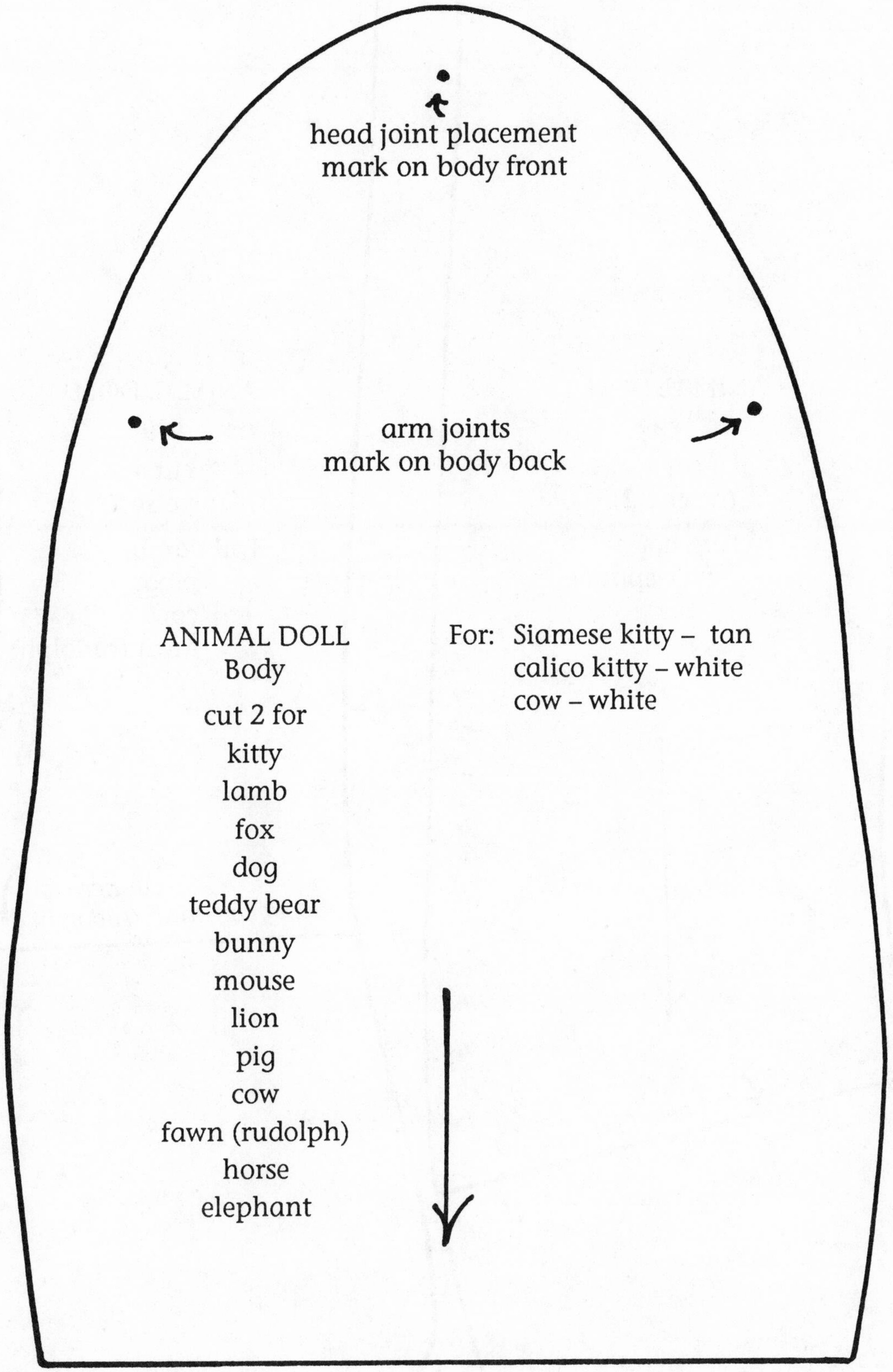

head joint placement
mark on body front

arm joints
mark on body back

ANIMAL DOLL
Body

cut 2 for

kitty
lamb
fox
dog
teddy bear
bunny
mouse
lion
pig
cow
fawn (rudolph)
horse
elephant

For: Siamese kitty – tan
calico kitty – white
cow – white

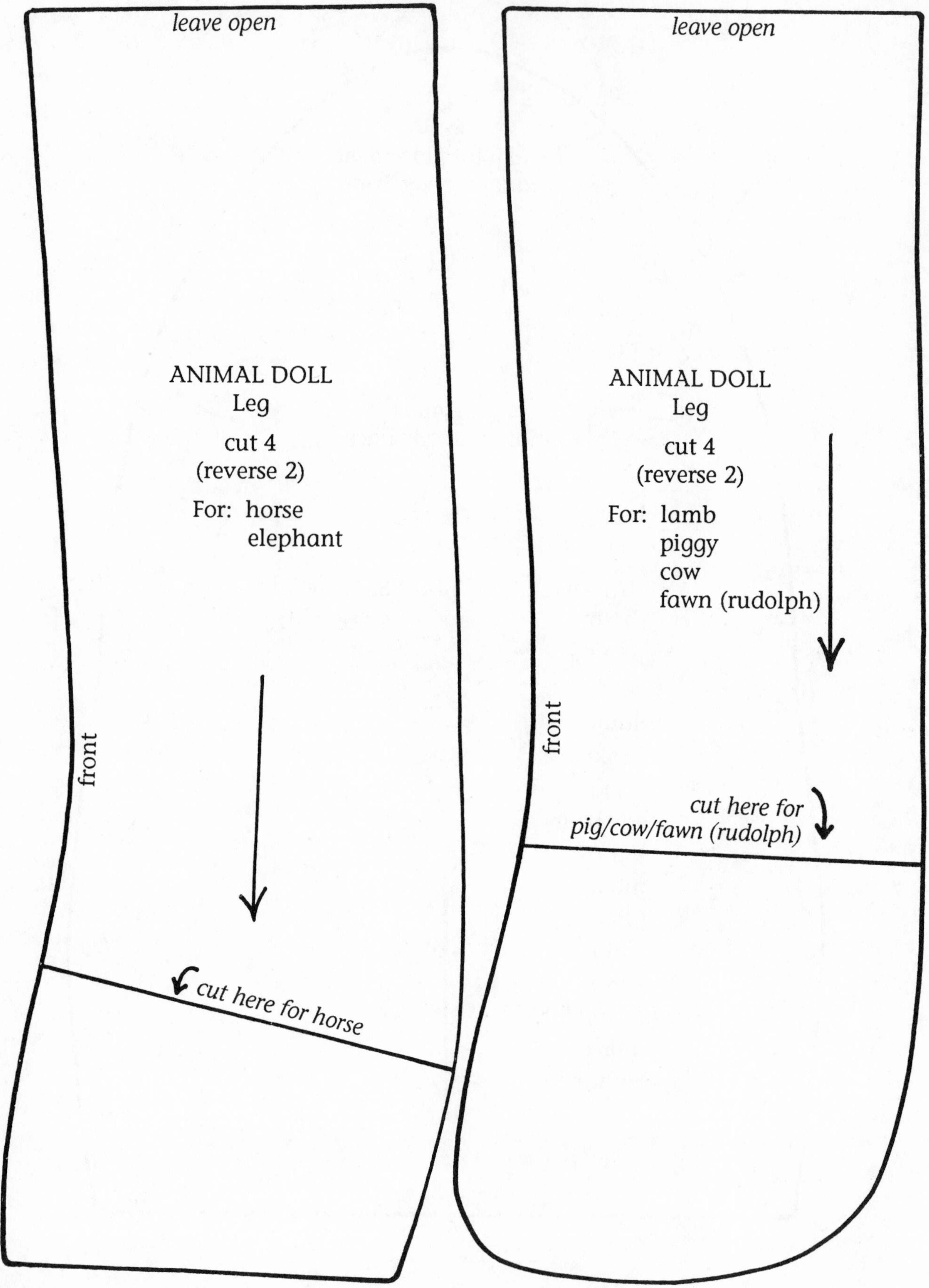

leave open

leave open

ANIMAL DOLL
Leg

cut 4
(reverse 2)

For: horse
       elephant

front

cut here for horse

ANIMAL DOLL
Leg

cut 4
(reverse 2)

For: lamb
       piggy
       cow
       fawn (rudolph)

front

cut here for
pig/cow/fawn (rudolph)

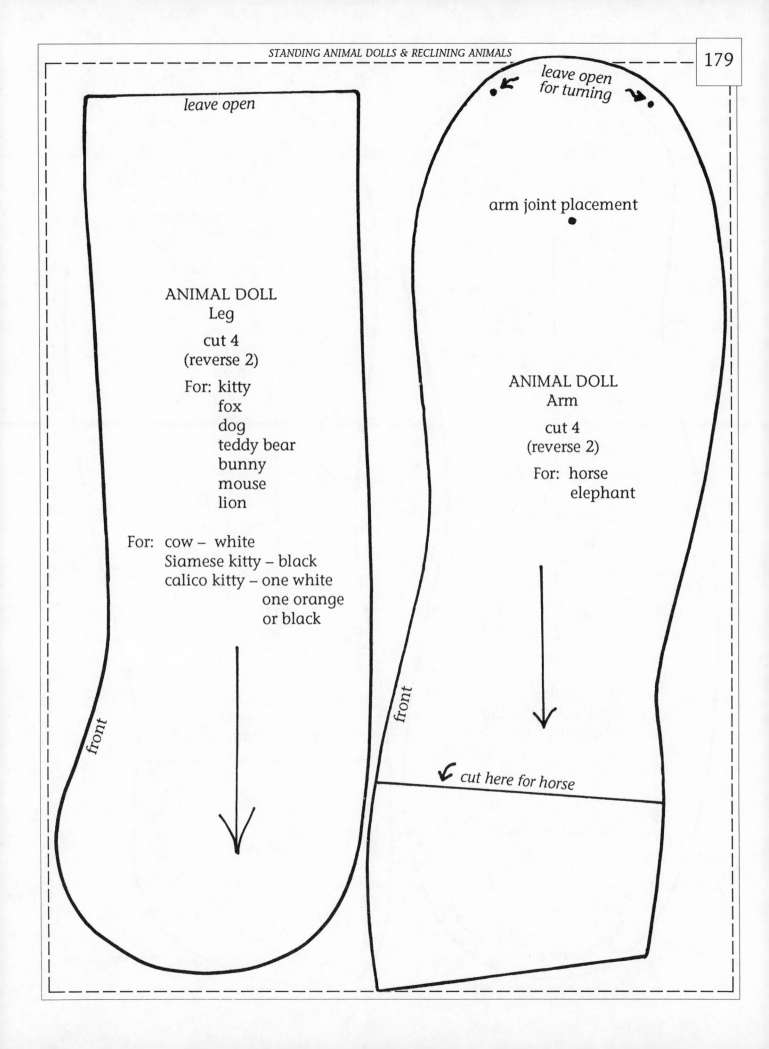

leave open

ANIMAL DOLL
Leg

cut 4
(reverse 2)

For: kitty
fox
dog
teddy bear
bunny
mouse
lion

For: cow – white
Siamese kitty – black
calico kitty – one white
one orange
or black

front

*leave open
for turning*

arm joint placement

ANIMAL DOLL
Arm

cut 4
(reverse 2)

For: horse
elephant

front

cut here for horse

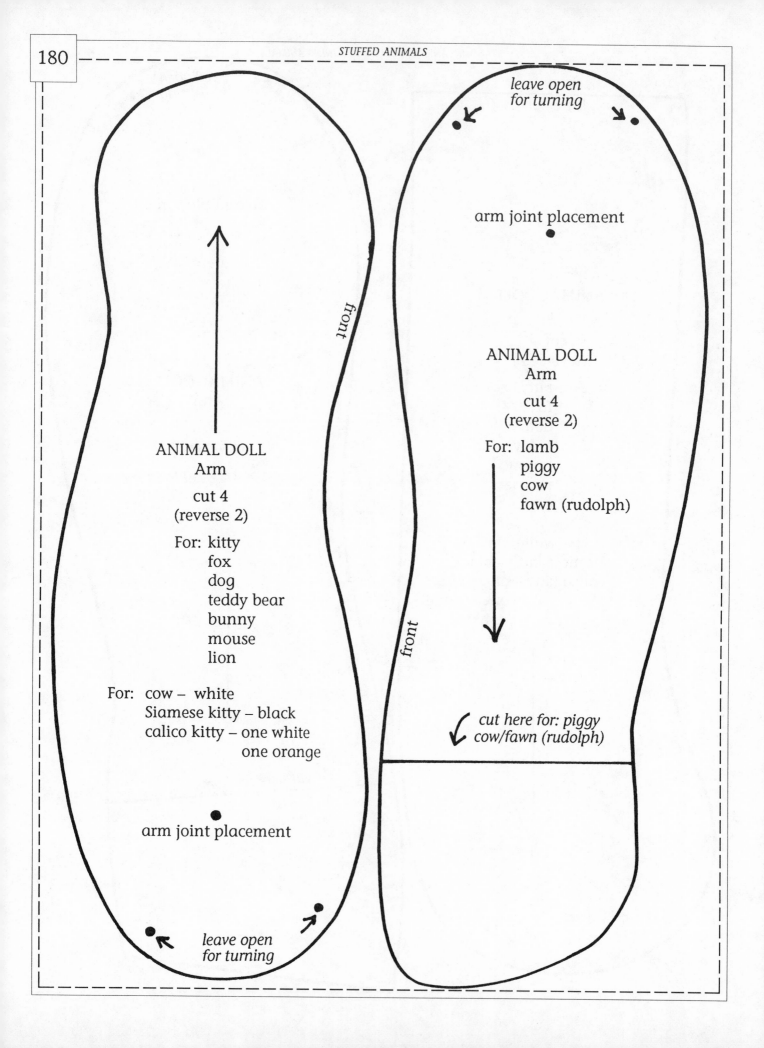

*leave open
for turning*

arm joint placement

front

ANIMAL DOLL
Arm

cut 4
(reverse 2)

For: lamb
　　piggy
　　cow
　　fawn (rudolph)

*cut here for: piggy
cow/fawn (rudolph)*

ANIMAL DOLL
Arm

cut 4
(reverse 2)

For: kitty
　　fox
　　dog
　　teddy bear
　　bunny
　　mouse
　　lion

For: cow – white
　　Siamese kitty – black
　　calico kitty – one white
　　　　　　　　　one orange

arm joint placement

front

*leave open
for turning*

GENERAL INSTRUCTIONS FOR RECLINING ANIMALS

INSTRUCTIONS

Note: All seam allowances are ¼" unless otherwise instructed.

As instructed on page 10, make patterns, cut and transfer all markings from the reclining animal body pattern pieces to the fur backing or "wrong" side of the fabric.

1. For black and white lamb: Pin black feet to bottom of legs on underbody, inner back legs, upper body back and upper body front. Stitch.

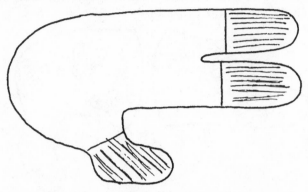

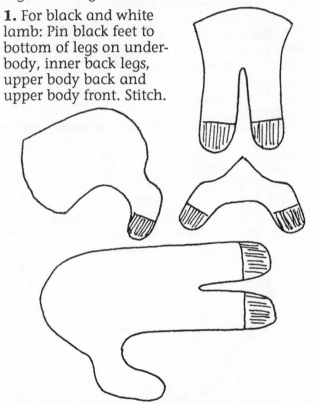

For calico kitty: Right sides facing, pin black upper body back part 1 to orange upper body back part 2, as illustrated, matching like lettered dots, easing part 1 to fit. Stitch. Pin white upperbody back part 3 to upperbody back part 2, as illustrated, matching like lettered dots, easing part 3 to fit. Stitch.

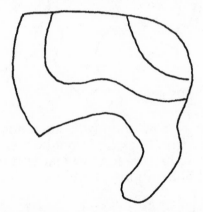

Right sides together, pin orange underbody part 2 to white underbody part 1. Stitch.

For Siamese kitty: Pin and stitch black Siamese kitty legs to reclining animal underbody, inner back legs, upper body back, and upper body front, right sides facing.

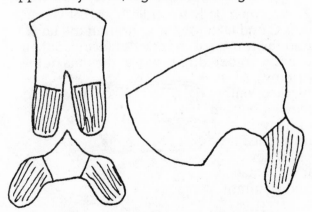

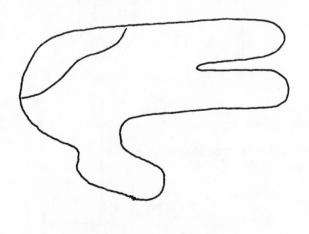

For cow: Turn to the pattern for the standing cow in chapter 2. Make several spot patterns, cut them from black fur and zigzag applique them to the reclining cow's upperbody back and upperbody front.

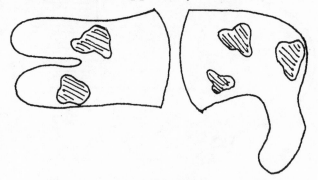

For fawn: Arrange the white fawn spots on the upperbody back in a random pattern, mostly at the top, rather than the sides.

2. For piggy, cow and fawn: Stitch hooves to bottom of legs. Back and front hooves are different, so be sure to follow pattern markings and illustrations carefully.

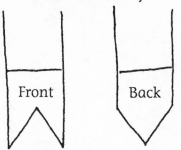

For horse: Stitch hooves to bottom of legs.

For kitty, lamb, fox, dog, lion and elephant: Omit step 2.

3. For all animals except horse: Baste the tail to the fur side of the underbody, between the dots, as shown.

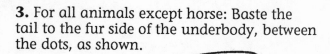

4. For all animals: Pin and stitch the upper body front to the upper body back as shown, matching center dots A and dots J, and K.

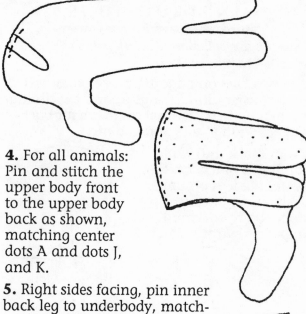

5. Right sides facing, pin inner back leg to underbody, matching dots D and C. Stitch between dots. For piggy, cow, fawn, horse and elephant: leave bottom of hooves open.

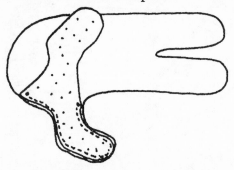

6. Pin other half of inner leg to upper body back, matching dots C and D. Stitch between dots, leaving the bottom of the hooves open for piggy, cow, fawn, horse and elephant.

7. Pin upper body to under body between dots C and D, all the way around the back and the front legs, right sides facing. Stitch, leaving an opening between the dots at the tummy, as marked, and leaving bottom of hooves unstitched for piggy cow, fawn, horse, and elephant.

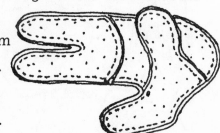

8. For piggy, cow and fawn: Stitch "V" in front hooves as shown.

Fold back hooves so seams match and stitch "V" as shown.

Trim seam allowances across points of hooves.

For elephant and horse: Pin foot soles to bottoms of feet, matching dots to seams. Stitch.

9. For all animals: Turn the body right side out.

10. Make a hole with a seam ripper at the dot on the upper body front for the head joint placement as marked. Push joint post protruding from head through hole, into body. From inside the body slip a large washer onto the post. Next snap a locking washer over the post, pushing as far as possible. As instructed in the section on jointing on page 13, add a metal lock-washer, pounding it securely in place with a hammer and socket or nut.

11. Stuff the legs very softly. Stuff the body a bit more firmly. Aim for the softness of a feather pillow. Use the method described on page 14 to stitch the opening at the tummy closed, easing the fullness of the upper body.

12. To finish, return to instructions for the specific animal you are making.

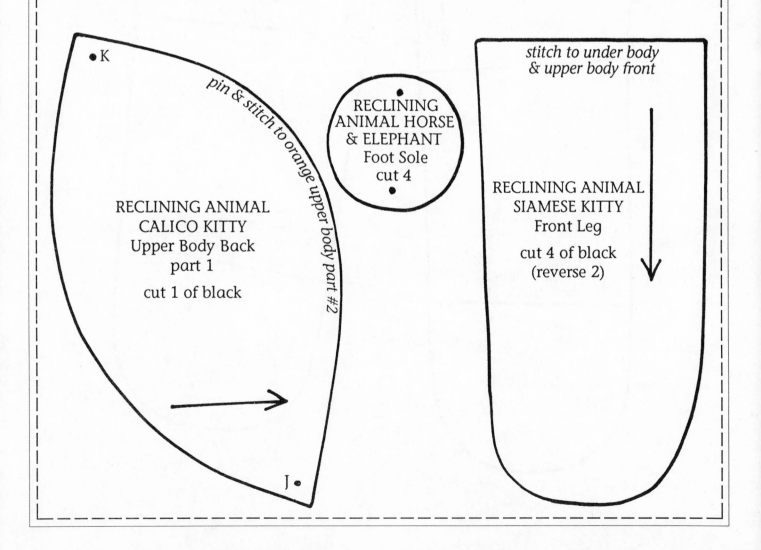

• K

pin & stitch to orange upper body part #2

RECLINING ANIMAL
CALICO KITTY
Upper Body Back
part 1

cut 1 of black

J •

RECLINING
ANIMAL HORSE
& ELEPHANT
Foot Sole
cut 4

*stitch to under body
& upper body front*

RECLINING ANIMAL
SIAMESE KITTY
Front Leg

cut 4 of black
(reverse 2)

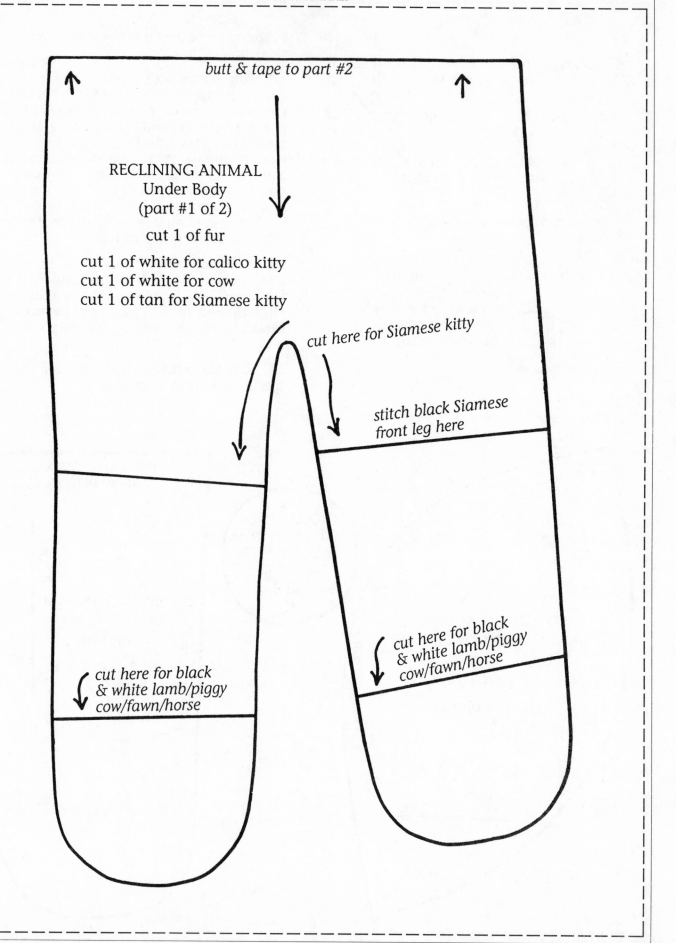

butt & tape to part #2

RECLINING ANIMAL
Under Body
(part #1 of 2)

cut 1 of fur

cut 1 of white for calico kitty
cut 1 of white for cow
cut 1 of tan for Siamese kitty

cut here for Siamese kitty

stitch black Siamese
front leg here

cut here for black
& white lamb/piggy
cow/fawn/horse

cut here for black
& white lamb/piggy
cow/fawn/horse

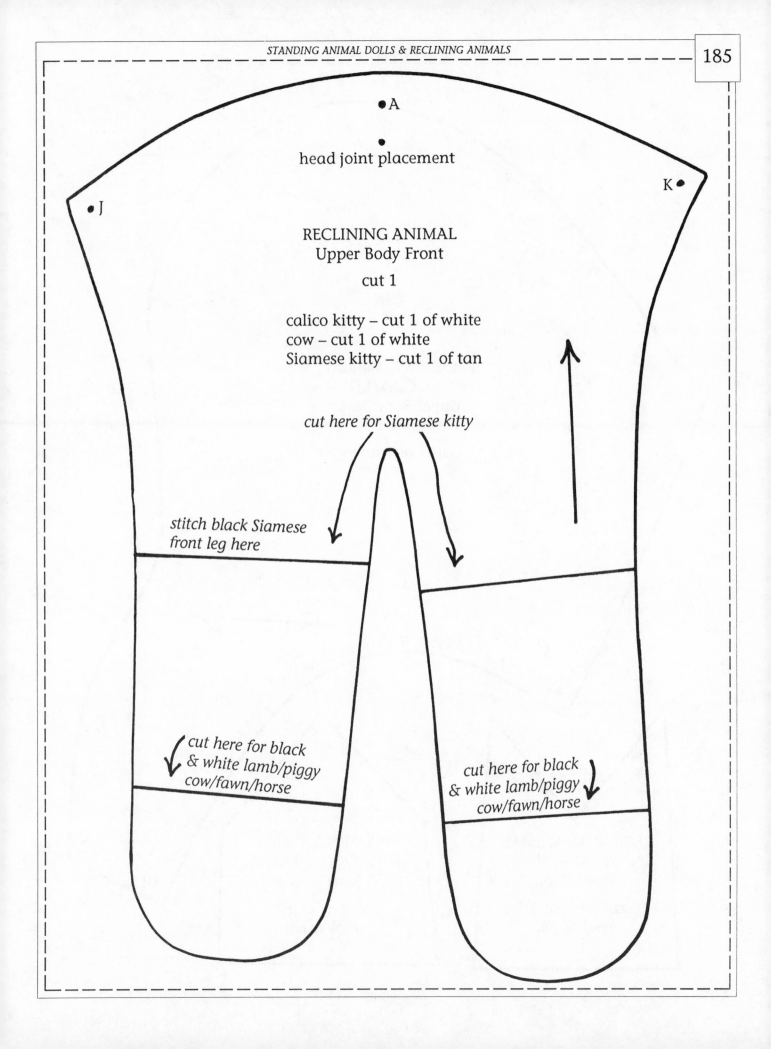

• A

head joint placement

• J

• K

RECLINING ANIMAL
Upper Body Front

cut 1

calico kitty – cut 1 of white
cow – cut 1 of white
Siamese kitty – cut 1 of tan

cut here for Siamese kitty

*stitch black Siamese
front leg here*

*cut here for black
& white lamb/piggy
cow/fawn/horse*

*cut here for black
& white lamb/piggy
cow/fawn/horse*

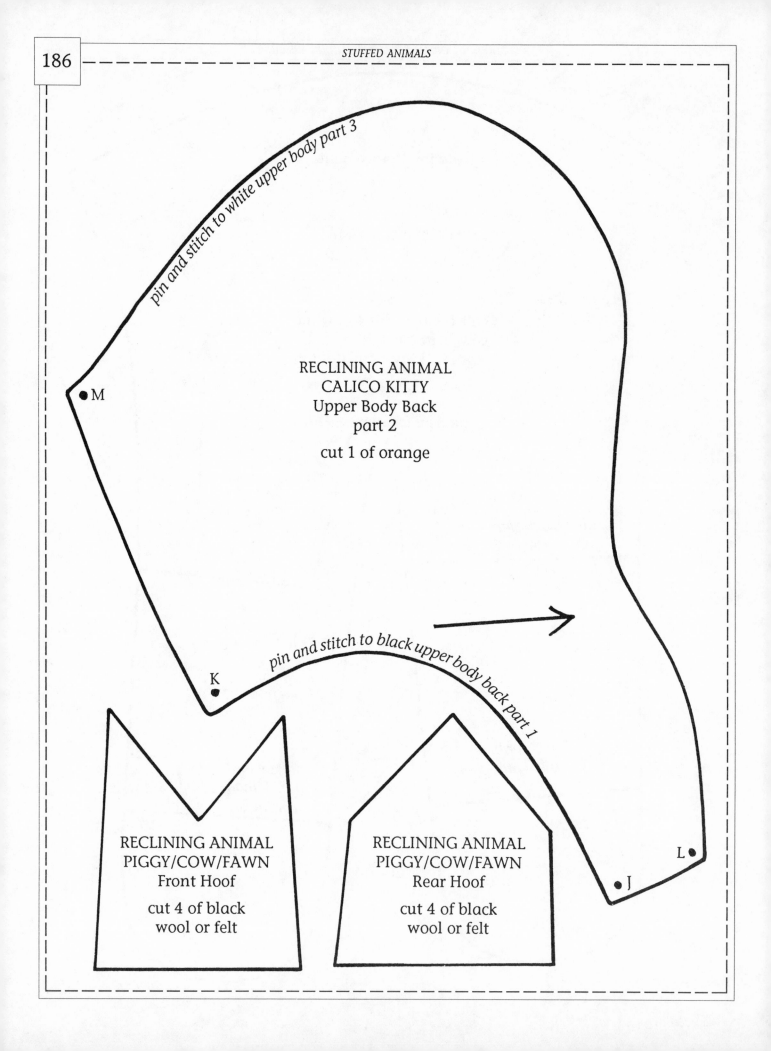

pin and stitch to white upper body part 3

• M

RECLINING ANIMAL
CALICO KITTY
Upper Body Back
part 2

cut 1 of orange

• K

pin and stitch to black upper body back part 1

L •

• J

RECLINING ANIMAL
PIGGY/COW/FAWN
Front Hoof

cut 4 of black
wool or felt

RECLINING ANIMAL
PIGGY/COW/FAWN
Rear Hoof

cut 4 of black
wool or felt

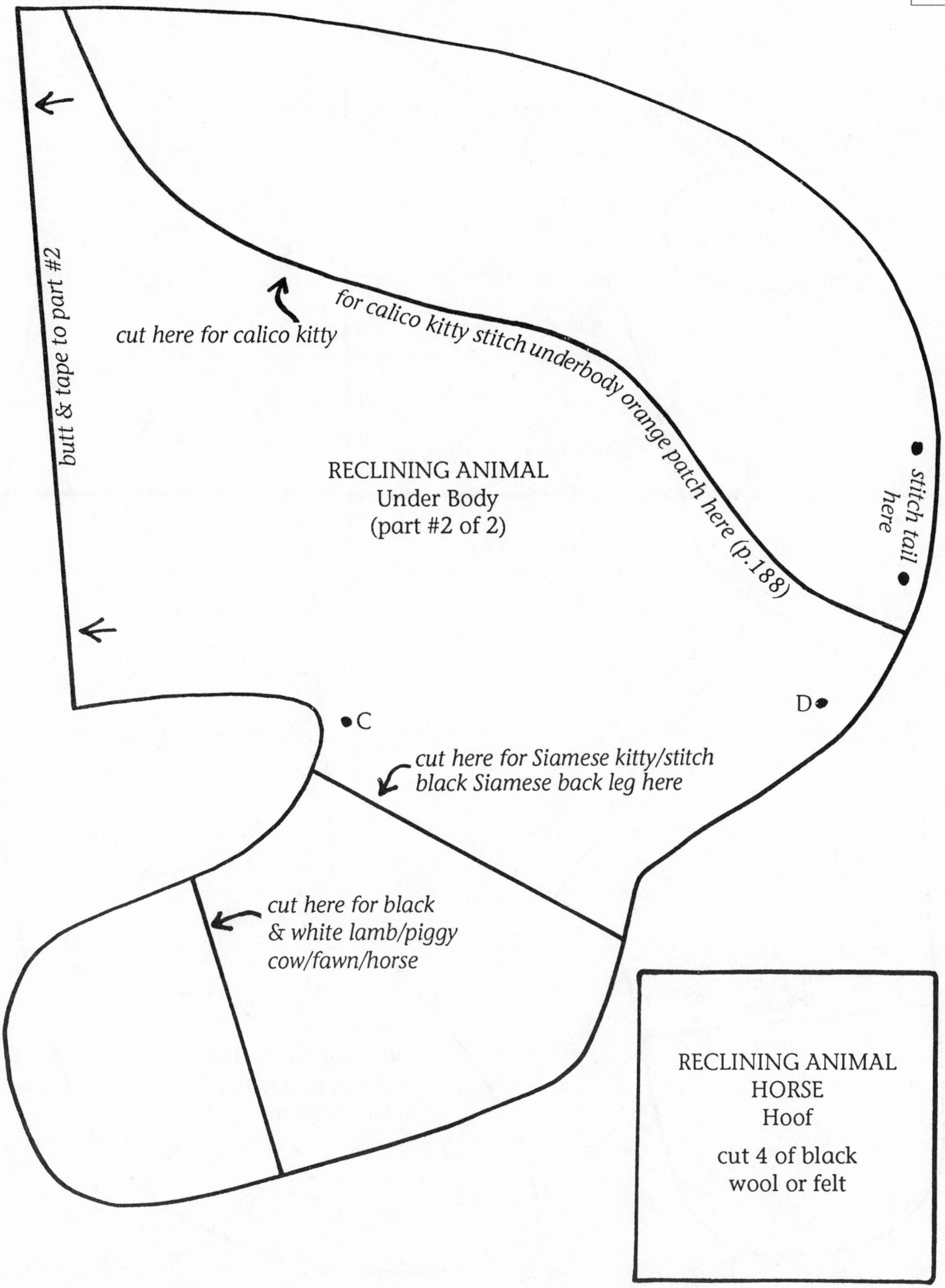

butt & tape to part #2

cut here for calico kitty

for calico kitty stitch underbody orange patch here (p.188)

RECLINING ANIMAL
Under Body
(part #2 of 2)

stitch tail
here

•C

•D

cut here for Siamese kitty/stitch
black Siamese back leg here

cut here for black
& white lamb/piggy
cow/fawn/horse

RECLINING ANIMAL
HORSE
Hoof

cut 4 of black
wool or felt

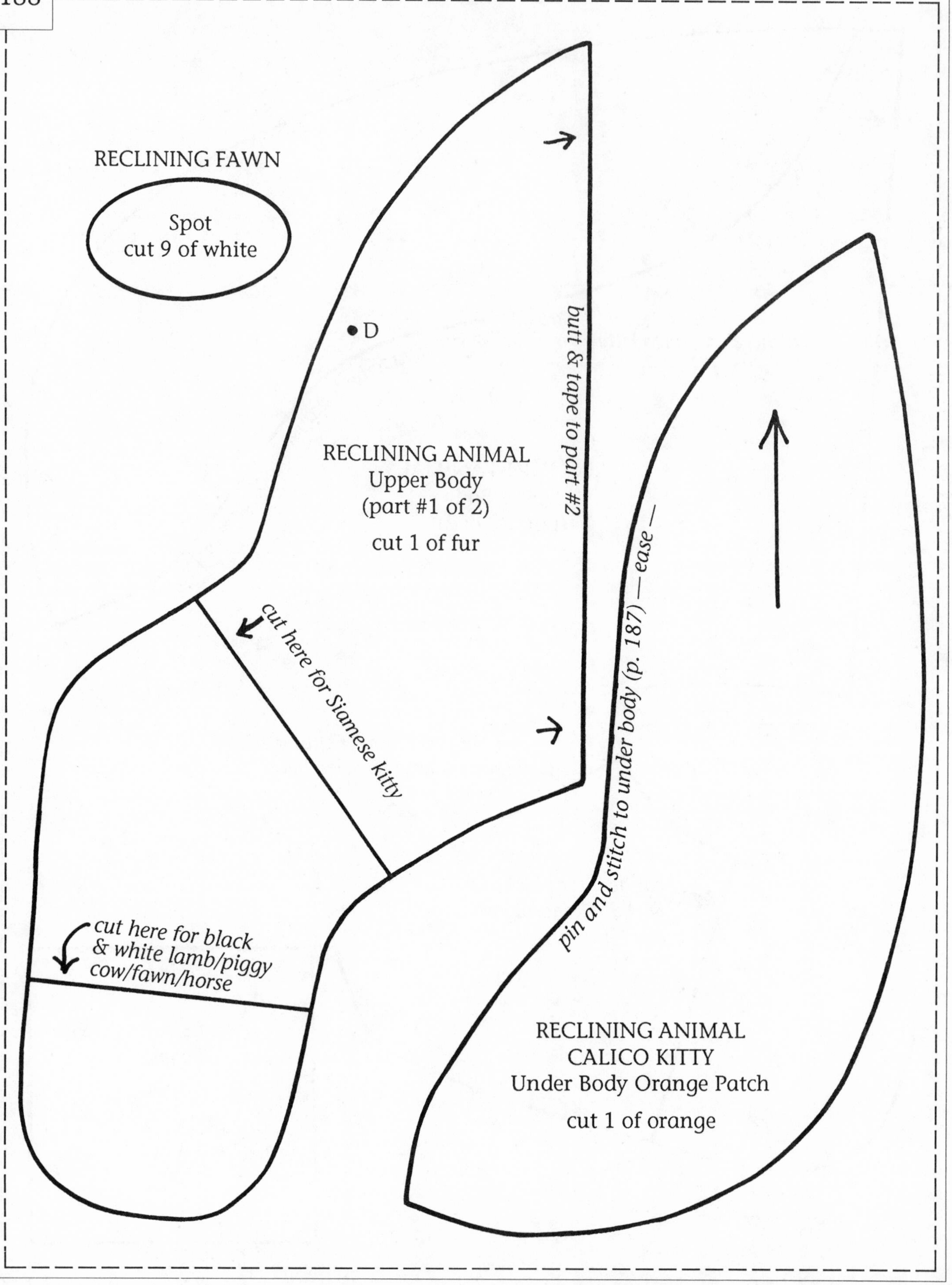

RECLINING FAWN

Spot
cut 9 of white

• D

RECLINING ANIMAL
Upper Body
(part #1 of 2)

cut 1 of fur

butt & tape to part #2

cut here for Siamese kitty

pin and stitch to under body (p. 187) — ease —

cut here for black
& white lamb/piggy
cow/fawn/horse

RECLINING ANIMAL
CALICO KITTY
Under Body Orange Patch

cut 1 of orange

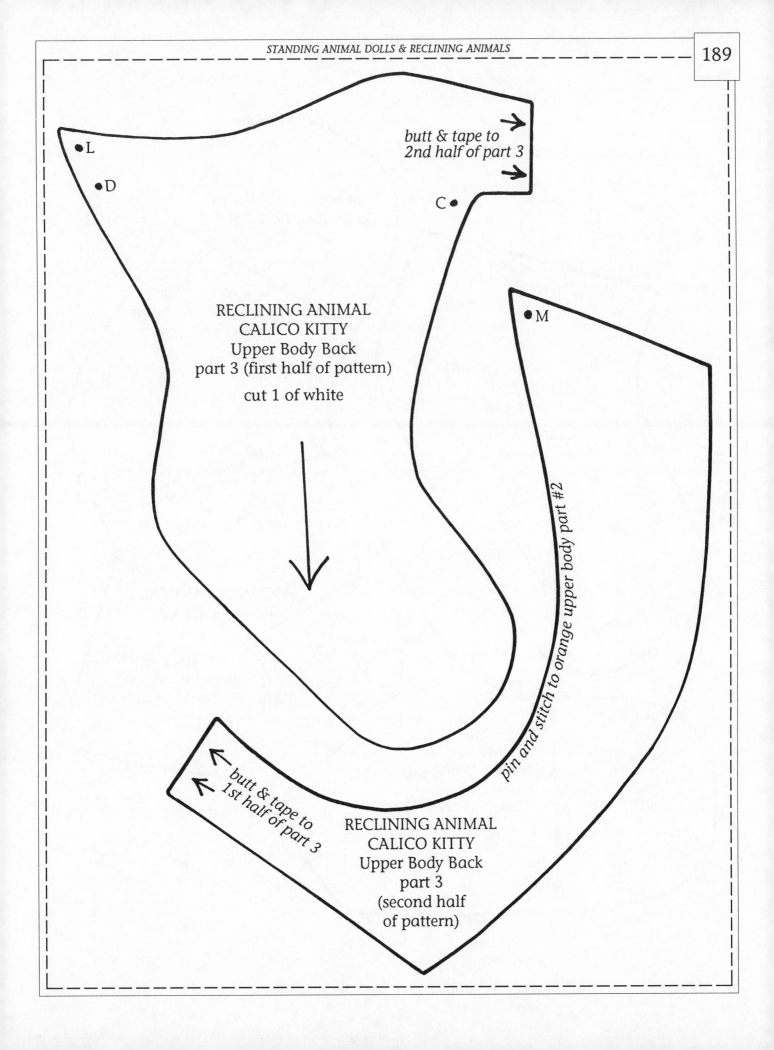

● L

● D

*butt & tape to
2nd half of part 3*

C ●

● M

RECLINING ANIMAL
CALICO KITTY
Upper Body Back
part 3 (first half of pattern)

cut 1 of white

pin and stitch to orange upper body part #2

*butt & tape to
1st half of part 3*

RECLINING ANIMAL
CALICO KITTY
Upper Body Back
part 3
(second half
of pattern)

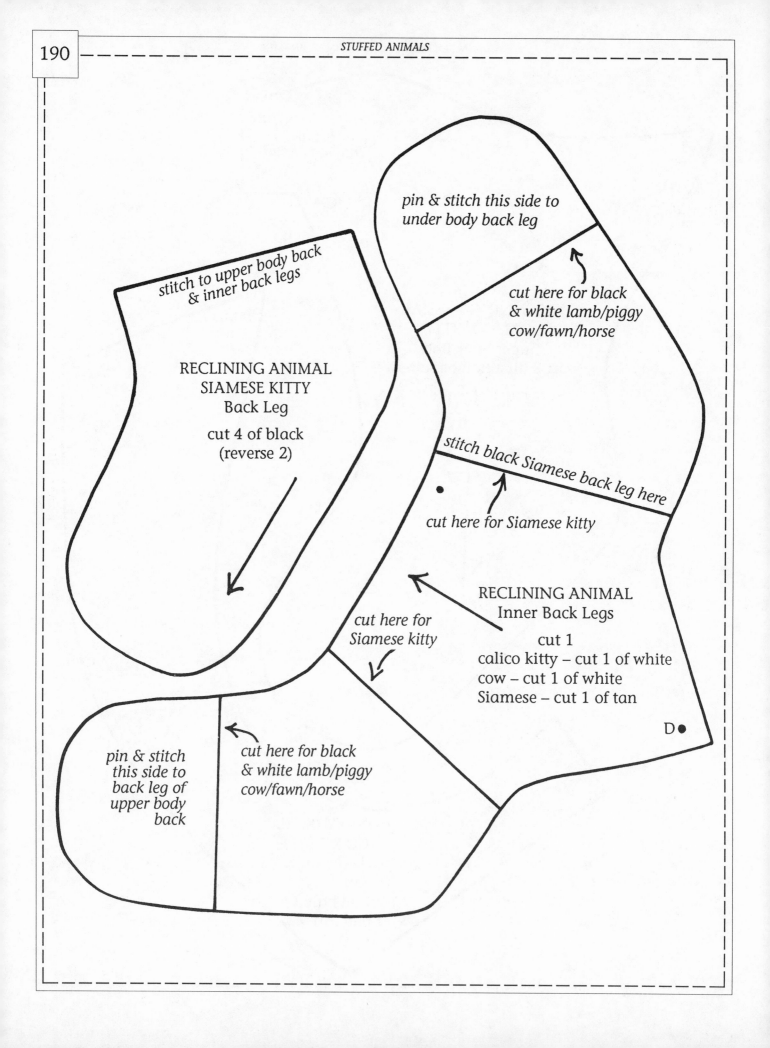

pin & stitch this side to under body back leg

cut here for black & white lamb/piggy cow/fawn/horse

stitch to upper body back & inner back legs

RECLINING ANIMAL
SIAMESE KITTY
Back Leg

cut 4 of black
(reverse 2)

stitch black Siamese back leg here

cut here for Siamese kitty

RECLINING ANIMAL
Inner Back Legs

cut 1
calico kitty – cut 1 of white
cow – cut 1 of white
Siamese – cut 1 of tan

D •

cut here for Siamese kitty

pin & stitch this side to back leg of upper body back

cut here for black & white lamb/piggy cow/fawn/horse

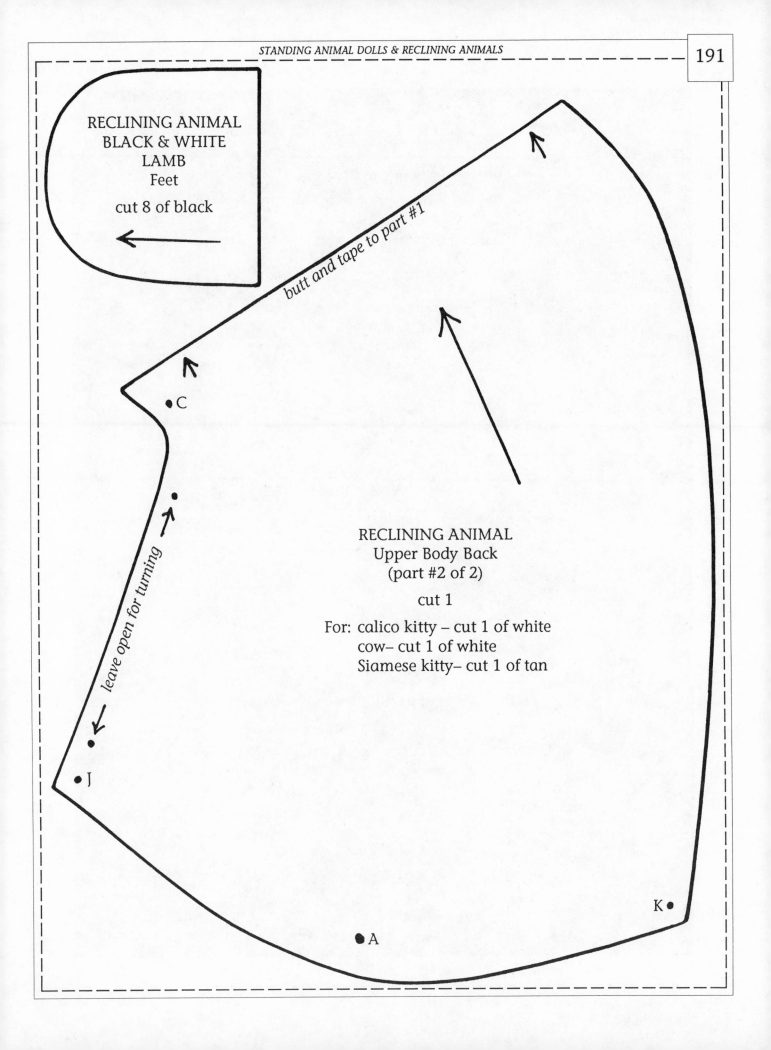

RECLINING ANIMAL
BLACK & WHITE
LAMB
Feet

cut 8 of black

butt and tape to part #1

•C

leave open for turning

•J

RECLINING ANIMAL
Upper Body Back
(part #2 of 2)

cut 1

For: calico kitty – cut 1 of white
cow– cut 1 of white
Siamese kitty– cut 1 of tan

K•

•A

♥ ♥ ♥ ♥ ♥

Animal Doll Clothing

You can stitch up the perfect outfit for any of your animal dolls with these easy patterns. The bodice and sleeves are the same for both the jumpsuit and the dress. Calico, corduroy and denim are natural choices for the outfits. Try combining fabrics for the pants and top of the jumpsuit and match fabrics for the dress, apron and bloomers. Turn to the sources section at the back of the book to order a pair of glasses or a hat to complete your animal's attire.

♥ ♥ ♥ ♥ ♥

MATERIALS

Dress

¹/₃ yard fabric

Matching thread

Three ³/₈" buttons or snaps

Apron

¹/₃ yard fabric

Matching thread

2 yards 1" wide gathered eyelet or lace

¹/₂ yard 1" wide ribbon

Bloomers

¹/₄ yard fabric

Matching thread

¹/₂ yard 1" wide eyelet or lace

¹/₃ yard ¹/₄" wide elastic

Jumpsuit

¹/₃ yard fabric (or smaller pieces of several fabrics)

Matching thread

Three ³/₈" buttons or snaps

INSTRUCTIONS

Note: All seam allowances are ¼" unless otherwise instructed.

Prepare, mark and cut fabric and patterns as instructed on page 10. For dress cut skirt 8" x 22".

For Dress and Jumpsuit:

1. Stitch both front bodice pieces to back bodice at shoulders. Repeat for second set of bodice pieces.

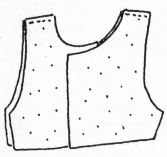

2. Right sides facing, pin bodices together at neck and back edges. Stitch.

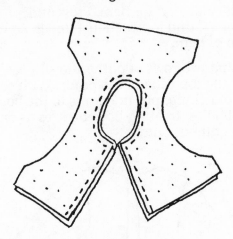

Trim corners. Clip curves.

3. Pin and stitch one long edge of sleeve to arm hole, treating the two layers of bodices as one. Repeat for second sleeve.

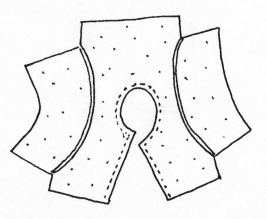

4. Pin and stitch sleeve and side seams, again treating the two layers of the bodice as one.

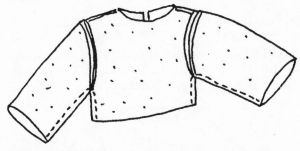

5. Press under ¼" at sleeve hems. Repeat. Topstitch just less than ¼" from edge.

6.. Turn right side out. Make buttonholes on one side of bodice back as marked on pattern. Sew buttons in place on other side at dots.

To finish, follow the instructions for the dress or jumpsuit below.

Dress

7. Right sides together, pin short ends of 8" x 22" skirt fabric together. Using a ½" seam allowance stitch center back seam, back-stitching half way, and continuing with a long, basting stitch. Press the seam open.

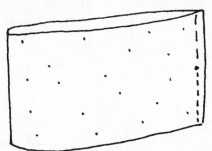

Turn under ¼" on each seam allowance. Press under another ¼". Topstitch a scant ¼" from both sides of the seam. Remove basting stitches from center back seam.

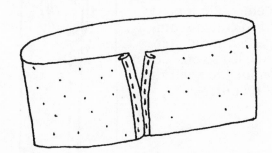

8. To hem the skirt, press under ¼" on the bottom (regular stitched end, not basted) of the skirt. Press under another ¼". Topstitch.

9. Using two rows of gathering stitches, gather the top edge of the skirt. With center backs matching, pin the skirt to the bottom of the bodice, treating both bodice layers as one. Adjust gathers. Stitch.

Jumpsuit

7. Stitch inside leg seams of pants. Press open.

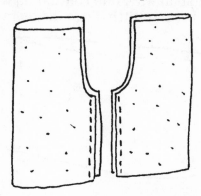

8. Turn one leg right side out. Put it inside other leg, right sides together. Pin long curved crotch seams together, matching inside leg seams. Stitch from one top waist to dot on other side.

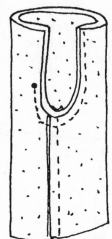

Turn right side out. On remaining raw edges of crotch seam, above dot, turn ¼" to inside. Repeat. Topstitch. This will be the back opening of the jumpsuit.

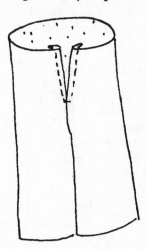

9. Press under ¼" for hem. Press under another ¼" and topstitch just under ¼" from bottom of hem.

10. Using two rows of gathering stitches, gather the top edge of the pants. With center backs matching, pin the pants to the bottom of the bodice, treating both bodices as one. Adjust gathers. Stitch.

Apron

1. Cut along the cutting line on the back of both apron pieces.

2. Pin eyelet or lace to edges of right side of one apron piece as shown. Make seams in lace where lace ends meet. Baste lace in place.

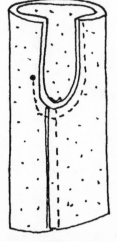

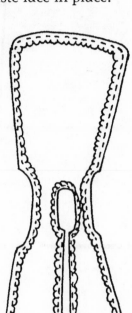

3. Pin second apron piece over first, right sides facing. Stitch all the way around leaving an opening between the dots at the bottom front as marked on pattern.

4. Turn apron right side out. Slipstitch opening at bottom front closed. Press. Put apron on animal, with opening at the back. Tie ribbon in bow around animal's waist.

Bloomers

1. Stitch inside leg seams.

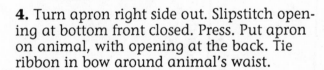

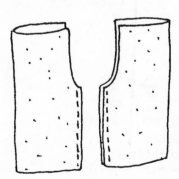

2. Turn one leg right side out. Slide inside other leg, matching inside leg seams and raw edges of crotch curve. Right sides will be together. Pin long curved crotch seams together, matching inside leg seams. Stitch from one top waist to dot on other side.

Turn right side out. On remaining raw edges of crotch seam, above dot, turn ¼" to inside. Topstitch. This creates an opening at the back of the bloomers from which the tail will protrude.

3. Turn bloomers right side out. Press ¼" to inside at top edge of bloomers. Press under another ½". Topstitch close to both folds, leaving a ½" wide gap in bottom stitching for inserting elastic.

Cut a piece of elastic 10" long. Attach a safety pin to each end. Insert one safety pin into the casing, run it all the way around, emerging out of the gap. Overlap ends ½" and secure with small stitches. Stitch gap in topstitching closed.

4. Press ¼" to inside at bottom legs of bloomers. Press under another ¼". Cut a piece of lace 10½" long. Right sides facing, seam the lace as shown.

Pin and topstitch the right side of the lace to the wrong side of the hem, right side of lace to wrong side of bloomers.

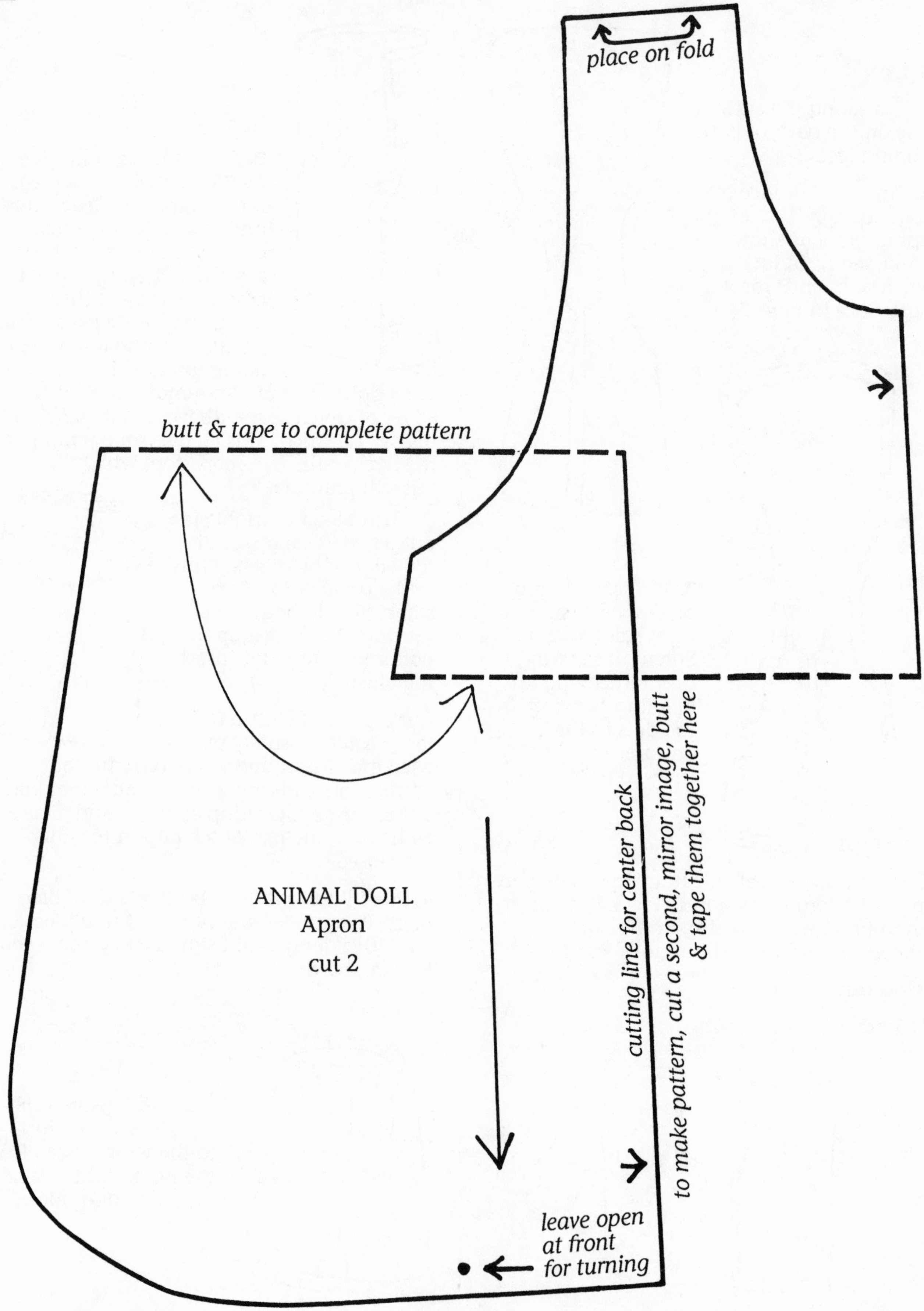

place on fold

butt & tape to complete pattern

cutting line for center back

to make pattern, cut a second, mirror image, butt & tape them together here

ANIMAL DOLL
Apron

cut 2

leave open
at front
for turning

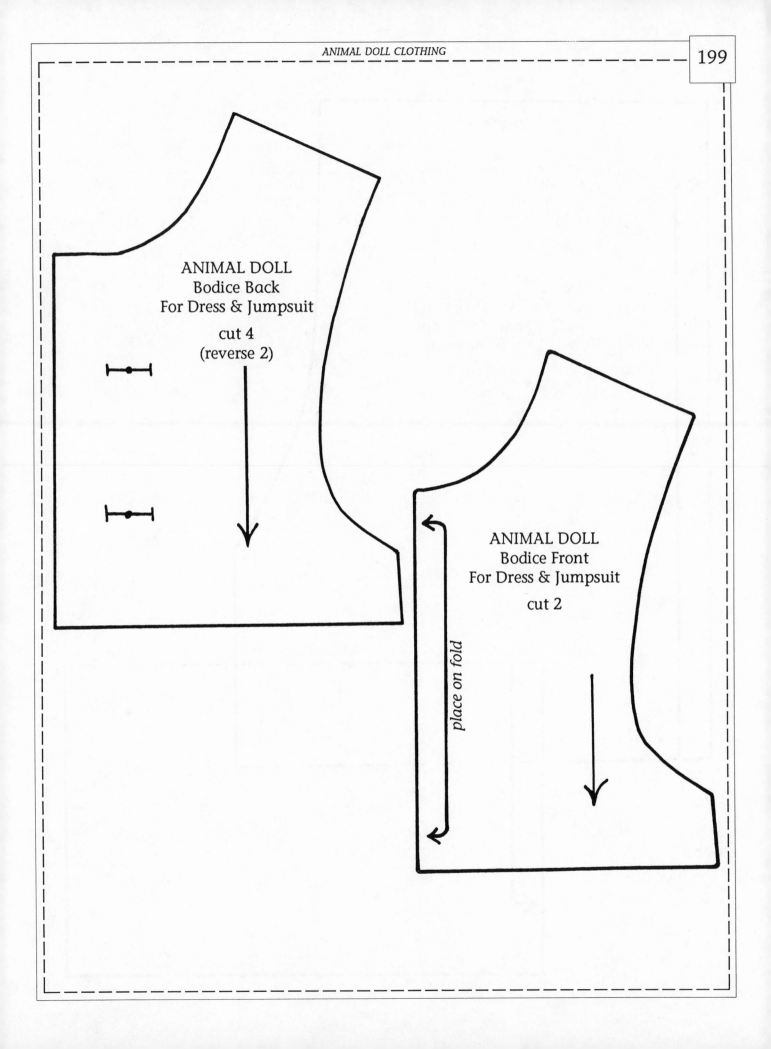

ANIMAL DOLL
Bodice Back
For Dress & Jumpsuit

cut 4
(reverse 2)

ANIMAL DOLL
Bodice Front
For Dress & Jumpsuit

cut 2

place on fold

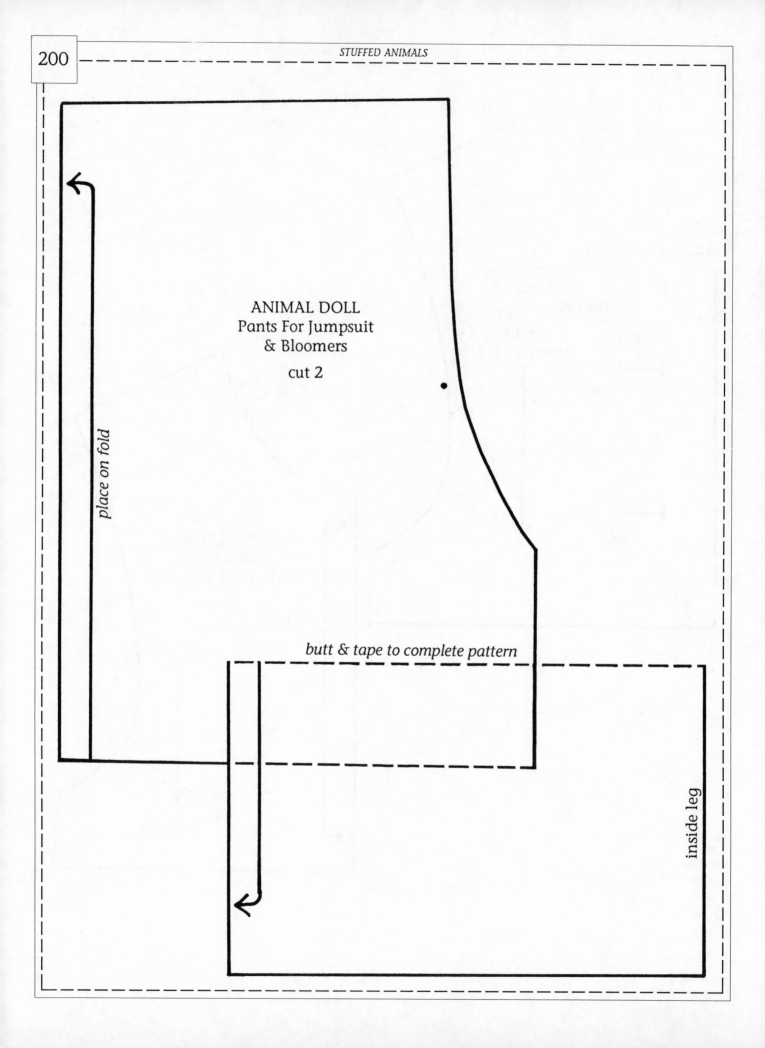

ANIMAL DOLL
Pants For Jumpsuit
& Bloomers

cut 2

place on fold

butt & tape to complete pattern

inside leg

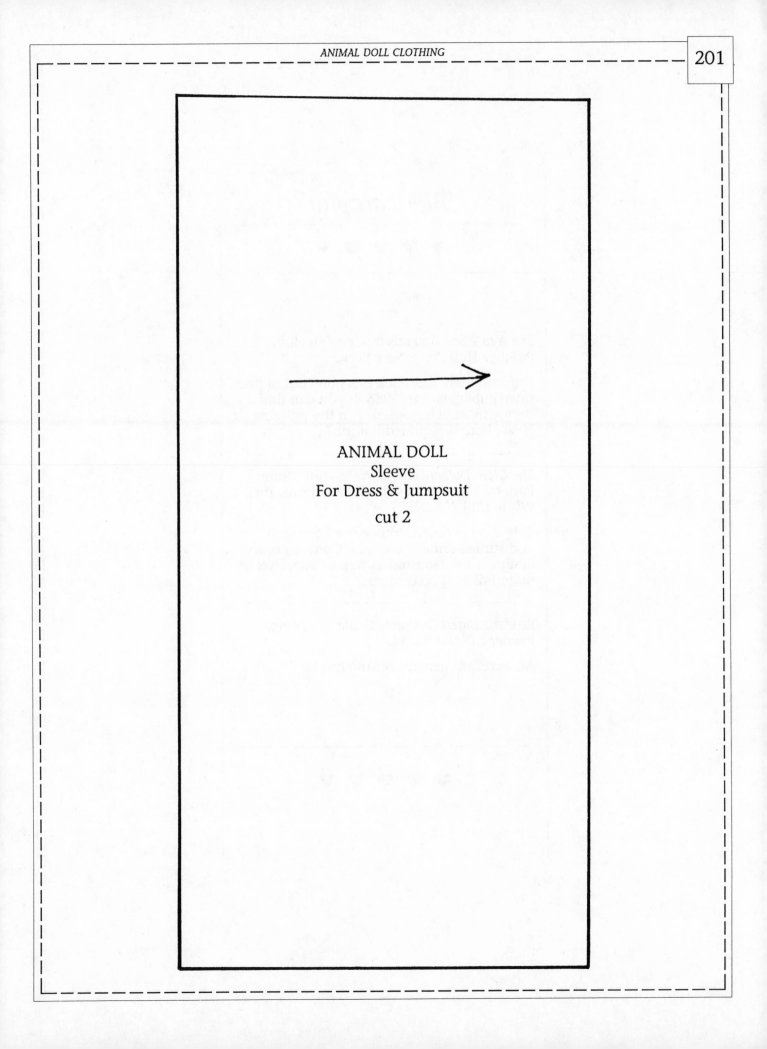

ANIMAL DOLL
Sleeve
For Dress & Jumpsuit

cut 2

Bibliography

The A to Z Soft Animals by Carolyn Hall, Prentice Hall Press, New York.

Unfortunately this book has gone out of print since publication in 1986. If you can find a copy you will be pleased with the patterns. How about a sequined iguana?

The Cloth Dollmaker's Sourcebook by Diane Patterson Dee, Betterway Publications, Inc., White Hall, VA 22987

This is an excellent source book for doll- and stuffed-animal making. Contemporary designers are featured as well as suppliers of materials and accessories.

Reader's Digest Complete Guide To Sewing, Reader's Digest Books.

An excellent general sewing guide.

Sources

by Diane
1126 Ivon Avenue
Endicott, NY 13760
Catalog: $1.50

Diane's catalog features patterns and kits for a zoo-full of animals, including more than two dozen teddy bears. She also offers most of the furs and everything else you'll need to make the stuffed animals starring in this book.

CR's Crafts
Box 8
Leland, IA 50453
Catalog: $2

In this wonderful source for general crafts supplies you'll find the joints, eyes, seam brush, Pretty Hair®, sheep and cow bells, kitty whiskers (212C or B), and fur mentioned throughout this book.

Edinburgh Imports, Inc.
P.O. Box 722
Woodland Hills, CA 91365-0722.
Price list: Two first class stamps

The source for top quality mohair and synthetic (woven backing) furs and all other supplies needed for bear making. You'll find the gray and white mohair for the jointed bunny here as well as the Edinbrush and perle cotton.

Home Sew
Dept. JD
Bethlehem, PA 18018
Catalog: Free

This is a must. You won't believe the low prices on basic sewing supplies as well as laces and ribbons.

Patterncrafts
Box 25370
Colorado Springs, CC 80936-5370
Catalog: $2

Color photos of more than 700 patterns, including dolls and stuffed animals, are featured in this extraordinary catalog of patterns collected from the best sources. Also carries Stuff-It® tool.

More good books from
WILLIAMSON PUBLISHING

To order additional copies of **Easy-To-Make Stuffed Animals &
All The Trimmings**, please enclose $13.95 per copy plus $2.50
shipping and handling. Follow "To Order" instructions on the last
page. Thank you.

Easy-to-Make TEDDY BEARS & ALL THE TRIMMINGS
by Jodie Davis

Now you can make the most lovable, huggable, plain or fancy teddy
bears imaginable, for a fraction of store-bought costs. Step-by-step
instructions and easy patterns drawn to actual size for large, soft-
bodied bears, quilted bears, and even jointed bears. Plus patterns for
clothes, accessories — even teddy bear furniture!

208 pages, 8½ x 11, illustrations and patterns,
Quality paperback, $13.95

Easy-To-Make CLOTH DOLLS & ALL THE TRIMMINGS
by Jodie Davis

Jodie Davis turns her many talents to making the most adorable and
personable cloth dolls imaginable. With her expert directions and
clear full-sized patterns, anyone can create these instant friends for a
special child or friend. Includes seven 18-inch dolls like Santa, Rag-
gedy Ann, and a clown; a 20-inch baby doll plus complete wardrobe;
a 25-inch boy and girl doll plus a wardrobe including sailor suits;
and 10 dolls from around the world including a Japanese kimono
doll and Amish dolls. Absolutely beautiful and you can do it!

224 pages, 8½ x 11, illustrations and patterns
Quality paperback, $13.95

Easy-To-Make ENDANGERED SPECIES To Stitch & Stuff
by Jodie Davis

Another wonderful book by the amazing Jodie Davis. Along with
making the most adorable stuffed animals such as a loggerhead
turtle, spotted owl and bald eagle, you can have wonderful wind
socks adorned with these fabulous animals that we all treasure so
much. Picture some playful pandas, gazelles, rhino, and monkeys
on a colorful windsock or a gorgeous scarlet macaw. Let Jodie show
you how with her step-by-step instructions and full-sized patterns.

192 pages, 8½ x 11, illustrations and patterns
Quality paperback, $13.95

CARING FOR OLDER CATS & DOGS
Extending Your Pet's Healthy Life
by Robert Anderson, DVM and Barbara J. Wrede

Here's the only book that will help you distinguish the signs of natural aging from pain and suffering, that will help you care for your pet with compassion and knowledge. How to help your older pet, how to nourish, nurture, and nurse your cat or dog, and finally when and how to let go. Medically sound with reasonable homeopathic remedies, too, mixed with practical advice and compassion. Every older pet deserves an owner who has read this!

168 pages, 6 x 9, illustrations
Quality paperback, $10.95

THE BROWN BAG COOKBOOK
Nutritious Portable Lunches for Kids and Grown-Ups
by Sara Sloan

Here are more than 1,000 brown bag lunch ideas with 150 recipes for simple, quick, nutritious lunches that kids will love. Breakfast ideas, too! This popular book is now in its ninth printing as more and more people realize how important every meal is to our health!

192 pages, 8¼ x 7¼, illustrations,
Quality paperback, $9.95

GOLDE'S HOMEMADE COOKIES
by Golde Soloway

Over 50,000 copies of this marvelous cookbook have been sold. Now it's in its second edition with 135 of the most delicious cookie recipes imaginable. *Publishers Weekly* says, "Cookies are her chosen realm and how sweet a world it is to visit." You're sure to agree!

176 pages, 8¼ x 7¼ , illustrations,
Quality paperback, $8.95

BUILDING FENCES OF WOOD, STONE, METAL & PLANTS
by John Vivian

Complete how-to on wood fence, stone fence, block, brick and mud fence, living fence and hedgerows, primitive fence, wire livestock fence, electric barrier fence, and classic horse fence. Next best thing to having a teacher by your side!

192 pages, 8½ x 11, hundreds of drawings, photos, tables, charts
Quality paperback, $13.95

THE KIDS' NATURE BOOK
365 Indoor/Outdoor Activities and Experiences
by Susan Milord

Winner of the Parents' Choice Gold Award for learning and doing books, *The Kids' Nature Book* is loved by children, grandparents, and friends alike. Simple projects and activities emphasize fun while quietly reinforcing the wonder of the world we all share.
Packed with facts and fun!

160 pages, 11 x 8½, 425 illustrations
Quality paperback, $12.95

DOING CHILDREN'S MUSEUMS
A Guide to 265 Hands-On Museums
by Joanne Cleaver

Turn an ordinary day into a spontaneous "vacation" by taking a child to some of the 265 participatory children's museums, discovery rooms, and nature centers covered in this highly acclaimed, one-of-a-kind book. Filled with museum specifics to help you pick and plan the perfect place for the perfect day, Cleaver has created a most valuable resource for anyone who loves kids!

272 pages, 6 x 9,
Quality paperback, $13.95

PARENTS ARE TEACHERS, TOO
Enriching Your Child's First Six Years
by Claudia Jones

Be the best teacher your child ever has. Jones shares hundreds of ways to help any child learn in playful home situations. Lots on developing reading, writing, math skills. Plenty on creative and critical thinking, too. A book you'll love using!

192 pages, 6 x 9, illustrations,
Quality paperback, $9.95

MORE PARENTS ARE TEACHERS, TOO
Encouraging Your 6- to 12-Year-Old
by Claudia Jones

Help your children be the best they can be! When parents are involved, kids do better. When kids do better, they feel better, too. Here's a wonderfully creative book of ideas, activities, teaching methods and more to help you help your children over the rough spots and share in their growing joy in achieving. Plenty on reading, writing, math, problem-solving, creative thinking. Everything for parents who want to help but not push their children.

224 pages, 6 x 9, illustrations,
Quality paperback, $10.95

THE HOMEWORK SOLUTION
by Linda Agler Sonna

Put homework responsibilities where they belong - in the student's lap! Here it is! The simple remedy for the millions of parents who are tired of waging the never-ending nightly battle over kids' homework. Dr. Sonna's "One Step Solution" will relieve parents, kids and their siblings of the ongoing problem within a single month.

192 pages, 6 x 9,
Quality paperback, $10.95

PRACTICAL POLE BUILDING CONSTRUCTION
by Leigh Seddon

Saves money, time, labor; no excavation. Complete how-to-build information with original architectural plans and specs for small barn, horse barn, shed, animal shelter, cabins and more.

186 pages, 8½ x 11, over 100 architectural renderings, tables
Quality paperback, $10.95

THE COMPLETE AND EASY GUIDE TO SOCIAL SECURITY & MEDICARE
by Faustin F. Jehle

A lifesaver of a book for every senior citizen — in fact every citizen — you know. Do someone a special favor, and give this book as a gift. Written in "plain English," here's all that red tape unravelled. Over 800,000 copies sold!

176 pages, 8½ x 11, charts and tables,
Quality paperback, $10.95

KIDS CREATE!
Art & Craft Experiences for 3- to 9-year-olds
by Laurie Carlson

What's the most important experience for children ages 3 to 9? Why to create something by themselves. Carlson provides over 150 creative experiences ranging from making dinosaur sculptures to clay cactus gardens, from butterfly puppets to windsocks. Plenty of help for the parents working with the kids, too! A delightfully innovative book.

160 pages, 11 x 8½, over 400 illustrations,
Quality paperback, $12.95

ADVENTURES IN ART
Art & Craft Experiences for 7- to 14-year-olds
by Susan Milord

Imagine an art book that encourages children to explore, to experience, to touch and to see, to learn and to create . . . imagine a true
adventure in art. Here's a book that teaches artisan's skills without
stifling creativity. Covers making handmade papers, puppets, masks,
paper seascapes, seed art, tin can lantern, berry ink, still life, silk
screen, batiking, carving and so much more. Perfect for the older child.
Let the adventure begin!

160 pages, 11 x 8$\frac{1}{2}$, 500 illustrations
Quality paperback, $12.95

To Order:

At your bookstore or order directly from Williamson Publishing. We
accept Visa and MasterCard (please include number and expiration
date), or send check to:

> Williamson Publishing Company
> Church Hill Road, P.O. Box 185
> Charlotte, Vermont 05445

> Toll-free phone orders with credit cards:
> 1-800-234-8791

Please add $2.50 for postage and handling. Satisfaction is guaranteed
or full refund without questions or quibbles.